# BONFIRE OF THE BRANDS

# BONFIRE OF THE BRANDS

## HOW I LEARNT TO LIVE WITHOUT LABELS

## NEIL BOORMAN

CANONGATE

*Edinburgh · New York · Melbourne*

First published in Great Britain in 2007 by
Canongate Books Ltd, 14 High Street,
Edinburgh EH1 1TE

1

# BONFIRE OF THE BRANDS

## 17 september 2006

**The Lacoste polo shirt or the Gucci: which one to choose?**

I normally wear Lacoste during the daytime, especially if I am feeling youthful or frivolous. The Gucci is more of a grown-up shirt, good for an informal meeting or drinks in a smart-ish pub. But now this distinction hardly matters. I grab them both from a selection of my polo shirts, all neatly folded for display purposes. Beside the shirts lie a dozen pairs of trousers, again, folded with precision and arranged atop each other so that I can see the label on the beltline of each pair, just as in the shops. Then jumpers, suits, coats and finally shoes; rows of trainers, smart leather brogues and lace-ups, boots and flip-flops, their pristine condition a testament to the love and affection I have poured over them since starting the collection some 20 years ago.

Polo shirts in hand, I stand up and face a mass of some 300 onlookers, pressed against a row of crowd-control barriers. Their mouths are wide open, cheeks all red, eyes bulging, as they roar in my direction. The sound should be deafening, but it has become a background white noise, drowned out by the thudding pump of my heart.

I turn and march away from the throng, triggering a sustained burst of flashbulb light from a gaggle of photographers who barge each other for space. From the corner of my eye, I see a man with a large TV camera tracking my every move, followed by a smart perma-tanned presenter who jabbers into a microphone. None of it matters.

The bonfire in front of me is huge. It burns so brightly that it is impossible to pick out separate flames, a towering triangle of orange blinding to the eye. The heat is like nothing I have experienced before, singeing the hair on my face as I move closer. At ten feet, the heat becomes too much to bear and I have to recoil a step or two. It's now or never. I pull back my arm and lob the polo shirts into the fire. They seem to evaporate on contact.

As I stride back to the pile of clothes, my tunnel vision subsides, as if a giant head-muffler has been removed, and suddenly I am very much aware of my surroundings. I am standing in the middle of a square in Central London, the material contents of my life laid out on the grass before a mob of people. Security guards prevent the crowd from jumping the fence and pyro-technicians buzz around me tending to the fire. A man in a blue boiler suit stands by with a sledge-hammer, waiting to destroy my Sharp LCD television and Technics turntable. Before he does, I must throw the rest of my wardrobe into the fire; the Helmut Lang shoes, the Louis Vuitton bag, the Vivienne Westwood suit. But now the moment has arrived, I don't feel much like throwing these things away. I would rather scoop the lot up and take them back home where they belong.

Standing before this circus, I wonder: how exactly, did it come to this?

Sports day 1982: all the boys dressed in branded gear – except me.

# BEFORE

## 2 march 2006

I am a half-eaten apple, a polo-playing horseman and a snow-capped mountain. When I am at work, I like to be thought of as a free-thinking creative. So I use an Apple Mac, which is what all the cool, artistic people seem to use. My polo shirt, made by Ralph Lauren, is common among council estate kids and I wear it to make me look just a little bit tough. All day I drink Evian water, not because it tastes especially nice, it's just that the label makes me feel healthy and, well, special. I am a white, lower middle-class Londoner, an ABC1. As a brand consumer yourself, you should be able to guess all this just by looking at me.

If you and I met at a party, you would probably ask me what I do for a living, what town I live in, perhaps the school I went to – the kind of questions that would help you to build a picture of who I am. I might ask the same of you, but probably I wouldn't be listening. It's more likely that I'd be looking at the label on your jeans, glancing at your shoes, eyeing up your mobile phone. These are the things that really tell me who you are. Of the myriad brands of clothes and phones available to buy, you chose those particular items. You chose them because they suited the person you think you are. Or perhaps the person you want to be. Considering the amount of time and money I spend on choosing the clothes I wear and the objects I carry, I sincerely hope you would notice the same things about me.

The truth is, I am a carefully considered collection of brands. These brands send out distinct statements to those who understand: statements about myself, my circle of friends, what we do and where we come from. It is no mistake that my phone is a Blackberry or that my shoes are made by Adidas. I have spent a great deal of time attaching myself to these brands. I want you to look at my phone, at my trainers and form an opinion about the statements they make. And to those who don't understand, well, that's okay. We'd probably never be friends anyhow.

I began to behave like this at a very early age. I remember the first day of junior school, standing alone in the playground desperately wanting to make friends. I headed straight for what seemed to be the most promising group of boys. They were clearly the most popular because they were talking to girls, trading football cards, eating luminous green sweets. They were doing all the things I wanted to do. As I attempted to mingle, one boy asked me, 'Do you support Tottenham Hotspur?' Another, 'Do you have any Scalextric?' A third, 'Are you into Michael Jackson?' I answered yes to them all, even though the truthful answer was no. Anything to prevent my having to stand alone in the playground during the afternoon break.

Things seemed to be going well until one of the boys caught sight of my trainers. I'd never thought too much about them before. They were just plain blue sports shoes Mum had bought for playing in the back garden. At once, a roar of disapproval broke out among the group. 'Where did you get those from? Oxfam?' Looking at the boys in bewilderment, I noticed for the first time that they all had similar shapes on the sides of their trainers where I had none. They were mostly ticks and stripes, like the ones on famous footballers' boots on television. It wasn't just their shoes; crocodiles, eagles and tigers sat on the breasts of their T-shirts, and every single boy seemed to have exactly the same school bag, a blue plastic holdall with a leaping puma in silver on the side. I slunk away dejected and confused. In this unexpected rude awakening I caught a glimpse of what was required if one was to be accepted in popular life. From that day on I resolved to be like them, if not more so.

I felt as if my parents had lied to me. Well, perhaps not lied, but withheld certain truths. Every boy in school seemed to have had the golden rule explained to them, and they were duly prepared; to be cool, to be 'in', to be accepted and popular, you needed the right gear. My parents must have known about this important rule, so why hide it from me? Throughout my short life, my mother and father had taught me the difference between right and wrong, and I had believed every word they said. I had placed complete trust in them to prepare me for the outside world, but on this occasion they had let me down, badly. They often told me how much I was loved, but it was clear now, they didn't love me enough to explain this vital truth. Thus began a growing resentment towards my parents and an almighty struggle to convince them of the need to have names and logos, the *right* names and logos on all my things.

Over the next few years, there were many battles with my parents. The bloodiest was over a Pringle jumper, a staple brand among the boys at school, that I simply had to have. The colour and design didn't matter. It just had to have the gold lion embroidered on the chest. Why, my mother asked, should she spend £50 on a jumper with a tiny logo, when Marks & Spencer made one exactly the same for half the price, only without the logo? Besides, wasn't it a well-known fact that famous name brands designed for Marks & Spencer on the quiet and it all came from the same factory? So really there was no difference between the two, bar Pringle's extortionate prices. This rationale missed the point on any number of levels. During trips to the shopping centre I would fly into a spectacular rage causing the gruelling school-jumper-for-Neil-mission to be aborted for another weekend.

After countless tantrums, I eventually won that particular war, one in a long line of hard-fought victories that I valued as sizeable deposits in the playground-status bank. I am not sure I ever fully explained to my parents the real reasons why wearing Adidas, Fila and Lacoste over Woolworth, M&S or BHS was so fundamentally important to me. To be honest I am not sure I necessarily understood the reasoning myself. I vividly remember praying to God and asking him whether we could make a deal; I'd do my homework and be nice to my sister, as long as I got the Puma football that I'd seen in Argos. The fact that I was useless at football, and rarely got picked to play for the school team wasn't an issue. All that really mattered was that I had the right gear.

I grew up in a period when English social structures were changing dramatically. Although I was blissfully unaware at the time, the Thatcher government of the mid-1980s was creating a new prosperity among the fringes of the lower middle class my family inhabited, and my parents (and thus their children) began to enjoy the luxuries of a larger house, a second car and the annual package holiday to Spain. But being a member of the middle class was nothing to be proud of at school. In comparison to me, the poorer kids were better at fighting, were allowed to rent 18-certificate videos, went to football matches and had girlfriends who seemed to wear the most jewellery and make-up. In addition they had all the right labels on their clothes, their bikes, even their lunchboxes. This was a continual source of confusion to me. If their parents had less money than mine, why did they have all the expensive gear? It wasn't that my parents were cruel or unkind. After all, I had the largest collection of Star Wars toys compared to anyone else. It was just my growing passion for brands they didn't understand.

At the age of 14, I was now wholly dedicated to observing the law of brands, although I sometimes felt uneasy about the way it would make me behave. Like most children in their early teens I would feel embarrassed when I was spotted in public with my parents. But somehow it was made worse by the fact that my parents were clearly uninterested in acquiring and wearing brands themselves. More alarmingly I was beginning to feel spite for other children who violated the rules. Social gatherings with my friends were the most important things in my mind, an opportunity to reaffirm my acceptance among the peers I so admired and cruelly sneer at those I did not. Now the twice-yearly school disco was looming and I demanded that my parents buy me a new pair of trainers. Miraculously, my mother agreed, although only on the condition that I would take my little sister to the disco and look after her throughout the evening. I agreed to the deal. What else could I do? My sister and I had played together happily for most of the time and loved each other without question. But as the date of the disco loomed, something changed; I began to see her in the same light as the unpopular kids at school. She didn't have the right trainers or the right kind of jeans. She wore funny dresses that Mum bought. She didn't seem to be interested in the right gear. A cold panic descended as it dawned on me that being seen with her would be the ruin of me. I'll never forget the look of disappointment she gave me as I abandoned her in the disco for my friends. Throughout the night, I could feel her watching me as I joined in the bullying and taunts my friends gave the unfortunate kids with 'square' clothes. The sense of betrayal felt awful. But I couldn't let that get in the way of my hard-won status of cool.

This struggle for personal identity became less tortuous as a late teen, when I began earning money working part-time in shops and bars. Now that I was largely responsible for my own income, there could be no debate over the choices in knitwear I made, or any other purchase for that matter. That's not to say my parents were any less despairing when I returned home from the local shops armed with expensive-looking carrier bags; I knew they disapproved, but this served only to further compel my burgeoning obsession with brands.

My friends and I spent all our free time at the local shopping centre. By now, I had climbed the social ladder high enough to mill around outside McDonald's with the popular set from school, and we would endlessly trawl the clothes stores for a glimpse of any new deliveries of trainers and tracksuits we could save up to buy. Photos taken around that time depict us as walking advertisements for sportswear brands, mostly obscure American companies that were endorsed by the big rap stars of the day. Our social tribe was built around the badges of these brands; one could not join the group unless you wore the same clothes (ours being Nike), which we made sure were different to rival groups in the town (mostly Reebok). I would draw logos on my textbooks, pinch advertising posters from bus stops and collect every sort of packaging or ephemera that I could. Nothing else really mattered, except maybe girls.

A classic example of my changing relationship with brands at this time was Technics, a symbolic brand throughout the early 1990s. Technics manufactured the 1200 turntable, which was standard equipment for all the successful DJs we admired at the time. To have a textbook emblazoned with a coveted Technics sticker was a coded message to likeminded people; you weren't a 'Goth' or a 'square', you were into black music, the coolest music ever. A seminal moment finally came when the posters of celebrities on my bedroom walls were replaced with those famous brands. Pride of place above my bed was a glossy picture of the 1200. To own a pair of Technics and become a DJ would surely be the height of credibility with anyone that mattered and I duly began acclimatising my parents to the idea of buying me some. The day that two friends and I finally persuaded our fathers to finance a pair was a sweet day indeed. No one at school could quite believe we had them. Within weeks, we were invited to play at parties for kids much older than us, our own gatherings were oversubscribed and, soon after, a large group of friends formed around our social nucleus. We'd previously been plugging away at our DJ careers on inferior turntables with little success, but no more; we were now generating our own popularity and we could choose who was accepted in the playground, which deep down was all that counted.

By the time I reached my twenties, the power to gain acceptance, and in turn grant acceptance to others, had begun to preoccupy my adult life. It's not unreasonable to say that my own sense of self-worth now depended on maintaining and exerting this power. To be admired and loved by people I respected gave me the confidence to be myself. With this confidence, I in turn granted acceptance to others, which filled me with a sense of self-importance. As a child, that Puma football I prayed for was finally bestowed on me by the gods, and as a result I was picked to play for a team. Later on, I even got to pluck boys out of the crowd to play for the team myself.

Over time, the methods of obtaining this power became more sophisticated, and the type of people I have sought out and to which I have awarded acceptance has changed. But the goal remains the same. Central to this process is branding. The logos I carry around day to day transmit carefully orchestrated messages, so that those around me can understand who I am. The manner in which they react to these messages also gives me clues about who they are. Emitting the right messages to the right people again fills me with happiness and confidence, and I feel sure that the greater clarity and sophistication my branded messages carry, the happier I will become and the more I will be liked. To explain who I am and what I do to every person I encounter day to day would be impossible but it is important to me that friends, acquaintances, colleagues and strangers receive these messages. This is why I use brands.

Along with the inevitable social and financial changes I experienced moving into adulthood, came changes in the brands I adopted, new aspirations calling for new badges of identity. But one particular brand has remained a permanent fixture throughout my life: Adidas. A German sportswear brand that has its roots, its 'brand heritage', primarily in athletics and football, Adidas has also been the unofficial clothing brand of black American music since the early 1970s (save a small blip in the 1990s when Nike muscled in). As an international brand, its position in the market and the signals it sends out vary in different regions throughout the world. Like most sophisticated brands these days, it tailors its marketing and product to suit particular territories. But as a white, middle-class young adult living in England, these are a few general meanings and signals that Adidas carries for me:

> I am aspirational: I share the same goals and ideals as the athletes (British Olympic team), musicians (Run DMC) and fashion designers (Stella McCartney) associated with Adidas. But not David Beckham.

> I am not the mainstream: although Adidas is one of the biggest sportswear brands in the world, it is not the largest. As an individual I want to fit in generally, but not be the same as everybody else.

> I am European: Adidas is not American. Although I am not nationalistic, I am proud of my heritage, and sometimes feel anti-American.

I am ethical: some rival sports brands are notorious for using sweatshops, which I disagree with. Although I cannot be sure if Adidas has a better or worse track record, to me they seem far more responsible.

I am not a slave to work culture; I am prepared to work hard when required, but I do not subscribe to the traditions of the workplace, choosing to wear sportswear over a suit to reinforce this.

By wearing the Adidas stripes on even the most minor piece of clothing, I hope to convey the idea that I am an aspirational, freethinking and autonomous European with some sense of moral structure and a worldwide political view. It's likely that I have never actually articulated these values to the people I know in any serious conversation, nor given much thought to acting on these supposed standards, but to acquaintances and strangers alike, these are the principles I wish to associate myself with, and I can articulate them visually by endorsing this one brand. Having been exposed to the same marketing and brand positioning, a stranger passing me in the street would hopefully catch sight of my Adidas trainers, remember the brand's values and then equate them with myself.

To someone with a little less zeal for brands, this proposition may sound far-fetched. But I believe that we all build meaning into the simplest things we buy, consciously or not. The successful conveyance of ideals during an interaction varies according to the passing stranger's age range (a person roughly the same age decoding the message far better). But any reaction from the stranger, positive, negative or indifferent, is a clue to who they are. It is important to mention here that the men and women at Adidas may not hold with one single brand value I have just listed but after exposure to the brand for the 30 years of my life, I have come to project my own self-serving understanding of its values, and have allowed it to become an emblem of my unique sense of self. Openly admitting this to my circle of friends would be an embarrassing admission of superficiality. Yet each of us knows we are thinking the same thing.

On leaving school, I had vague ideas about the working life I wanted to pursue. Like the majority of young people then and now, I fancied a job in the media, and subsequently drifted into work placements for television production companies. Working behind the scenes on shows was hard, low-paid work. But this was supposedly compensated by the glamour of working with celebrities. I did indeed meet some famous people – Roger Moore, Naomi Campbell, Joan Collins – although I very much doubt they would remember me. For all the expectation built around celebrity, I was surprised how little effect meeting the likes of Robbie Williams had after the initial 'wow factor'.

Once I realised that the fringe benefits of television held no currency for me, I returned to the trusty turntables (I still owned the same pair my father had bought me) and began throwing regular parties around London, eventually establishing myself as a promoter. During the late 1990s, British club culture was in full swing. Although a relatively new phenomenon, it attracted young beautiful punters, career-minded DJs and opportunistic marketing men, the latter of which were keen to attach their brands to the intoxicating hedonism they had seen reported on the news. As a club promoter, I duly provided 'platforms' for brands to connect with young people through sponsorship deals, often tailoring events to the appeal of the brands as much as to the paying customers. I managed to slip branded beer bottles into the hands of the illustrated girls on flyers, re-name established events to incorporate a product's strapline and get every smoking punter coughing on the same brand of cigarettes for extra funding. I considered myself an expert in subtly shoe-horning corporate partners onto club flyers, and, in a curious way, having a major brand attached to an event gave it some sort of validation, the events somehow being more culturally relevant if they had the seal of approval of the marketing department of a well-known company. I would occasionally moan to other promoters that these companies were taking advantage of our newfound youth culture. But in truth I was irresistibly drawn to the power and influence these brands appeared to have. Compared to my brushes with minor celebrity, the sponsorship meetings I attended at Diesel Jeans and Coca-Cola were

15

far more exciting. Here was an opportunity to really understand a brand, meet the creators behind the scenes and find out what plans they had for the future.

The day I was called in to speak to Adidas was, as you might imagine, a jubilant one. By now I had started working in publishing, editing youth magazines (not a dissimilar trade to promoting, for one is largely managing and feeding off other people's talent). I was writing endlessly about the trends of young consumer culture, working closely with brands whose product releases I regarded as important news. To the delight of these companies, my reverence for brands would inspire me to produce features that pored over the history and culture of their products, as others would an artist or a performer. I would regularly meet with brand managers to discuss how their companies would like these 'news stories' to be written. And so the day came when I finally met the men at Adidas.

At the age of 26, I was climbing the stairs to their office, diligently attired head-to-toe in three-striped gear. My hands were sweating, my pulse racing, as if I were about to take tea with royalty. The office was an Aladdin's cave of merchandise; product posters signed by stars, limited edition trainers in glass boxes, rails upon rails of un-released clothing samples, and there, in front of a giant logo on the wall, sat the brand managers of Adidas UK. They too were resplendent in the company uniform, some items of which I would have moved mountains to obtain for myself.

As the meeting began, it became clear these men were wholly dedicated to the brand. They spoke about the culture of Adidas with a fervour that far outstripped my own, which initially I found impressive but soon became increasingly unsettling. It seemed to me that the only aspects of culture that held any relevance to them were the ones that the brand sponsored, or 'owned'. Rival brands, the people that wore them and the culture they enjoyed, were not to be spoken of in the room. Here was the unsavoury side of brand obsession, tribalism gone mad; for the first time in my life, I found myself thinking, 'It's only a pair of trainers'. Despite my obsession with these organisations, I'd never quite understood 'company men', people who devoted themselves to working for an organisation as if it were their own. Elvis Presley once explained that he preferred not to tour abroad and meet his fans, fearing he might not live up to expectations. I had built up the men at Adidas to be demi-gods over the years, and, to be fair, nothing short of a miracle would have met my expectations. But this unpleasant experience sparked a gradual turning point for me, at which I began to question the levels of attention I afforded these brands.

During the early stages of my magazine editorship, I would regularly fill with a sense of pride that these companies were interested in talking to me, showing me their unreleased merchandise, tipping me off about trends to come and, best of all, giving me things for free. Later those relationships would become strained when I couldn't give my clients enough attention, and they would begin to behave like needy children. I had to call upon the skills of a mother of 20, affording the same love and affection to competing brands like there was no other; to wear Reebok at a meeting with Nike would be a serious *faux pas*. Even to mention a competing brand in conversation would cause sparks to fly. All the while it was clear that, as advertisers, they were indirectly paying my wages and so demanded the respect they felt was their due.

The culmination of these events amounts to the person I am now; one of the most branded individuals you could meet. Almost every product that I buy is a carefully considered lifestyle choice, and it is with a confusing mixture of pride and embarrassment that I admit to appearing in books and magazines that celebrate these choices. From the tea I drink in the morning to the sheets I sleep on at night, these are consumer decisions that I make in a perpetual mission to reinforce my identity. This, you must understand, is undertaken with a certain degree of subtlety; I cannot appear to try too hard, for that would not be cool.

Cool, by its very essence, is effortless; one does not attempt cool, one *is* cool, without thinking. These emblems of self must appear to collect themselves around me in the most natural way. Like a magnet, I must naturally attract symbols that reflect positively on my character, all the while repelling those that I believe to be negative. The avoidance of certain brands is an art in itself. Discriminatory brand choices, being seen *without* brands, can be more powerful than positive choices, especially during a consumer epidemic. For example, I have studiously avoided the temptation to join the worldwide iPod tribe. iPods are produced by a brand I regard highly. They are beautifully designed and really very useful. In short they are exactly the kind of thing I should like to cherish in my pocket. But their ubiquity is such that to wear the white headphones in the street, or have it on display by my glass at the bar, would be to join a tribe so large, so ordinary and easily identifiable that my individual identity would be jeopardised.

Circumnavigating mainstream trends, however irresistible they appear to be, is an important part of a painful but worthwhile process. Better to have a less common, potentially inferior mass-produced music player in one's pocket than to follow the herd.

If I pick over the minutes of any given day, it is frightening to realise how many of my actions and choices are dictated by brand values. Even more frightening is the fact that I've actually devoted a major part of my life to mulling over the options as lifestyle choices. This is how the average morning in Boormanland pans out:

07:00   Woken by alarm on Blackberry – a device that can send and receive emails on the move. (Go-getting business people use them and I like to be thought of in the same vein.)

07:10   Put on Adidas Y3 tracksuit. (Y3 is a luxury extension of the Adidas brand, and I like to devalue it by slumming around the house in it.)

07:15   Boil water in Kenwood kettle. (Fashionable kitchens commonly have a Dualit kettle, but they're too common now, so I opted for a lower-ranking brand as an act of rebellion.)

07:20   Pour boiling water into Bodum teapot. (Nice understated German brand, or is it Swedish?)

07:21    Add Yamamotomata green tea. (Not sure if it's the best brand available but it's difficult to get hold of in London, so no danger of having a cliché in the tea cupboard.)

07:25    Switch on Roberts radio. (Quintessential English radio, one of the few things that makes me feel proud to be British when I look at it.)

07:26    Listen to BBC Radio 4 *Today* programme. (I trust the BBC, and it is impressive to quote from later in the day.)

07:40    Switch on Mac. (Entry-level iBook G4, anything more pricey would be an overstatement.)

07:45    Boot up Word. (I'm not supposed to like Microsoft, according to the newspapers, but I can't remember why. Still, everyone uses it, and so must I.)

08:00    Turn on AEG oven. (Not keen on that brand. It was left in the flat when I bought it. Must get a new one.)

08:05    Open Liebherr fridge. (Important to avoid Smeg, which, like Dualit, is a try-hard kitchen cliché.)

08:10    Make porridge with Quaker Oats. (The old boy on the box looks trustworthy enough, and I think they're organic.)

08:15    Take Solgar vitamins. (Don't know if they really work but esteem-wise, I feel better for taking them, as they cost so much more than the regular brands.)

08:16    Eat from IKEA table, cutlery and plate. (Nothing about IKEA makes me happy, but I haven't invested the necessary time/money into acquiring a better brand.)

08:25 Shower with Simple soap. (Their slogan is 'Not coloured, not perfumed, just kind'. It makes me feel pure.)

08:25 Shower with Aveda shampoo. (As a man, expensive statement cosmetics like this are a little OTT, but I'm happy to use the girlfriend's stash.)

08:30 Dry with towel from John Lewis. (Although clearly founded by a man, this brand feels like a trusty old auntie with whom I can cuddle up. Also, their slogan is 'Never knowingly undersold' which I would be proud of if I owned a store.)

08:32 Clean teeth with Colgate brush and toothpaste. (The ads always mention something about dentists preferring Colgate, so it must be a good choice.)

08:35 Apply lashings of Simple deodorant. (Unlike people who use Lynx, I'd rather not be overtly defined by my deodorant, so this is a bit more understated.)

08:40 Put on Calvin Klein underwear. (Don't really like Calvin Klein as a brand. Every man and his dog wears them. But I'd be letting myself down if I wore a no-name brand, and I can't find a better alternative.)

08:42 Put on Ralph Lauren socks. (It doesn't get more ridiculous than branded socks, but this over-attention to detail makes me feel better about myself. Should I be run over and admitted to hospital today, the nurse would be impressed by the footgear.)

08:45 Put on Levi's jeans. (Jeans brands come and go, but Levi's offers a little less faddish transience. If I need to make a special statement with a piece of clothing, I'll do it with something more classy than jeans.)

08:46    Put on Ralph Lauren polo shirt. (Such is my devotion to this brand, I'm thinking of setting up a fansite called ralphie.com. I'm sure it would be popular among city barrow boys and ironic fashion students.)

08:47    Put on Adidas trainers. (If there was one piece of clothing by which I would define a person, it would be their shoes. Hence my limited edition 1980s reissues imported from the States.)

08:48    Put on Helmut Lang jacket. (There's no overt branding for anyone to see, but I know who it's made by, and that fills me with a quiet satisfaction.)

08:55    Stuff Moleskine notebook into North Face rucksack. (Pablo Picasso and Bruce Chatwin used Moleskine apparently, which can only be good. The North Face is a bit too outdoorsy for my taste, but they make sturdy rucksacks and for once I have relented to practicality.)

09:00    Jump on Trek bike to work. (Don't know much about the brand but the cycle couriers in town seem to approve when I ride by.)

09:20    Visit newsagent for *Guardian* newspaper and Evian water. (Can't stand the people that read it, yet I seem to buy a copy almost every day. Feel healthy just looking at Evian water.)

09:21    Stare at Marlboro Lights behind shop till. (The gold-and-white box reminds me how much more contented my life would be if only I bought another pack.)

09:22    Pull out Louis Vuitton money clip. (Nice piece of luxury in my pocket. It makes me feel rich, even though I'm not.)

09:23 Pay for goods with Co-operative Bank Visa card. (The bank with an ethical policy, it tells cashiers I'm a thoughtful consumer, although joining the bank is really the only ethical thing I've ever done.)

09:26 Open office with Vivienne Westwood keyring. (I wasn't old enough to be a punk, but I'd like to think I would have been one in another life.)

09:28 Sit at IKEA desk. (Them again, must commit to an IKEA purge *asap*.)

And so on . . . Remarkably, this is only my two-and-a-half-hour morning ritual from home to work. The day's list of branded thoughts and acts, too tedious to fully outline here, is seemingly endless, and these are only the branded decisions I *choose* to make. I have omitted the brands I came into contact with on the Internet, on the radio, in the street, in the store and in the newspaper. If pressed, I'm sure I could express an opinion, a preference, an emotion towards those too.

I am not a shopaholic, I am not an extreme narcissist, but I am involved in a succession of real, evolving relationships without which I would be completely lost. These very public affairs abound until I tire of their flaws, or I catch them with an undesirable other. I'll then disown them, and pretend we never met. I've even been known to spite old flames by jumping into bed with their ardent enemies. As a child, I felt forced into these relationships in order to gain acceptance. As a teenager, I used them to create a newfound sense of identity. Moving into adulthood, brands have become a tool by which I reinforce my identity and articulate aspirations of the future me. I have grown to depend on these brands to reassure every aspect of my self-esteem.

This system of values is of course not only applied to myself but to all those around me. I pride myself on an ability to form instant personality profiles on this basis; I will make detailed judgements about perfect strangers within seconds of meeting them, as long as they have some visible branding. A woman sits opposite me on the bus, drinking from a certain coffee-chain cup, reading a certain newspaper, a certain phone ringing in a certain handbag. Assumptions are made, opinions are formed and, on some occasions, actions result accordingly. Those who do not display any branding are sources of confusion to me, and require only a brief conversation ('Lovely bag, that, where's it from?') if their identity is to be revealed. Very rarely will you come across a person without branding. In today's world it's practically impossible. However, a person with no discernable brands upon them would still project a message to me – non-conformer, hippy, alien from a distant planet – although as such he has no language with which to speak it. At this particular point in my life, I should very much like to meet an unbranded person like this.

You might assume that a person with standards as precise as mine would be scathing of those that do not wholly match my own rigorous expectations, that my circle of friends would all carry the same symbols of membership to a unique tribe. But you'd be wrong. Perversely, it is the people with the very same (or uncomfortably similar) emblems as my own that provoke knee-jerk reactions of distaste and anxiety. I call them PLUs – People Like Us – and they are, to my continuing displeasure, all around me. They wear my jeans, they ride my bike, they read my paper. Quietly, I feel they are stealing my hard-won identity from under my nose. Even worse, when they pass me in the street, they seem to smile as though they recognise this blatant theft of my identity. Why on earth would one person wave hello to another if they should happen to drive past in the same model of car? Who would be so shallow as to make detailed assumptions about strangers based on the labels they wear? Oh, that's me.

Finally, it has dawned on me that this value system by which I judge myself and those around me is entirely hollow. Throughout my life, I have carved out a sense of self through a series of artificial relationships with brands, and while this has afforded me acceptance in peer groups and opportunities in my career, it is becoming apparent that it has not provided me with any sustainable form of contentment. I should be happy. I live a comfortable life with my partner whom I love very much. Both my parents are alive and remain happily married, giving me a vital base of stability. I have a wide circle of friends, I have an interesting career, and it goes without saying that I possess a lot of nice, branded things. I should be happy. Instead I feel empty, cheated and disillusioned.

At the age of 30, I have come to understand that these relationships, into which I pour so much energy, are a complete sham. I am beginning to wake from a long daydream. Semi-conscious of my predicament, I have been sleepwalking through life, only occasionally waking to consider why, after devoting so much attention to these relationships, I am not as happy as I thought I'd be. With every considered purchase, I have attempted to make myself more like me, assuming this would bring fulfilment to my life. With an encroaching sense of numbed dissatisfaction, the reality is only just becoming clear; with every new emblem of identity I add to my collection, I lose a piece of myself to the brands. They cannot reciprocate the love I give. They cannot transport me to the places I'm promised exist. I am not, nor will I ever be remotely similar to the people that appear in their ads. It is a lie, a lie I have believed in for too long.

Reading this confession, you must feel that I am one of the most shallow, judgemental people one could ever meet. But I promise you, I am truly a decent individual. I wouldn't refuse to open a door for you if you had the 'wrong' mobile phone, and I wouldn't consider not being your friend because you read the 'wrong' newspaper. I might think slightly less of you, but I would most likely never tell you so. Please believe me, I don't know how I allowed myself to become so superficial. All I ever wanted was to love and be loved, and these damn labels seemed to be the best way of achieving it. Only now, after 30 years of buying myself back from brands, is it becoming clear: I literally have no idea who I am.

# 10 march

My great epiphany came to me one morning as I was sitting on the toilet at home. My partner Juliet had left a dog-eared copy of John Berger's *Ways of Seeing* lying on the cistern. In no great hurry to get into work, I started to thumb through it:

> It is true that in publicity one brand of manufacture, one firm, competes with another; but it is also true that every publicity image confirms and enhances every other. Publicity is not merely an assembly of competing messages: it is a language itself, which is always being used to make the same general proposal . . . It proposes to each of us that we transform ourselves, or our lives, by buying something more. This more, it proposes, will make us in some way richer – even though we will become poorer by having spent our money . . . The purpose of publicity is to make the spectator marginally dissatisfied with his present way of life. Not with the way of life of society, but with his own within it. It suggests that if he buys what it is offering, his life will become better. It offers him an improved alternative to what he is . . . All publicity works upon anxiety. The sum of everything is money, to get money is to overcome anxiety. Alternatively, the anxiety on which publicity plays is the fear that having nothing, you will be nothing.[1]

Thus came the epiphany, crashing around my ears. For the first time, I became aware of the subconscious emotions that I experience when I see an advert for a brand. A decadent, beautiful woman stares at me from a billboard and the glamour of the image is exciting. There follows a crushing sense of inferiority; I am not as appealing as her, and therefore less satisfied in life. I could never be part of her world, unless I make amends. This anguish turns to dogged resolve; I will do whatever it takes to become as happy as her, I will buy the same things that she has. If I cannot afford her lifestyle, I will work harder so that one day I can. Perversely, the anxiety gives me a sense of hope; it sets me on the road to self-betterment. But the goal towards which I must stretch my aspiration moves ever further away. I must keep up.

I see so many adverts during the day, and experience this rush of emotion so often, that my constant state of anxiety has become normal, something which I have never questioned, until now. The anxiety is seductive because it offers a vision of a more likeable me; likeable to others, but mostly to myself. I realised that I was turning to the very source of this anxiety as an antidote to the anguish it caused; shopping for brands as leisure. Idolising and publicising brands at work; stroking the hand that kills me. People who habitually behave in a way that they know to be self-destructive are called addicts. I am a brand addict.

'What are you up to in there?' asked Juliet knocking at the door.

'Er, just reading . . . out in a second.'

'Well, hurry up, there's someone from Levi's wanting to speak to you on the phone.'

It is an uncomfortable experience, coming to terms with an epiphany that contradicts your system of belief. I believed that buying and using things with conspicuous labels attached to them would give me satisfaction; it was one of the primary motives in life, a reason to get up and go to work, to work as hard as I could to earn as much money as I could, so I might have the material things that I wanted. Disillusionment came first. In the days that followed, I would stare at the panorama of my environment, the consumer paradise that is Central London and see only one agenda: consumption for happiness. Now I realised that I, along with the tens of thousands of other shoppers on Oxford Street, had been told a lie. But by whom? Or perhaps we were all complicit in denial; all of us aware that this consumption was self-destructive but was too convenient to give up. This new sense of self-awareness, a kind of existentialist angst, was both confusing and frightening.

Throughout this period, my level of consumption remained unchanged. I would visit Selfridges department store to gaze at the shoe collections, then offset the guilty feelings by purchasing a copy of the anti-consumerist magazine *Adbusters*. Conscious of the hypocrisy, I would return home to charge myself with militancy by listening to

Gil Scott-Heron's 'The Revolution Will Not Be Televised' on my expensive audiophile stereo system.

Disillusion turned into denial; had I along with the rest of the Western world really become a brand-obsessed consumer madman? Were we not simply enjoying the fruits of capitalism, something which millions around the world were not fortunate enough to enjoy themselves? This rationale held purchase for a while. But I soon realised I was simply giving myself more reasons to shop.

The helplessness finally spilled over into anger. I was angry with myself for being so shallow; that I had wasted so much time and money pursuing such empty goals; I was angry at 'the system', whatever that was, for peddling the agenda of consumption everywhere I turned.

Whichever emotional state I happened to be in, I would express it by buying things. I would cheer myself up with a new pair of trainers when disillusioned, wear ever more garish brands when I was in denial, and bought copies of Naomi Klein's *No Logo* and the 1960s anti-advertising bible *The Hidden Persuaders* when I felt angry. The only way I knew how to express myself was through consumption.

I tried moderation for a few months, limiting myself to a couple of frivolous purchases every few weeks alongside the regular food and cleaning supplies. But shopping was only a small part of my brand addiction; it was the meaning and the status that these brands held that I valued so highly. Some people play happy music when they want to cheer themselves up, or eat a nice meal when they want to feel special. For these occasions, I used my brands.

As any addict knows, moderation is very rarely a viable solution to a problem. Each time I opened a magazine, I saw new opportunities to buy things that would make me happier. Each time I turned on the television, I saw people surrounded by those same things, and they did indeed look much happier than me. Each time I left the flat, there were shops nearby with tantalising window displays, inches from my grasp. Moderation felt like impossibility when the culture around me was forever chipping away at my resolve. How exactly does one moderate a habit of buying things that one doesn't need? To imagine a life without my Adidas, Nokia and Apple was to imagine a grey and drab life, disconnected from the Zeitgeist, from my social network, from my hard-won status; ultimately, disconnected from happiness.

This fear was not altogether unfamiliar. At the age of 23, I realised that I had developed a problem with alcohol. Working in clubs, socialising at parties and just living in London, surely one of the booziest of cities, my drinking had finally caught up with me and I checked myself into an alcohol advisory clinic. One of the first steps, my counsellor told me, was not simply to admit to myself that I had a drink problem, but to explain the problem to the important people around me. Seven years later, I am going to have to make another declaration, only this one sounds far more preposterous than before:

I am addicted to brands.

I am dependent on them to make me happy, to prop up my self-esteem.

I am going to give up brands in the same way that I did alcohol.

For the time being at least.

On the day I gave up drinking, I had poured my supply of booze down the drain and destroyed the empty bottles and cans in an iconic gesture to remember each time I was tempted to drink again. This new amnesty would require a similarly grand gesture, to prove to myself and others that I was serious.

'You're going to take every branded thing out of the flat and destroy it, are you?' asked Juliet, when I first explained the plan.

'I can't see any other way,' I said. 'I'm serious, this is a problem that I have to deal with.'

'You can't put it into storage, until you get better?'

'No, I've got to do something drastic, make a statement. Smash it all up or burn it.'

'You're going to burn all your stuff?'

I have a habit of doing this – arguing myself into a corner and trumping the situation by making a ridiculous pledge.

'Yes, that's right,' I said. 'I'm going to burn the lot. That's settled then'.

'You do what you want, Neil, but just *your* stuff,' said Juliet. 'My brands are staying right here where they belong.'

# 16 march

*Brand* is a word that has come to be so ubiquitous in our lives that we often use it without understanding what it really means. We buy things that are 'brand new'. We express our preferences for things as 'my brand of . . .'. Often we refer to a product or a service not by the name of the thing, but the name of the brand that is attached. In business meetings I hear people talk about brand value, brand personality, brand extension, without really understanding what these terms mean. When protesters say that they are anti-brand, are they anti the company or the brand that it owns, or the science of branding or capitalism in general?

Having lived with brands all of my life, I wonder exactly how and when they came into being? How exactly do these companies manage to make their logos mean so much – after all they are just the logos of companies that make products and services. To understand where my obsession originated from, I needed to know how brands came into being. Surely there was a time when the buying and selling of things meant a lot less? I have enrolled at the British Library to find out. Throughout my short academic life, I moved mountains to ensure that I spent as little time as possible reading books, preferring to work at part-time jobs so that I could buy more at the shopping centre. Now I find myself willingly entering a place of learning, researching the history of branding. This in itself is a giant leap for me.

It's hard to imagine a single action we undertake in our daily lives that does not involve brands in some way, whether we care about them or not. They are in the home, at the office, wherever we choose to relax; they accompany us in public and during the moments when we are at our most private. They are attached to all the things that make our lives easier to live; the benefits of living in a modern, industrialised society. To imagine a life without cars, computers, nice food, decent shops and services, is to imagine a life in the Dark Ages. Cultures without access to these things are considered undeveloped.

Brands are part of the fabric of daily life. Each day, we consume them in their hundreds. They help us to make quick decisions, speeding the pace of life. Brands are central to the Zeitgeist; if one wishes to keep up-to-date or be in the know, it is helpful to talk about them. People who take up new brand trends ahead of the pack are called *opinion formers* in the marketing industry. Those who are slow to accept new products are referred to as *late adopters*. Brands have become attached to so many different things (goods, services, places, even people) that the distinctions between brand, product and producer have become blurred.

## PRODUCT
A product is something of monetary value, which you buy and use.

## BRAND
A brand is the name, term, sign or symbol that determines the origin of the product it is attached to.

## COMPANY
The organisation that produces the product and owns the rights to the use of the brand.

In the most basic terms, companies that trade products and services use brands to identify and promote their goods. Wherever there is competition in the market place there is branding, that is to say whenever two or more products exist that fulfil the same need, manufacturers, retailers and consumers need brands to identify their origin. Where there is choice, there is branding.

Essentially, a brand is a promise; a promise of protection to both the consumer and the manufacturer. To us, the consumer, they make a promise that the product is authentic in origin and therefore distinguishable from similar products on the market. Based on this promise, we can hold the manufacturer responsible for the quality of the product, and through experience we can make quick decisions on this basis when we are faced with a variety of choices on the store shelf. In other words, brands help us reduce the risks involved in buying a product. Without the promise of authenticity, we cannot be sure if a product will perform to our expectations, be worth the price we pay for it, or if the product will cause us harm or embarrassment. In buying a branded product, we accept the manufacturer's promise that these risks will be avoided.

For the manufacturer, branding is an identifying mark of ownership that acts as a safeguard of investment. A firm that spends its assets on developing and refining the quality of a product can protect its investment by registering ownership via trademarks, patents and packaging designs. By maintaining the quality of a product and promoting its virtues through advertising and marketing, a firm can use its brand to create an expectation of quality and prestige, which ultimately justifies the product's price. Through clear branding, satisfied customers can easily identify the product and choose to consume it again.

On a basic day-to-day level, this system allows us to make a large number of safe decisions that can be undertaken almost on autopilot. Without brands, our lives would certainly be much slower. Consider the following two interactions with your local shopkeeper, and the time each would take, in worlds with and without brands:

**WITHOUT BRANDS**
I would like to buy some mint-flavoured chewing gum. The flavour has to last a long time, and it has to be sugar-free. Also, I don't really want to spend more than 50p. Which type would you recommend?

**WITH BRANDS**
Give me a pack of Extra.

Beyond the physical logo and package designs, brands are largely intangible, existing in the minds of the producer and consumer. The mental image of a brand is built up from layers of experiences connected with the product. According to the branding guru Kevin Lane Keller, 'it is necessary to teach consumers "who" the product is – by giving it a name – as well as "what" the product does and "why" the consumers should care.'[2] Brands are mental structures that help us to organise our knowledge and feelings towards a product. Ultimately, for the producer, branding must enable consumers to perceive differences among competing brands; the strength of that perceived difference gives value to the brand.

Some products that compete against each other on the shelf are so similar it really is only their brands that separate them. Take bottled water, for instance. With hundreds of different brands of water on the market, we are faced with a dilemma of choice. By and large, all bottled water tastes the same, quenches thirst in the same way and barring the odd mineral trace is made of the same stuff. The only discernable difference is the source of the water and the manufacturer who bottled it. When ordering drinks at a bar or in a restaurant, we do not ask to see the water menu. Unless you are particularly patriotic in your spending habits (buying French Evian over Belgian Spa) or are aware of the magical purity of one particular water region, the only possible reason one would buy a certain 'type' of water over another is connected with one's perception of the brand. Is the brand good value for money? Does it guarantee good quality? Is it a brand that we are happy to be seen in public with? The choice has almost nothing to do with the product itself, rather the identity and associations we have made around the bottle it comes in. These associations, or brand attributes, are a combination of personal experiences and memorised perceptions that have been built up through exposure to advertising and marketing. That we choose to pay for bottled water when we could drink it from the tap for free, at the point of consumption at least, is a testament to our belief in the promises that the brands like Evian make.

Beyond logos and packages, a modern brand identifies much more than the products and services to which it is attached. Brands embody a whole range of associations, meanings and emotional triggers that collectively make a product more attractive and saleable to the consumer. A brand identifies the people working for the company and the spirit that sustains it (brand image). A brand may also embody the 'vision' of the company and seek to establish values and attitudes that are consistent with the target audience of the products it sells (brand positioning). It is through these ideals that a brand will begin to connect with the consumer, beyond the practicalities of *need* to the aspirations of *want*. Virgin boss Richard Branson is clear on the vision that a successful brand must embody:

A product or service only becomes a brand when it is imbued with profound values that translate into fact and feeling that employees can project and customers can embrace . . . It is feelings – and feelings alone – that account for the success of the Virgin brand . . .[3]

To the consumer, a brand must project identity and position in the market, together with a set of appealing values and core beliefs – the brand promise. To the producer, the brand is central to the decisions it makes and the values it holds, thus enabling employees to deliver that promise.

When I buy a branded product myself, I very rarely choose on the basis of craftsmanship or value for money. Rather, I choose a brand that speaks to me best. Sometimes, the product becomes supplemental to the brand that it is attached to. Although the size of my shoe collection would most likely last me a lifetime, I continue to buy new pairs simply to associate myself with the brand. The shoes cease to be objects with which to protect my feet, and become devices from which I can display my affiliation to the values that Richard Branson talks about. For reasons that I do not understand, I would much prefer to fly Virgin as opposed to British Airways.

# COUNTDOWN

## 17 march 2006

## 186 days to bonfire

In 15th-century Italy, priests would regularly lead public burnings in local squares to destroy mirrors, fine clothing and cosmetics; sinful items of vanity in their day. Six months from today, I am going to hold my own bonfire of the vanities. Every day that passes is another day towards freedom (or one less day of comfort, depending on the swings of my mood). I have nearly 200 days in which to wind down my conspicuous consumption and carve out a brand-free lifestyle, which in practical terms seems realistic.

When I look around my flat, I suddenly recognise that my spending on branded luxuries has been out of control for some time. Clothes, gadgets and furniture are here in large volume. But also branded boxes, stickers, swing tags, all sorts of trophy ephemera that seem to have an enormous personal value to me. I have always collected things, from Star Wars toys when I was a boy to records when I was a teenager, but I only ever considered it a hobby, nothing more sinister than that. All this branded stuff piled into corners of the flat represents much more than a hobby though. The process of searching, selecting, acquiring, consuming and displaying of brands occupies my thoughts, all the time. I am constantly on the lookout for new things to buy. But these things must fit a bewildering array of criteria: Where does it come from? What does it mean? What type of person uses it? Is it me? How will I feel when I use it? What will other people think? Having met my stiff guidelines, the product is added to my mental shopping list, and I have to buy it, as soon as I have the time and money. I begin to feel anxious if the period between wanting and having goes on too long. I see something and I have to have it right away. There can be no waiting for the sales, or shopping around to see if there's a cheaper alternative.

Is this an addiction to shopping? An obsession with status? An unhealthy admiration for brands? I have a feeling it is all three.

## -182 days

How does a person announce to his friends that he is addicted to branded consumerism and will shortly be burning the majority of his worldly goods? Again, the situation drew parallels with my giving up drinking; shortly after I attended my first alcoholics' meeting I made a series of announcements to friends, family and colleagues that my consumption had grown beyond my control and that I was attempting to give up. Reaching out to these people, I told them that, even though the road to recovery was going to be tough, I knew I could count on them all for support. I couldn't have been more wrong.

In declaring that my level of drinking was becoming a negative part of my life, I was also casting aspersions on the drinking habits of many of the people around me, who were drinking at much the same level. First they would tell me not to be so stupid, I didn't have a problem, cheer up and have a drink. Then once they realised I was serious, the disbelief turned to scepticism; even if I did have a problem, I'd never be able to give up, me of all people. Finally, it morphed into rejection: I was no fun to be around; I was taking things too seriously; I made them feel uncomfortable. Invitations began to dry up. The support I was counting on soon evaporated among certain circles of friends and a distance began to grow between us; we would continue to work and sometimes socialise together but there was a distinct feeling that I had cancelled my membership to some sort of club, a dissenting voice against fun.

At least alcoholism is taken seriously. This new, self-diagnosed condition, a kind of obsessive branding disorder, is going to be a tough concept to sell. The declaration, which I start to make to friends as they cross my path, is met with the same, understandable scepticism:

'You of all people will never see it through.'

'What are you going to wear instead, a sack?'

'You can't live brand-free, it's impossible.'

'You're better off staging the fire with dummy gear and hiding the good stuff away.'

'Can I have your Helmut Lang jacket before you destroy it?'

The general reaction is well-meaning bemusement at best, and knee-jerk anger at worst. There is also some dispute as to what constitutes a brand in the first place – 'Everything is a brand, Neil. What are you going to do, live in a cave naked and starve?'

One slightly more open-minded couple – he is a journalist, she is a documentary researcher – begin to pick holes in the idea over dinner, and I start to panic that I've set myself an impossible task, a futile gesture at best.

'What do you classify as a brand then?'

'Well, anything with a well-known label attached to it.'

'What about supermarket own-brands? A can of Tesco Value Beans may not be as fancy as Heinz or some organic variety, but it's a brand all the same.'

'Technically you're right, but there isn't really any aspiration attached to buying own-brand products, is there?'

'What about buying non-branded things from a branded shop?'

'Uh, well, I haven't thought about branded shops just yet . . . I'll have to make some sort of ground rules.'

These two are among the most branded couple I know. He was a big Prada Sport man when I first met him, and he still has an eye for the sports end of the luxury brands market (Comme des Garçons, Missoni, Evisu). You have to look hard, or ask, for the logos, but when you do, it is always quietly confident, the right side of bling.

She used to be purely mass-market, but since getting together with him, she's been banned from the high street and now it's all Marc Jacobs and Vivienne Westwood. A bit try-hard but she wears it well. Do I like them that little bit more for continually impressing me with their quietly ostentatious branding? Probably, yes. Being with people like this makes me feel better about myself, as though some of the goodness of their brands rubs off on to me. Not sure about his Nike sandals though.

It is clear that I must set out stiff criteria for this task, if only to halt the endless debate as to what constitutes a brand.

Over the next week, I decide upon the goals that I must achieve and the ground rules that I must follow:

**THE GOALS**
1. Replace the branded products in my life with non-branded equivalents.
2. Stop using branded products.
3. Burn all branded goods.
4. Live brand-free for six months.

**THE RULES**
Products permitted for consumption:
- Any product produced by small-scale/local/independent traders that carries no visible branding.

Products not permitted for consumption:
- All branded goods, including supermarket 'own-labels'.
- Chain stores that use discreet branding, such as Muji or Uniqlo.
- Products that have had the labels/logos removed.

**EXCEPTIONS**
Where there is absolutely no non-branded alternative to essential utility services, an ethical replacement must be found.

## -180 days

My writing agent suggests that I publish this diary as a book. I feel slightly uneasy that strangers might potentially read these rather shallow declarations of mine. But a public record of the events moves the whole thing out of my head into the real world; this is not some paranoid delusion in my over-marketed head, but a real life event. Once the declaration has been made public, I really cannot go back on my word. Juliet jokes that a book deal would help me to recoup some money, should I wish to buy my branded self back after the bonfire.

I duly start a blog, an online version of the diary that will record the de-branding events as they unfold (and help in the search for a book deal). The first blog post is a statement of my intent, which I email to my old paymasters in journalism, fashion and advertising, together with several hundred marketing websites and anti-corporate blogs. I wonder if anyone will care to read it?

## -178 days

Saturday. Shopping day. There is nothing I like more than to spend a sunny afternoon like today, wandering around the shops in Central London, looking for things to buy. The level of expectation I reach before buying these brands is ferocious, as if something desperately important is missing from my life, something that must be acquired immediately, which will make me feel more relaxed, more comfortable, more confident about myself. Juliet likes to go shopping too, but the emotional stakes are nowhere near as high for her. I have to subdue my child-like enthusiasm when shopping with a partner, which negates the primary motive for going in the first place, so I will often peel off mid-shop to go foraging on my own.

I put on a smart outfit – dressing for the shops is essential, but nothing too showy, you don't want to look like a tourist – then march into town and head straight for the shop in question; this is shopping with a purpose. I usually straighten my posture and take in a good, deep breath as I enter the shop; I look the assistant in the eye and say hello with a certain confidence that lets them know that I mean business, I know what I'm doing and I don't need any help. I'm in full hunter-gatherer mode now, scanning the store for the item in mind. I am usually peaking as I grab said item and walk to the till; this thing is going to be mine and I'm going to be so much happier for it.

As the assistant taps the details into the till, I pull out my money clip and prepare to pay. The euphoria dips from here on in. I start to dwell on the price. Do I really need the item? Is it really me? A sense of dread washes over me as I realise I'll likely be told off by Juliet for bringing yet more stuff back to the flat. But then the assistant neatly wraps and bags the goods – I like it when they seal the bag with a sticker, it stops you peeking at the things before you get home and raises the expectations again – and my mood bounces back as I stroll past the store staff, out of the shop and into the street. That's right, I made a purchase, I can afford it, I'm worth it. This little purchase? Oh, nothing really, I just popped out for a loaf of bread, and, well, you know how it is.

I'm actually swinging the bag as I walk, whistling to myself and keeping an eye on passing shoppers to see if they are seeing me with my big shiny bag of brand new stuff. Nothing feels better than walking home with expensive shopping bags on each arm; I'm on top of the world.

It's only when I return home that the dopamine levels begin to dip again. Unpacking the goods, I quickly discard the packaging and bags so that Juliet won't see that I've bought more stuff when she comes home. I try on/out/pore over the items for a while, waiting for them to work their magic, to make me feel more whole than before. After all, that's what I thought they would do, make me feel more like me. I begin to feel sheepish, sheepish about the money I've just spent, that I got so overexcited about buying this stupid stuff, sheepish that it's just going to be thrown onto the pile of forgotten expensive things in the spare room within days. The crazy thing is, I knew this would happen. I've known for ages that I don't need any more stuff, that it doesn't make me happy, and that I should be saving my money for something more worthwhile. I'm not sure how this happens. I just seem to go into a trance.

It is only now, as I take the initial steps to disconnect from these brands, that I realise the extent to which they occupy my life. I honestly do think about brands all the time; I seem to be hyper-receptive to their calling. In the cinema I notice that George Clooney is using the same Blackberry as me and I feel pleased that we share the same taste in mobile technology. Although I claim never to watch much television, I am usually familiar with every advert that airs on the main channels. Once, a market researcher cold-called me at home, to ask if I would complete a survey on music in TV adverts; they played the jingle and I had to say which brand it belonged to. I got 18 out of 20; the woman said that was the best score she'd had all week. I actually felt quite proud, and told my then-partner. She wasn't as impressed as I hoped she'd be.

In the street, I observe every passer-by and the brands that they carry. In the distance, it's difficult to see exactly what logo is embroidered on the chest of an oncoming male, but I will not avert my gaze until the logo comes into view and I register just what it is. It is fair to say, I am not one of those people that stares at the pavement in the street (unless guerrilla marketers have sprayed some brand message on the concrete). When I visit people's houses, my branded eye is continually scanning for information, like Arnold Schwarzenegger in *The Terminator*, registering marks of good and bad taste.

## -176 days

Sitting on a crowded bus today, I spotted the most beautiful woman amongst the crowd. Huge dark eyes, the most delicate lips, and rich thick hair; if I were single, perhaps I'd have been attempting some sort of breezy, nonchalant come-on (or thinking about it at the very least). As it is, I am very much not single, so I just sit back and admire her from afar. Some people, astonishingly, need exert no effort in radiating beauty, they just are. A faint pout of the lips, a flick of the head, a twitch of the nose. Suddenly, the bus pulls into a stop and the deck clears, leaving only her in full view. Disaster. She's wearing Pumas; to me the all-time most rubbish sneaker brand money can buy. The brand that says you'd like to be cool, you'd like to be adventurous, but you've neither the confidence nor the flair to see it through. Think Puma, think James Blunt, think Saturday nights at Pizza Express, think *Friends* DVD box set. The woman's spellbinding beauty evaporates and, deflated, I turn to the window to stare at something less boring instead.

Destroying my emblems of status is only part of the journey towards a brand-free existence. No less daunting or unsettling is my coming to terms with the way I judge those around me. I wonder, how many personal relationships of mine are built on these shaky foundations? More to the point, how many meaningful encounters have I denied myself on the basis of branded footwear of all things? I'd like to think that I was bigger than that. But on days like today, I can't be sure.

## -170 days

My research on the history of branding is throwing up some interesting parallels with modern life. Where we willingly emblazon logos on our chests today, early man was forced to bear marks as a sign of ownership or character. To early European slave traders, a burnt mark on the skin legally dehumanised a person to mere livestock, owned and sold for arbitrary use and abuse. The term *brand* originates from the ancient Norse term *brandr*, meaning literally 'to burn'. The Ancient Greeks marked their slaves with the letter *delta*; the Romans used a branded *F* as a permanent criminal record on fugitive slaves, commonly on the arm, neck or calf. Convicted criminals destined to battle in the gladiatorial arenas were branded on the forehead. The Anglo-Saxons later adopted the practice, and vagabonds, gypsies and brawlers were branded with a large *V* on the breast. Branding was abolished in England in 1829, except in the case of army deserters, who were marked with the letter *D*, by tattooing with ink or gunpowder. Notoriously bad soldiers were also branded with *BC* (indicating bad character), a practice only phased out in 1879. Accounts of modern human branding are confined to the initiation rights of US street gangs and underground fetish groups. However, it has been widely reported that when US President George W Bush was a member of the Delta Kappa Epsilon chapter at Yale, it introduced a practice in which fraternity pledges stripped to be branded on the buttocks with a hot coat hanger bent into the shape of a capital delta.[4]

Of course it was not only people who were branded. Logos began to appear on manufactured goods during the reigns of the Greek and

44

Roman empires. Clay potters were among the first, marking their goods with crosses or symbols of fish at the request of traders who were distributing their goods to increasingly far-flung territories, beyond the local reputation of the craftsmen. Counterfeiting was a problem even in 50 BC as inferior factories attempted to pass off their produce with identical marks, eventually forcing Roman law to recognise tradesmen's marks as legitimate tools of business. With the fall of the Roman Empire, tradesmanship receded in sophistication and geographical scale, and thus trademarks continued at a local scale. Medieval craftsmen began to brand furniture, porcelain and paper in order to identify origin and quality for the patronage of monarchs, who increasingly sought to enforce monopolies via makers' guilds. As the scale of trade increased, producers needed to be held accountable for their goods and in the 13th century, breadmakers were required to stamp each loaf of bread with a maker's mark.

Laws enforcing the hallmarking of silverware were passed and rigidly enforced in the 17th century to allow customers greater confidence in the product. The case of *Southern v. How* (England, 1618) is regarded as one of the earliest court cases of trademark infringement, whereby the manufacturer of high-quality cloth sued an inferior competitor who used the marks reserved for a quality that was not being met. In Europe and North America, all manner of goods from tobacco to medicine were being traded overseas, and with competition among producers increasing, product branding took on a new level of sophistication. Portraits of the manufacturers began to appear alongside the company mark, and the products themselves began to inherit their own names and identities, aside from that of the company that made them.

Modern branding, it seems, was born in the 19th century during the manufacturing and consumer boom of the Industrial Revolution. New industry drew rural populations to the cities in search of work, away from their largely self-sufficient lifestyles. The newly created workforce was unfamiliar and wary of mass produce and so turned to the promises of quality that began appearing alongside branding on packaged goods. Improvements in production processes made it possible for manufacturers to produce high volumes of goods in sophisticated individual packages that allowed greater scope for lavish branding, essential in the increasingly competitive marketplace. Improvements in transportation allowed greater reliability in international trade and the reputation of some manufacturers began to spread around the globe. Around 1850, the soap and candlemaker Proctor & Gamble noticed that dockhands were branding crates of their candles with a star as a means of identification. Traders who relied on the star as a symbol of quality soon began to refuse shipments of candles without the mark and so the company began to formally mark their packaging with the symbol and call the product 'Star'.

Unprecedented sums of money were now being invested in new production facilities, and with the continued rise of counterfeiting, industrialists began to demand some form of legal protection for their investments. Thus the United States passed federal trademark legislation in 1870 with Europe quickly following suit. In the same year, Averill Paints received the first modern US trademark and, in 1876, the Bass Brewery red triangle became the first trademark ever registered in the UK. By 1890, most countries had passed trademark acts, establishing brand names and logos as legally protectable assets.

The average Western family was becoming more affluent. Steady work in the factories created disposable income and, away from the labours of the field, leisure time was also increasing. The notion of shopping as leisure began to develop, and with it came new demands on manufacturers to produce non-essential products (to which they duly responded). Newly opened department stores and mail-order catalogues were filled with multiple choices of seemingly identical products, and the consumer was now faced with a real dilemma of choice. Many of the new brands of packaged goods were unfamiliar to a customer base that had traditionally bought local goods, and it became necessary for manufacturers to convince the buying public that the new non-local brands were names that they could trust. Thus the practice of product marketing was born.

In 1877 in New York, J Walter Thompson founded what is arguably the world's first advertising agency, promising to build the reputation of any business that was committed to spending assets on promotion. In a booklet published in 1911 called 'Things To Know About Trademarks',

Thompson outlined the discipline of trademarking in the first known commercial explanation of what we now know as branding:

> The trademark is the connecting link between the manufacturer and the ultimate consumer. By use of trademarks, widely advertised, manufacturers are able to build up a trade that comes to mean a certain standard of quality, workmanship and material.[5]

Thompson personally bullied newspaper and magazine publishers to print product advertisements alongside their editorial. Print media had until then subsisted on newsstand and subscription revenue but Thompson saw their huge audiences as the perfect vehicle for commercial advertising, the practice of which he evangelised as an essential aspect of modern commerce:

> Advertising capitalises on human faith, and faith is a mental impression. It is a quality of the human mind that the most profound impressions are made by things – not by abstract ideas. Consequently, successful advertising must be tied hard and fast to a name (or trademark) and this trademark must be distinctive, and not easy to confuse with something else.

With new platforms from which to advertise, branded products soon became household names in domestic and international markets. Having established basic recognition and trust in their trademarks, companies began to specialise in more sophisticated aspects of marketing in the face of ever increasing competition. Design professionals were enlisted to create corporate and product identities, salesmen were carefully trained to understand the market of their products and advertising creatives began to use more persuasive slogans, encouraging customers towards brand loyalty. A 1912 advert for Woodbury's Facial Soap featured a man seductively caressing a woman's arm and kissing her hand underneath the slogan 'A skin you love to touch'. The overt sexuality triggered a hostile reaction from some readers of *Ladies' Home Journal*, who promptly cancelled their subscriptions.

But the campaign launched one of the most successful selling techniques of all time.

By the early 1920s, radio networks were springing up in Europe, the BBC being the first, broadcasting to London in 1922. In the same year, WEAF in New York broadcast the first radio commercial. The new medium was pounced upon by the advertising industry, and by 1929 radio accounted for $10.5 million in advertising in the US.

Manufacturers and their advertising agencies began to commission market research studies and employ behavioural psychologists to understand their customers better and turn need into product. John B Watson, who worked at J W Thompson in the 1920s, claimed that human beings are capable of three basic emotions – love, fear and rage. Thus, advertising campaigns began to capitalise on notions of status, sexuality and insecurity. Sigmund Freud's nephew, Edward Bernays, an early pioneer of industrial public relations, applied principles of psychology to clients such as American Tobacco, General Electric and Dodge Motors. In his influential 1928 book *Propaganda*, he argued that it was right and proper to use sophisticated techniques of persuasion in both commerce and government:

> The conscious and intelligent manipulation of the organised habits and opinions of the masses is an important element in democratic society . . . We are governed, our minds are moulded, our tastes formed, our ideas suggested, largely by men we have never heard of. This is a logical result of the way in which our democratic society is organised.[6]

Looking around my flat, it is clear to me that I have spent thousands of hard-earned pounds on things which, at the time of purchase, appeared to be things that I desperately needed, but were in fact of very little use at all. Some of these items – a leather Roberts radio, an oversized Prada keyring – are proudly displayed on shelves like trophies I once felt rather proud to own. To gaze at them now makes me feel rather ashamed. How exactly did I come to decide that I *needed* an £80 ashtray from Heal's?

Pick a brand, any brand, and I bet you I can give you an informed opinion on its values, a memory of its advertising campaigns, and its status among other brands and within society as a whole. I say 'informed', even though I've probably not purchased or indeed shown an interest in many of them before.

Here's a mini-test. I'll think of half a dozen brands starting with the letter *B* – not *A* because that takes in Apple and Adidas and you'll be sick of hearing about those by the end of the book – and give you my first thoughts and impressions.

### BENSON & HEDGES

*Council estates, surreal adverts, Brut Aftershave, smoking drugs*

Gold packets of fags that used to have baffling but very cool adverts on billboards next to my school. B&H and Silk Cut were the Coke and Pepsi of cigarettes, but then somehow they both became a bit common, and now everyone smokes Marlboro instead. I think of B&H during my childhood and I think of men with moustaches and gold sovereign rings who could have been porn stars on the quiet, which was quite cool. I think of B&H now and I think of dodgy teenagers in hoodies in newsagents asking for 'ten Benson and a pack of Kingsize Rizla'. You always see packs of Bensons on the dashboards of builders' vans; if a friend of mine pulled out a packet, I'd be surprised, and interested to know why they were smoking them. Some ironic reference to the 1980s perhaps?

### BP

*Green logo, pollution, Ginsters pasties, naked women*

Their logo has changed from a shield to a green and yellow flower, which makes the company look a bit more environmentally friendly, even though it remains the world's second largest oil supplier, which isn't green at all. When I was younger, I used to feel proud seeing the BP logo when I was travelling abroad, flying the flag for Britain and all that.

BP stations are the home of road-trip junk-food brands like Pringles and Ginsters pasties. As a teenager, BP became synonymous in my mind with porn; the local 24-hour BP being en route from the pub to the parental home, where I would drunkenly order one of their '3 for 2' value packs of previously unsold issues of *Hustler* and *Leg Show*; not a core brand value for the company, I would imagine.

## BBC
*The truth, posh headmasters, Roberts radios, imperialism*
*(in a positive, benevolent way)*

When I think of the BBC, I feel secure, enlightened, proud, protective and grateful. Like BP, I used to feel proud that people abroad had heard of the BBC, but never personally watched it, because ITV always had the best US imports like *Knight Rider* and *The A-Team*; the Beeb was always a bit dusty and establishment. Not enough guns and car chases for my liking. But now I've grown up, I understand; the BBC is an uncommercialised marvel that I cherish every day, suspecting that it will eventually fall foul of the government and the commercial sector. Ignoring the rubbish they export as entertainment, the BBC's news, music and digital services enrich my life on a daily basis.

## BACARDI
*Girls in short skirts, the bat logo, luminous orange, vomit*

Bacardi has always been for girls. As the oldest-looking 16-year-old, I was always landed the task of buying alcohol from disreputable off-licences, and the girls always asked for a quarter bottle of Bacardi (Tennent's Super Lager for boys). Since the company extended the brand to sickly sweet alcopops, I think of badly dressed drunken girls swaggering down the high street at night slurring old Oasis hits at the top of their voices. And the generic Latino adverts that do their best to remind us that Bacardi is from somewhere near Cuba. Not that anyone really cares.

## BRITISH TELECOM
### *Kafkaesque call centres, family advertising, Maureen Lipman, rage*

From the cosy Maureen Lipman cross-generational ads of the 1980s to the current campaign featuring a beleaguered step-dad of three, BT's marketing reminds me of the generic blandness that England has perfected so well. If there is one company that has been capable of reducing me to tears of boredom and angry rages, while reminding me that I am not an individual but an insignificant number amongst a hundred million other suckers who signed up for misery, this is the one. The day I disconnected my BT line and moved elsewhere was a triumphant day indeed (although the operator at the BT call centre did not appear to register this triumphalism).

## BRANSTON PICKLE
### *My mother in the kitchen, school lunchboxes,*
### *brown and yellow jar, cheese on toast*

Only good things come into my mind when I think of Branston. It reminds me of the love I feel for my mother, who used it liberally when making my sandwiches for school – which I would munch two hours before lunchtime. I think of the hours I have spent scraping out the last bits from the bottom of the jar, or escaping from the cold weather and making tasty and satisfying cheese on toast with pickle on top. It can only be good. Every time I take a jar out of the kitchen cupboard, I involuntarily mumble the strapline 'Bring out the Branston'. Does everyone feel the same way about Branston Pickle? I imagine so.

Perhaps the most significant *B* brand in my life right now is Blackberry, the hybrid phone/email device that is so 'useful' that its community of owners have renamed it the Crackberry, on account of it being so addictive. After seeing dynamic-looking businessmen and can-do creative people fiddling about on them, I bought one myself, because I wanted to be as connected and resourceful as them. I was also looking for a new clique to join, and the Blackberry, being a serious piece of kit for grown-ups, was an exit from the polyphonic 3G WAP madness of the 'high street' phones, that are, let's face it, designed for children.

Crack is the right drug to associate with this gadget. I have been trans-fixed by the thing for over six months now, continually glancing at the screen, flicking around the emails and text messages. It never leaves my right hand. It has invaded my whole life, eroding any boundaries between work and play, to the extent that on a deserted beach in southern India, I was caught on camera by my girlfriend aimlessly wandering in the sea, holding the Blackberry to the sky to get a signal. 'Blackberries used to be things we picked along country paths in September and made into a crum-ble,' wrote Tom Hodgkinson in the *Guardian*, 'nowadays, they are no longer a free source of pleasure, but a very expensive source of pain.'

## -166 days

My agent sets up a meeting with a publishing house interested in the diaries. Like most people, I sense that they do not wholly believe that I will go through with this project, even though I would be paid money to write about the thing. During our discussion, in what appears to be a bluff-calling exercise, the publisher suggests that I burn one of my most valued branded objects as a dummy run. A test of mettle. Without blinking I agree.

As soon as I leave the office, I begin to think about the branded possessions that I cherish the most. I know deep down what they are, but I can't bring myself to even imagine them going up in flames, my life without them would surely be worse off, emotionally as well as financially. After some serious soul-searching, I narrow the long list down to three items:

### LOUIS VUITTON DAMIER CHECK SHOULDER BAG
One of the first luxury items I bought myself back in 1999, when I first had some money in my pocket. Spending £400 on this bag was a symbolic act of financial freedom after leaving home. Everyone I knew thought it was a crass gesture, but I read this as jealousy, which made me flaunt the thing even more. It has lasted me for six years, and is not in production any more.

## ADIDAS 'ADISTAR RUNNER' TRAINERS

Not a particularly rare pair of trainers, but these particular shoes were given to me when I first met the brand managers at Adidas UK. I seem to walk taller in them whenever I put them on. They are delicately cleaned and Scotchgarded after every use.

## BLACKBERRY

I have a love-hate relationship with this thing. The constant connection to email, text and phone has enslaved me to 24-hour working days. But there's no mistaking the effect it has on people when you pull it out of your pocket. It makes me look and feel confident, dynamic, adult. It shows, quite literally, that I mean business.

The more I think about this list, the more I realise that the most symbolic of my enduring love for inanimate objects (and the people that make them) are the Adidas trainers. To the fire they will go. I allow myself a seven-day period of grace, during which time I will wear the things day and night; a fitting send-off for something I love so much.

# -164 days

A television company has invited me to their offices. There is some interest in filming the bonfire. One producer in the meeting asks me if people themselves can become brands? The likes of Jennifer Lopez, Jamie Oliver and David Beckham market every aspect of their lifestyles and attitudes, selling products from perfume to cookbooks to trainers off the back end. So in a sense they are.

'Your partner works at a big art gallery, doesn't she?' he asks. 'Is she part of your collection of brands?'

'Yes, I suppose she is. But she's exempt from the fire, of course.'

'Would you have been attracted to her as much, had she not been working in such a cool job?'

That's a bit below the belt. There follows a pregnant pause, and I blush at my apparently shallow nature. The meeting ends soon after, as do my chances of TV stardom.

As part of my research into the history of brands, I have contacted Adam Curtis, a British documentary maker who produced an astonishingly sinister film about consumerism called *Century of the Self*. Much of the film centres around Edward Bernays, widely celebrated as the godfather of PR. Curtis considers Bernays as the pioneer of manipulative marketing, giving rise to a culture of selfish individualism. Today an email arrives with some of his notes on the subject:

Edward Bernays was the first person to take the ideas of Freud and use them to manipulate the masses. He showed American corporations how they could make the public want things that they didn't need, by linking mass-produced goods to their unconscious desires. Out of this would come a new political idea of how to control the masses; by satisfying their innermost desires, one made them happy and thus docile. It was the start of the all-consuming self, which has come to dominate our world today.

One of Bernays's early clients was George Hill, president of the American Tobacco Association. Hill asked Bernays to find a way to break the taboo of smoking among women in America. Together with early American psychologist A A Brill, Bernays found that cigarettes were a symbol of the penis and male sexual power. If he could find a way to connect cigarettes with challenging male power, then women would smoke, because they would have their own penises. Bernays decided to stage an event at New York's Easter Day parade, in which he persuaded a group of rich debutantes to hide cigarettes under their clothes. They should join the parade and at a given moment, they should light up their cigarettes dramatically. Meanwhile he informed the press that a group of suffragettes were preparing to protest by lighting up what they called 'torches of freedom'. News of the event promptly filled the papers across America and the event became a great success.

What Bernays had created was the idea that if a woman smoked, it would make her more powerful and independent, an idea that still persists today. He realised that it was possible to persuade people to behave irrationally, if you linked products to their emotions and feelings. It meant that irrelevant objects could become powerful emotional symbols of how you wanted to be seen by others.

After the First World War, the system of mass production was flourishing and millions of goods were pouring off the production line. These producers were frightened that there would come a point when people had enough goods, and would simply stop buying. Up until now, the majority of products had been sold on the basis of need – shoes, stockings and even cars were promoted for their function and durability, and the aim of most adverts was to show the public the product's virtues, nothing more. Corporations realised they had to transform the way that Americans thought about products. Edward Bernays's role was critical in this process. He was employed by publisher William Randolph Hearst to promote a new range of women's magazines, and Bernays glamorised them by placing articles and advertisements that linked products of his other famous clients to film stars such as Clara Bow, who was also his client.

But Bernays's role was not limited to magazines. He also began the practice of product placement in films, dressing film stars in clothes and jewellery from other firms he represented. He was, he claimed, the first person to tell car companies they could sell cars as symbols of sexuality. He employed psychologists to issue reports claiming that products were good for you, and then pretended they were independent studies. He organised fashion shows in department stores and paid celebrities to repeat the new and essential message; you bought things not just for need but also to express your sense of yourself to others.

It is hard for me to think of very many products that are marketed simply on the basis of what they do. These products seem rather dull and ordinary in comparison to the apparently life-changing properties of so many brands advertised on TV. One advert, for Ronseal fence varnish, is conspicuous in its honest banality. A workman holds a tin of the stuff to the camera and simply states: 'If you want to protect your wood, use Ronseal wood protecting varnish. It does exactly what it says on the tin.'

## -162 days

The week's farewell to my beloved Adidas is over. I have worn them around the house, to meetings and out to the shops. With all the wear, they have become quite grimy, so I clean them with Foot Locker Sneaker Refreshing Mousse one last time. It really is awful to see them go, pathetic really. Feeling both sadness for the loss and loathing for myself, it is safe to say this is not one of the happiest days of my life, and my mood is compounded by the relentless drizzle of spring rain. I trudge around the backstreets of my neighbourhood, looking for somewhere suitable to make my first sacrificial burning, away from any CCTV or nosy passers-by. Eventually I find an old Edwardian stairwell leading to a bridge, a frequent stopgap for those of no fixed abode, judging from the acrid-smelling, piss-stained floor. Perfect then, for this initial act of brand cleansing. Just like the tramps, I am about to piss on my own doorstep.

Stooping in the stairwell-cum-urinal, I take the shoes from their original box and begin to douse them with lighter fuel. Despite their years, the things still look pretty crisp. With one final loving glance, I take a match to the laces and the flames engulf the shoes then the box with a soft *whoosh*.

The laces disintegrate almost immediately and the rubber soles slowly curl up at both ends, the suede and nylon uppers soon forming a black charred mush. I am standing in a street burning a perfectly good pair of trainers. In a matter of months I will be doing the same to almost every possession that I own. Perhaps it's not too late to pull out? The flames look like they might grow out of control, so I douse them with water (Evian, since you ask) and a nasty chemical-smelling steam rises from the disintegrating plastic.

As the smoke clears, my sense of alarm subsides and I breathe a sigh of relief. What exactly was I mourning here? Not the financial cost, even though I am by no means rich. No, it is the emotional connection. To a pair of trainers. This can only be a positive thing; my first step to a new life. The things you own end up owning you, so I once read, and these stupid trainers had owned me for far too long. One day soon, I'm going to be free of all this. It's surely just a case of re-programming my mind. I can love myself and be lovable to others without these brands. I can work towards goals that stretch beyond the hoarding of things. I can learn to look at another person and make judgements aside from their badges of self. Or better still make no judgements at all.

## -158 days

I have a book deal. This personal journey has suddenly become very public indeed.

## -155 days

I recount on my blog the story of the beautiful Puma-shod woman on the bus and within two days, a PR Manager at Puma is in contact:

> Neil,
> Your comments on PUMA are very interesting – particu-
> larly interesting to me as you spent most of last year
> sitting in our reception telling us how wonderful PUMA
> was and your magazine (which no longer exists . . . for
> some reason?). I obviously spent a lot of money with
> you on the basis of you telling us both magazine and
> brand worked well together. I'm assuming that if you
> ever work on another similar title you will not want
> the advertising money of PUMA????
> Let me know your thoughts

A fair point. During my tenure in style magazines, I often felt disingenuous going begging for advertising money from brands that I personally disliked (rendering me, as an editor and publisher, unfit for the purpose). Half-truths and false friendships are the essence of most relationships in business, but brand managers are a different breed of employee altogether. Brand managers such as this don't simply treat their jobs as a means to pay the mortgage, do the bare minimum and sneak off home early. They are the most fanatical company men and women you could ever meet. They commonly stay with the same company for years on end and treat the promotion of their brand message as some sort of crusade. This is why the staff take the criticism so personally. It is also why I am leaving the business and writing this book; brands such as these are not holy icons. They just manufacture and sell shoes.

## -149 days

Adidas hear about my project and invite me to their offices to explain exactly what I am up to with this bonfire. Adidas – my all-time favourite brand, the company that spent the most money on my magazines, and in the UK at least, the most powerful sportswear brand in terms of popularity in the market and influence in the industry. I come running like a trained monkey.

As I walk into their press office, I suddenly feel uneasy, as if I were stepping into the no man's land of this private war I have started. But the paranoia quickly subsides at the sight of their new product lines, surrounded by promotional posters and brand memorabilia that had been lovingly collected over the years. Apparently the Adidas trefoil logo represents the continental plates coming together in the spirit of the Olympics.

'What's all this about then?' says one of the two brand managers, jolting me out of my three-stripes daydream. I gingerly give them the spiel . . . branded from birth . . . no sense of self . . . burning the lot . . . wholesome new life. I feel like a Catholic standing up in the middle of church to declare I am becoming a Jew. It's clear they've invited me in to size up the situation but to my surprise they are nodding in all the right places and laughing at some of my jokes. They make the usual critiques – burning everything is a waste, you'll never see it through, it's impossible anyhow, and what's so wrong with brands in the first place? But it isn't until I recount my infamously shallow Puma-shod-girl-on-a-bus story, and the fury it elicited from Puma UK, that the meeting livens up.

'You were absolutely right about that woman,' says one manager. 'She wears Pumas because she thinks they're cool, and that she is cool. You think that Puma is anything *but* cool, and from looking at her shoes, you can tell that straightaway. Those shoes saved you the effort of getting to know her and finding out, much later, that you weren't compatible. Think of all the time you would have wasted. That's why you need brands.'

I find it hard to disagree. The brand choices we make simply reflect the people we are. Is there really a problem with that? I myself have often enjoyed a sense of security, solidarity even, being part of a branded tribe. It grounds me. I know where I belong in life. Perhaps this project *is* a mindless waste of time.

I imagine the brand men are delighted with the negative publicity Puma are getting as a result of my blog – a sizeable number of fellow-bloggers confirmed their mutual dislike for the brand on my site. I wonder how they'd react if the boot had been on the other foot. Still, that's to be expected. Changing the subject, one of the managers asks if I would like some free gear to take home with me. Clinging for dear life to my new principles, I refuse. Well, I had to, if I wanted to walk out of there with any dignity. We all know I am on the waver. It is written on my face.

Having discussed the book, our meeting quickly trails off to an end. Not being a style journalist any longer, my use to them is now minimal, and this meeting feels like a friendly send-off into obscurity. As I stumble out onto the busy street lined with shops, happy people streaming in and out with bags of fresh consumer kill, I feel very, very low. My professional bridges are being burned to the point of no return now. I look around me and everyone, it seems, is getting on quite contentedly with their branded lives, working hard to make money to spend on the things that make them happy. Clothes, cars, phones, food; everywhere I see brands and people enjoying them as if there was nothing wrong at all. Perhaps there isn't. I don't want to be marginalised from society, disengaged from reality like some paranoid schizophrenic on the run from 'the system'. Is it too late to back out?

My childhood memories of the 1980s are littered with brands. In summer sports camp, I remember playing tennis under a giant poster of John McEnroe, dressed in a Sergio Tacchini outfit. Björn Borg stood beside him, at the Wimbledon arena, dressed in Fila. At weekends, I would watch motor racing on TV, the cars identifiable not by the drivers but by their sponsorship deals with Marlboro and John Player Special. During the family holidays to Tenerife, I would watch girls walk up and down the beach resplendent in fake Gucci T-shirts and Hugo Boss caps bought from the local tourist-driven markets. The ultimate goal in life was to own a gold Rolex Oyster watch. Brands certainly seemed much more brash, more ostentatious, than they appear today. A few days in the library reading about the history of the 1980s advertising boom would seem to bear this out.

During the early 1980s, manufacturers became aware that the myriad choices available to the consumer had become bewildering. Crowded markets had to rely on strong branding to stave off waning customer loyalty and, in reaction to shareholder pressure and shrinking market shares, the private sector elicited a boom in advertising to build their brands' values, filling print and broadcast media with ads to the point of saturation. Companies began to promote their products based around the heart and soul of the brand, the brand's *essence*, in marketing speak. Often this amounted to bombastic visions of a better world, made all the more enjoyable by the existence of their products. Consumers were no longer buying a branded product, but a set of values, and with it a whole new way of life, as the evolving slogans of Coca-Cola from the nineteenth to the twenty-first centuries show:

1886　'Drink Coca-Cola'

1900　'For headache and exhaustion drink Coca-Cola'

1906　'Thirst-quenching – delicious and refreshing'

1923　'A perfect blend of pure products from nature'

1943  'It's the real thing'

1957  'Sign of good taste'

1971  'I'd like to buy the world a Coke'

1976  'Coke adds life'

1989  'Can't beat the feeling'

1993  'Always Coca-Cola'

1998  'Thirsty for life? Drink Coca-Cola!'

2001  'Life tastes good'

2006  'The Coke side of life'

Brands seemed to be uniting the world. A person in China could enjoy the same soft drink as an individual at the opposite side of the globe in Puerto Rico. In 1988, McDonald's, now a feature on most high streets around the world, proudly announced their first store openings in communist Hungary and Yugoslavia, prior to the collapse of the Soviet Union. The image of the all-powerful consumer was mirrored by the growing importance of the individual in conservative political ideology, spreading as it did to the UK.

> A man's right to work as he will, to spend what he earns, to own property, to have the state as servant and not as master, they are the essence of a free economy and on that freedom all our other freedoms depend.
>
> *Margaret Thatcher, Conservative Party Election Broadcast 1987*

Nothing exemplified the 1980s economic boom quite like the luxury-brand market, which broke out of its upper-class demographic to become mainstream objects of desire. Such was the worldwide cultural value of traditional European luggage brands (Gucci and Louis Vuitton) and the new American fashion houses (Hugo Boss and Calvin Klein) that any product carrying their brands (perfume, watches, underwear, sunglasses) would sell at the highest possible premium, regardless of the quality of product. There followed a surge in counterfeiting as the working classes sought to appropriate the symbols of the super-rich, a phenomenon that later become known as *brand hijacking*.

With the increasing reliance on branding to sell products, the global financial community began to value brands as a tangible asset. Western financiers sought out companies with undervalued brands for potential takeover; the belief being that strong brands resulted in better profit performance and therefore greater value for shareholders. In 1988 the British confectioner Rowntree's tangible assets were valued at $900 million. But in the same year, Nestlé acquired the company for $4.5 billion. It was the intangible value of Rowntree's famous brands – KitKat, Polo and Smarties – that commanded the premium. There followed a frenzy of mergers and acquisitions across the world market, with nearly $50 billion trading hands in exchange for household brand names.

To the consumer, branded products were now valued more for their meaning than their actual use as advertising delivered wave after wave of epiphanies and life goals. Branding had become so emotional that some loyal consumers were beginning to display affection beyond all reason. In 1998, when Kellogg's changed the name of its cereal from Coco Pops to Choco Krispies in the UK, there followed an outcry. One newspaper held a national poll, in which nearly one million people voted, with 92 per cent in favour of a return to Coco Pops. After sustained pressure from consumers, Kellogg's relented and changed the brand to its former glory. Rebranding was viewed as no less than cultural destruction to some. Coca-Cola was accused of destroying the American way of life by loyal customers who disliked the improved recipe of 'New Coke'. Margaret Thatcher famously covered a model of British Airways' new branding with a handkerchief in disgust. A consumer survey in the United States claimed that trust and credibility in brands such as Coca-Cola, Microsoft and Ford

Motors rated higher than Amnesty International, Greenpeace and Oxfam.[7] Susan Fournier of Harvard Business School attributed the phenomenon to a general yearning for meaningful relationships:

> Relationships with mass brands can soothe the 'empty selves' left behind by society's abandonment of tradition and community and provide stable anchors in an otherwise changing world. The formation and maintenance of brand-product relationships serve many culturally supported roles within postmodern society.[8]

The turn away from labelled ostentation finally arrived in the early 1990s. However fanatical some brands' markets had become at their core, the wider market was developing a world-weary attitude to advertising. The brands' stampede to be heard loudest and longest certainly had a negative effect, but a downturn in the world economy brought about a new trend for real quality and value for money. The retail trade began to undercut the value of big brands with new discount warehouses and own-brand supermarket products, the biggest upset arriving in April 1993 with 'Marlboro Friday'. Losing market share to discount brands, Philip Morris, then the world's largest consumer products group, slashed the price of its bestselling cigarette by 20 per cent. Philip Morris shares, along with those of many other consumer goods companies, promptly collapsed. *The Economist*, along with many business commentators, promptly forecast the demise of major brand companies.

> From Marlboro to Kellogg's, big brands are under siege from supermarkets' own-labels. Many brands will perish or never be so profitable again.
>
> The Economist, *June 1993*

A less boisterous, more caring type of company branding emerged in the form of The Body Shop and Aveda, while outlet malls and discount chains flourished. But the big, emotional brand was not dead yet. New markets for life-affirming, aspirational branding developed as governments dismantled monopolies, creating a plethora of new companies in the deregulated market. Intangible services such as energy, healthcare and telecommunications required emotion in their marketing to lend the products real value. And so brands such as Enron, The Co-operative Bank and Orange were born.

By the new millennium, anything previously unbranded now was. Pharmaceutical brands such as Viagra and Prozac were extensively marketed and became household names. NGOs followed political parties in branding themselves and their ideals, notably Amnesty International and Oxfam. People themselves became brands proper and industries were built to capitalise on the celebrity of personalities such as Martha Stewart, while David Beckham was immortalised in his own logo, designed by Adidas. Entertainers, sportspeople and politicians were all carefully marketed to embody a coherent set of commercial values that could be used for sale in the marketplace, controlling their appearance and behaviour in line with their expertly defined audiences.

With prolonged economic growth and emerging international markets to conquer, branding returned to full strength. Old heritage brands such as Burberry and Gucci that were long missing, presumed dead, staged a comeback in the reinvigorated luxury market, while mega brands grew in size and influence to such an extent that they began to 'own' their culture. Nike *was* sport, Microsoft *was* computers. Saturn car owners built a society around the company's traditional principles. Starbucks created an in-store dialect around their products with Baristas and Grande Frappucinos. Disney created a sterilised community by building a gated town called Celebration. At the beginning of the 21st century, it was now possible to live a complete lifestyle around a brand.

## -139 days

The blog is only a few weeks old, but the traffic is building and spreading onto other sites. The dialogue posted by visitors is two-thirds positive encouragement and one-third angry mob, the ferocity of which takes me by surprise:

YOU ARE AN IDIOT!!! Go you Neil, to the bonfire!

I wanna kick your spoilt resource-wasting ass.

Let's just not mention that this whole thing is one big branding effort for Mr Neil Boorman. So it's to be self-immolation, is it then?

Taking on 'the brand' in order to change the economic order is like ending racism by getting a haircut.

The angry bloggers feel that there are poverty-stricken people around the world who would benefit from having my gear, that I should donate the lot to charity rather than burn it. There is also great concern that the bonfire will contribute to global warming. To top it all, I am being *paid* to write a *book* about the whole thing, which just goes to prove what a shallow person I am. A journalist posts a note congratulating me on getting so many people riled, as if that were the object of the exercise.

My bonfire is a personal cathartic act, I argue, which I am making public in order to raise publicity about the emotionalism of branded goods and consumerism. Yes, there is a book being published and, like every commercial author, I am being paid to write the thing. But the people who read the blog or come to see the bonfire are not obliged to buy the book. It seems ludicrous to me that a celebrity can appear across the media to promote their latest million-dollar film/record/sponsorship deal without question, yet an average guy who wishes to make a serious point and receive a modest reward is opportunistic, having ideas above his station.

Giving my collection of things to charity might seem like the most ethical thing to do but long-term will a few extra T-shirts sold at Oxfam make much of a difference? It would be better surely to grab the news agenda away from Kate Moss's love life for just one day, and talk about the damage that consumerism might be causing. In my opinion, the exercise would be neither personally cathartic nor press-worthy, were it called *Donation to the Charity Shop of the Brands*.

I am not completely sure why I chose to be an Apple or an Adidas person when I was younger. The brands just seemed to appeal to me on an instinctive level, summing up the person that I aspired to become. But what about the more ordinary things in life, such as peanut butter or toilet paper? I trust and rely on so many brands without giving them a minute's thought but I don't recall ever having studied the toilet-roll market to make an informed choice on price or quality. Google is the default web page that flashes up as I boot up my Mac, although I cannot remember consciously choosing that search engine over Yahoo! or Ask.com. The Visa credit card? Lurpak butter? The Bic pen? These logos are comfortingly familiar aspects of my daily rituals. But I have no idea how they got there.

I pay a visit to the business section of my local Borders bookshop and I am surprised at how many brand manuals there are on the market. Even more surprising is the evangelical tone that these books take, openly espousing the best ways to manipulate the consumer market. In his book *Lovemarks*, Saatchi & Saatchi CEO Kevin Roberts claims that the way to a consumer's heart is by triggering the emotions of mystery, sensuality and intimacy:

> For great brands to survive, they must create loyalty beyond reason. This is the only way to differentiate themselves from the millions of going-nowhere 'blands'.[9]

*The Culting of Brands* explains how to build consumer tribes using fanatical sects as case studies. In *Emotional Branding* one can discover which of the consumer's feelings are best exploited. Within *360 Degree Branding* lies a manifesto for saturating the consumer environment for total penetration. There are literally dozens of these books claiming ownership to the secrets of so-called 'loyalty beyond reason'. The brand as a ritual; the brand as a system of values; the brand as belief and the consumer as worshipper . . . these books might be written in outlandish hyperbole but, astonishingly, each one is written under the basic assumption that the consumer is an easily malleable dupe; merely fodder for sustained economic growth. Perhaps we are.

## -124 days

I discuss the ethics of these brands manuals on the blog, and a journalist, Matthew de Abuita, posts a timely comment:

> If you replaced every logo, advert and brand image you see on the high street with a quote from the bible, you would feel that you were living in an intolerably strict religious state. I mean, if you took all the billboards and put Jesus on them, there'd be a revolution. If you replaced the icons of one ideology with the icons of another, you realise the absurdity you've been living with, everyday, your whole life.

## -123 days

Since the early 1960s baby boomers, each generation in the West has been given a demographical name – Generation X, Generation Y and so on. However, the current generation is the first to be named after a brand. Such is the ubiquity of Apple's iPod and the general importance of branding in youth culture that the current crop of 16 to 25-year-olds will be referred to as the iGeneration. Meanwhile, a report in the *Sunday Times*[10] notes that Generation Y, to which I belong, is statistically the most selfish yet. Showing the most extreme traits of self-absorption in history, 52 per cent believe that the quality of life in Britain is best improved by putting the individual first.

## -121 days

This Saturday afternoon, Juliet and I fulfilled every cliché that accompanies a person in my marketing demographic (Social class C1, accounting for 21.9 per cent of the population). Being a lower middle-class, urban male employed in the creative industries, I cannot help but conform to the consumer stereotype. We visited an art gallery and bought a copy of the *Guardian* newspaper. We visited an upmarket supermarket (Waitrose) and bought organic food. We spent time in an interiors shop (Habitat) and purchased unnecessary designer knick-knacks for the home. This day hadn't been planned as such; Juliet and I started the day intent on visiting several galleries, then perhaps strolling around a park. Along the way, however, we came across so many opportunities to buy things we didn't realise we needed, that we seemed to drift, quite effortlessly, towards our natural consumer types and soon we were laden with shopping bags, the brands of which succinctly encapsulated our lifestyles. It felt pleasingly comfortable, natural even, browsing for ergonomic fish steamers. Then at the bus stop heading for home, we were confronted with our Doppelgängers. Waiting there for the bus was another thirtysomething, centre-left, white professional couple who, dressed in similar clothes, wielding an almost identical collection of carrier bags, had obviously been out shopping for entry-level designer home furnishings and reassuringly overpriced consumables of token ethical value.

Throughout my life, I have sought to express my individuality through branded gear, my particular combination of things making me unique in the eyes of all that should like to witness it. The only problem with expressing your individuality through brands is that the stuff is mass-produced, pretty much negating the uniqueness – unless one purchases a 'limited edition' product, which might narrow the odds of seeing a contemporary in the same outfit from a dead cert to a sporting chance. You could argue that the uniqueness is in the choosing of the product, not the product itself. One cannot purchase individuality from a factory that makes 10,000 editions of the same thing each day. How this paradox has eluded me for so long, I do not know. Part of the self-esteem I derive from brands is feeling that my stuff is more individual than everyone else's; I now understand that, far from being a freethinking consumer, I routinely conform to demo-graphic stereotype. I am a walking cliché with average aspirations and a limited understanding of my lot in life. After a week of diligent hard work, I like nothing better than to fritter my time buying things that make me feel good about myself, just like everybody else. Atop the bus, other people like me take out and unwrap the day's purchases, touching and feeling the branded trophies from a successful day's hunt.

## -120 days

According to current thinking on my blog, I should give the stuff to the homeless of London, or fly out to Ethiopia and hand out the stuff personally, or just shut up and be grateful for my lot in life. One much needed note of support does arrive:

> Neil, you have to burn it. There is no aesthetic charge in recycling. Protests require fire, as the self-immo-lations of Buddhist monks attest. The bad information must be destroyed, not recycled.

## -116 days

I meet with a close friend for a drink. Simon is somebody I should aspire to be like: clever, articulate, funny and of a gentle nature; one of life's good guys.

'I would have worn my new Puma trainers out tonight, Neil, only I read your blog and thought better of it.'

'I, er, oh. Sorry'.

'No, that's fine. I'll make sure that I never wear them when you're around. I wouldn't want us to fall out over a pair of shoes.'

'Come on, Simon, I don't mean it like that.'

'No, Neil, I think you do.'

## -115 days

'Think of a colour,' says Jim.

'Red,' I say.

'Okay, now look around you and try to remember all the things in this room that are red.' He gives me 30 seconds to make mental notes;

chair, ring-bound folders, stapler, pens. 'Now, close your eyes and think hard. Tell me all the things in the room that are blue.'

'I . . . er, I can't think of any.'

'That's how brands work – selective filtering. The conscious mind tells the unconscious mind what to focus on. You see less of one thing and more of another, even though they're both there together. Part of branding is training customers to filter out the competition.'

I am sitting in the offices of ESP, a research and communication consultancy that specialises in psychographic research. Companies such as these deconstruct the psychology of consumer markets and try to understand the unconscious desires that motivate us to buy. Armed with this knowledge, they can help companies increase customer loyalty and satisfaction. Basically, these people can map the personality of consumer archetypes, and determine what type of branding they respond to best. I stumbled upon the company online and wondered if a psychometric test might help me to understand my attraction to certain brands. Why exactly am I so fiercely loyal towards one shoe manufacturer over another? If anyone can find out, it has to be these people; they work for BMW and Tesco most of the time.

'It's all about rapport, Neil. Brands attempt to match and mirror your own rapport, in the same way that we do with body language. Have you ever noticed how you copy the posture that your friends adopt when you talk to them in the pub – crossing your legs, rolling your shoulders, that sort of thing? Well, we do the same, bonding people with brands. When people are like each other, they *like* each other. You know what the definition of rapport is in neuro-linguistic programming? The unconscious acceptance of suggestion.'

For the next four hours, I undergo a series of interviews and questionnaires, some under hypnosis.

**When recharging your batteries, do you prefer to be alone or with people?**

*Alone.*

When you come into a situation do you usually act quickly after sizing it up, or do you complete a study of all the consequences and then act?

*Act quickly.*

If someone you knew well said to you 'I'm thirsty', would you find the comment interesting, but probably do nothing about it, or would you feel really compelled to do something about it?

*I'd feel compelled to do something.*

Order the answers to the following statements according to preference (4 being the closest to describing you, 1 being the least descriptive).

During an argument, are you most likely to be influenced by:
- the other person's tone of voice                                    *1*
- whether or not you can see the
  other person's point of view                                         *4*
- whether or not the person has
  facts or a logical case                                              *3*
- whether or not you feel in touch
  with the other person's true feelings                                *2*

It is easiest for me to:
- turn on a stereo system and find the
  ideal volume                                                         *2*
- select the most intellectually relevant
  point concerning a subject                                           *3*
- select the most comfortable furniture                                *1*
- select rich, attractive colour combinations                         *4*

I am shown diagrams of boxes of varying sizes and positions, and asked to comment on them. There are no right or wrong answers, I am told. Then we move on to life values. What is important to me in life? What is its purpose? What does life give me? Not ever having properly thought about it, I give them the first thing that comes into my head, which is good apparently. We come to a hierarchy of my consumer values:

1. Contentment
2. Satisfaction
3. Happiness
4. Excitement
5. Amusement
6. Identity

The interviews draw to a close, and, from collating the results, Jim says he has mapped my profile; he now knows which subconscious values drive my behaviour, and he could guess quite accurately which brands I would respond to best. Over time, he would be able to manipulate the way I feel about a brand by mirroring, or even changing, the values that drive my subconscious through advertising.

**Neil Boorman's Psychometric Profile Summary**

**Introvert**
I prefer to be alone and process information internally. I tend to make decisions by myself, as opposed to extroverts, who are more instinctive and will be influenced by the opinions of others. Sixty per cent of the nation is introverted.

**Big Picture**
I prefer the top line overview as opposed to the specific detail. I like to think how to apply things to the future. Only 25 per cent of the national market are Big Picture thinkers.

The majority are Detailed thinkers, who prefer more information and need to know the practicalities.

### Feeler

I am empathetic, socially minded and use past events as a frame of reference. I make decisions, often unconsciously, based on gut instinct and personal experience, as opposed to Thinkers, who are more objective, less loyal and tend to shop around.

### Impulsive

I am flexible and open to suggestions, but I do not like them forced upon me. Planned people on the other hand are more resistant to sudden change.

### Visual

Brands that look good appeal to me as opposed to those that feel good, sound good or make sense. I am bored by long verbal instructions. Other people may respond better to touch, sound or logic.

### Loyalty

I score highly, appreciating loyalty from brands and am fiercely loyal in return.

'I bet you only ever use Apple computers,' says Jim.

I hadn't mentioned a single brand preference during the time I'd been here, and I'd left my laptop at home. Amazing.

'How on earth did you know?' I ask.

'You're a Big Picture consumer, just like me. You have a rapport with Apple because it represents personal freedom, style and individuality. They are the brand values of Apple. For Microsoft on the other hand, the values are more logical. They concentrate on what's inside the computer, not what the computer looks like.'

Apple is the only aspirational computer manufacturer on the planet, so perhaps Jim's guess wasn't so amazing. To test out the theory, I ask him why I have such a strong loyalty to Adidas over any number of lifestyle-defining sports brands.

'If you're so loyal to Adidas, you've probably been anchored when you were in a highly suggestible state. Brands are an external stimulus that trigger internal reactions. When you hear a certain piece of music, you will instantly remember a time or an event in the past associated with a strong emotion. Brands anchor themselves to a particular moment in your life and act as a trigger in the same way as music. Every time you see the brand, it triggers an emotion. Tell me about your earliest memories connected to Adidas.'

I recount memories from pop videos, watching Olympic athletes on TV, secretly falling in love with an older girl at school who had an Adidas tracksuit; none of these experiences seem to make sense. Then I remember the first day at school, being ostracised from the playground gang for not having the right gear; they were all wearing Adidas.

'That's it! Adidas is anchored to the feelings you felt that day. You were highly suggestible, you had a need for external connection and you saw the brand as a means to personal growth. When you see Adidas, you remember how it feels to be rejected, and it offers the possibility of acceptance. To you, Adidas *is* acceptance and love.'

## –110 days

I am frantically rummaging around the flat for the 'right' plastic bag to carry some books into work. That I am 20 minutes late for a meeting seems less important right now. One of the many supermarket bags clogging up my kitchen drawer would do the job just fine but it seems important that the bag carries a logo that is the most 'me' – Selfridges over Sainsbury's, if you will. Except I'm not really a Selfridges person. I wonder whether we have a John Lewis bag or something from Harvey Nichols? A sense of self-awareness only comes when I notice Juliet staring in disbelief.

'Neil, why are you ransacking the house?'

'I'm looking for the right bag.'

'And what's wrong with the ones you've left lying on the kitchen floor?'

'I told you, I'm looking for the *right* bag.'

She turns and leaves for work, leaving me to consider my situation, amid a sea of trophy carrier bags.

Let's get this situation into perspective. I am a habitual shopper and I think about the meanings of brands, a lot. Shopping is the national pastime in the UK, so I am not alone. But my habits border on the obsessional; when I'm not shopping, I am planning the next trip to town, dreaming up endless lists of things that I absolutely must have. I recently spent a week saying farewell to *a pair of trainers* and then burnt them in an act of revenge. In a few months' time, I am going to be setting fire to all my possessions in public. Obsession. Irrational behaviour. Revenge. Arson. This is not normal behaviour. Towards the end of my alcohol treatment, my counsellor suggested that I might benefit from long-term psychological treatment. Now is the time.

## –109 days

Often when I read anti-consumerist material, I am troubled by a nagging feeling that the writers might be just a little paranoid, prone to conspiracy theories that make for good stories, but little else. Then I come across quotes in the library, written by well-known, legitimate businessmen that are terrifying to me. This is one of them:

> We must shift America from a *needs* to a *desire* culture. People must be trained to desire and want new things even before the old are entirely consumed. We must shape a new mentality . . . man's desire must overshadow his needs.[11]
>
> *Paul Maser, Lehman Bros, 1924*

Having grown up knowing only a desire-based culture, these quotes come as genuine epiphanies to me.

## -108 days

I am standing in the toothpaste aisle in the supermarket. There are hundreds of brands to choose from. Amongst others, I see a tube with the Arm & Hammer logo. I remember an advert saying something about Arm & Hammer making baking soda. The packaging tells me there is baking soda in the toothpaste. I remember from the advert that baking soda is good at removing stains without damaging teeth. I also remember the ad was American. Americans have lots of good products, some of which we don't get here in England. *It must be good*. I look at the price and compare it with other brands. It's expensive, but not the most expensive on offer. I want it to clean my teeth but making them whiter would also be good. People with white teeth are more attractive. Film stars and television presenters have white teeth. If I had whiter teeth, people might find me more attractive. I like feeling attractive, it makes me feel more confident about myself. I want to feel confident. I'm going to buy the toothpaste.

This is the thought process I go through when choosing a new branded product. My brain executes this thought process in a split second, in the unconscious part of my mind. I'll likely make a hundred similar decisions while I trawl around the store. As consumers faced with the dilemma of choice, we all undertake these decisions day to day. Granted, some of us resolve the dilemma on the basis of price, others on the look and feel of the packaging. But the choice remains constant, as does our reliance on branding to help us decide. I am sure that I spend rather too much time making these choices.

## -107 days

Often when I discuss this project with people, they argue that, while some of the purchases that we make are based upon desire, most of the time we consume things rationally, based upon need; after all, how aspirational can a tube of branded toothpaste be? It would appear that some products are purely functional. But, according to the marketing manuals I have found, this clearly isn't the case. There are a range of needs that must be fulfilled before we make the purchase, some more humdrum and practical, others more exciting and emotional. In general, there are four criteria:

Functional attributes: what the product is made of

Functional benefits: what the product will do

Emotional benefit: how the product will make us feel

Aspirational benefit: how the product will change our lives

Of course, not all of these benefits will be of equal importance in each case. If we fall in love with a pair of shoes or a special type of gadget, we are unlikely to spend much time checking what the shoes are made of or what's inside the gadget. Conversely, we won't spend an incredible amount of time contemplating how much happier we will become if we buy a certain brand of toilet cleaner. But, during even the most banal of decisions, each of these criteria comes into play. It is fair to say that the greater emotional and aspirational benefits we associate with owning a branded product, the greater monetary value we also attach. We spend very little time aspiring to keep our toilet sparkly clean and so the financial value of the average toilet cleaner is very low. Saying that, I am sure that it is possible to buy a high-end cleaner for upmarket loos.

COLGATE TOOTHPASTE

| | |
|---|---|
| Functional attributes | *cleaning agents, fluoride, minty fresh flavour* |
| Functional benefits | *make teeth white, protect from decay, freshen breath* |
| Emotional benefit | *confidence of having bright, sweet-smelling smile* |
| Aspirational benefit | *more dynamic in social situations* |

MERCEDES CAR

| | |
|---|---|
| Functional attributes | *well-designed and manufactured components* |
| Functional benefit | *reliable, comfortable private transport* |
| Emotional benefits | *confidence from safety and prestige of the brand* |
| Aspirational benefits | *better driver, more attractive/successful to onlookers* |

| Functional attribute | *technologically advanced cushioning for feet* |
|---|---|
| Functional benefit | *provide comfort and stability while running* |
| Emotional benefits | *feeling properly equipped, more confidence in achieving goals* |
| Aspirational benefits | *become more like the Olympic runner in the adverts* |

The majority of consumer decisions we face each day are of the functional variety – which sandwich, which loo paper, which shampoo? But even these basic choices are subject to emotional and aspirational considerations, somehow reflecting the type of person we are. How exactly did the purchase of shampoo come to mean so much? David Ogilvy, founder of the O&M advertising agency, once noted that reason plays little part in our decisions at the till:

> The greater the similarity between products, the less part reason plays in brand selection. There really isn't any significant difference between the various brands of whisky or cigarettes or brands of beer. They are all about the same.[12]

In general, the functional differences between the competing products that we see on the supermarket shelf are few and far between, save a trace of ylang ylang here, an organic peptide there. For the most part, competing products perform the same task, and perform them well. The difference then is in the way we perceive the products; often we cannot reasonably discriminate between identical goods, so we are assisted in doing so in an unreasonable way. In their marketing, manufacturers promise that we will gain some emotional benefit from buying their products. They promise that we will feel better in some way for having bought the product. Ultimately, this is the role of the brand.

## –105 days

The British Association for Counselling and Psychotherapy has put me in contact with Carol. She is a therapist used to handling cases that will appear in the media (I tell them the sessions will appear in a book), having worked on several daytime chat shows. In the days leading up to our first meeting, I begin to worry that I'll be wasting this lady's time and my money. I am in a steady relationship; I have good friends; my parents are still happily married; I am not rich but life is comfortable, comfortable enough to support a burgeoning collection of upper to mid-market brands. What exactly is there to complain about? My condition will sound like self-referential navel-gazing, I'm sure.

Carol is a warm, confident middle-aged woman, dressed in Converse, Gap trousers and a top which I imagine comes from Next or Warehouse; growing old gracefully, but keeping an eye on what the kids are up to. By the time we meet, she has read the blog and is familiar with my self-diagnosed addiction and impending bonfire.

We begin to trawl through the back catalogue of events that have impacted on the 30-odd years of my life: kicked out of grammar school for laziness; worked in nightclubs instead of going to university; fell into journalism; in a steady relationship (although I wish I'd had more casual sex before).

'Let's talk about your compulsion to burn things,' says Carol. 'Have you burnt a lot of things throughout your life?'

'Well, on the cover of a magazine I edited, we once burnt an image of Posh Spice; we were calling for an end to celebrity culture. As a teenager, I would burn all the fluffy toys and Valentine cards that girlfriends had given me after we'd broke up. Nothing else really destructive. My friends and I used to spend our weekends drinking beer and smoking fags around fires on brownfield sites, before we were old enough to go into pubs. I would become transfixed by the flames, and stare at them for hours.'

'Interesting. I wonder where the current urge to burn all of your things comes from? Let's move on for now . . . I'd like to know some more about your family background. Tell me about your father. What does he do for a living?'

'He designs fire alarms.'

The conversation stops still. This is an epiphany for both of us.

'That's all we have time for, Neil. See you next week.'

I spend the rest of the week skulking about the flat, making a log of all my branded possessions destined for the fire, while mulling over the points Carol raised in our meeting. Why does therapy always seem to focus on the relationship we have with our parents? Surely no one has the perfect upbringing, but does that mean we are all plagued psychologically with 'issues'? It must be a common reaction of the patient to reject these theories when he or she is unearthing painful truths. But, still, my parents always cared for me, they never abused me; my grounds for complaint are few, beyond their refusal to buy me Adidas on demand. The connection of my father's business to the bonfire feels a little simplistic to me. Am I really seeking to start the one fire that my father cannot put out?

It is a miserable business indeed, logging each of my lovely branded possessions for imminent destruction. I find unworn clothes, still in their bags, stuffed behind boxes and furniture. No one knows I have these things but me; I could easily stash them away for use in the brighter, branded future when this insane project comes to an end. But what would be the point? If the therapy and the bonfire achieve what I hope, I won't care where my clothes are from. Much.

BRANDED ITEMS TO BE DESTROYED

| CLOTHES | | |
| --- | --- | --- |
| TOPS | | |
| 14 x | Ralph Lauren shirts | £910 |
| 2 x | YSL T-shirts | £150 |
| 2 x | Judy Blame T-shirts | £200 |
| 3 x | Lacoste polo shirts | £150 |
| 2 x | Vivienne Westwood shirts | £200 |
| 3 x | Siv Stoldal tops | £210 |
| 3 x | Nike T-shirts | £150 |
| 1 x | Kappa T-shirt | £40 |
| 1 x | Diadora tracktop | £40 |
| 2 x | Kilgore shirts | £240 |
| 2 x | Bernhard Willhelm sweatshirts | £300 |

| | | | |
|---|---|---|--:|
| 1 | x | Gucci T-shirt | £80 |
| 1 | x | Sergio Tacchini tracktop | £80 |
| 1 | x | Sergio Tacchini polo shirt | £70 |
| 1 | x | Kim Jones T-shirt | £50 |
| 1 | x | Gucci polo shirt | £60 |
| 2 | x | vintage Gucci sweat tops | £120 |
| 1 | x | Gucci shirt | £120 |
| 1 | x | Raf Simons T-shirt | £50 |

## JEANS / TROUSERS

| | | | |
|---|---|---|--:|
| 1 | x | Lee jeans | £60 |
| 3 | x | Levi's jeans | £180 |
| 2 | x | Adidas tracksuits | £200 |
| 1 | x | Lacoste tracksuit | £50 |
| 2 | x | Ralph Lauren shorts | £100 |
| 1 | x | Diadora shorts | £20 |
| 4 | x | Adidas shorts | £80 |
| 1 | x | Sergio Tacchini bottoms | £50 |
| 3 | x | Helmut Lang jeans | £600 |
| 1 | x | Ellesse trackpants | £30 |
| 2 | x | Siv Stoldal cords | £200 |
| 1 | x | YSL jeans | £180 |

## JUMPERS

| | | | |
|---|---|---|--:|
| 3 | x | Vivienne Westwood | £450 |
| 2 | x | John Smedley | £200 |
| 2 | x | Lacoste | £120 |
| 3 | x | Clements Ribeiro | £500 |
| 4 | x | Ralph Lauren | £500 |
| 1 | x | Bernhard Willhelm | £300 |

## COATS

| | | | |
|---|---|---|--:|
| 2 | x | YSL jackets | £400 |
| 4 | x | Lacoste jackets | £350 |
| 1 | x | Raf Simons bomber | £200 |
| 1 | x | Burberry overcoat | £300 |

| | | | |
|---|---|---|---|
| 1 | x | vintage Christian Dior mac | £80 |
| 1 | x | Bernhard Willhelm bomber | £120 |
| 1 | x | vintage Pierre Cardin bomber | £70 |
| 1 | x | Dolce & Gabbana blazer | £150 |

## SUITS / TIES

| | | | |
|---|---|---|---|
| 1 | x | Vivienne Westwood suit | £400 |
| 1 | x | Joe Casely-Hayford suit | £400 |
| 1 | x | Vivienne Westwood tie | £50 |
| 1 | x | Daks tie | £40 |

## SHOES

| | | | |
|---|---|---|---|
| 11 x | | Adidas | £770 |
| 2 | x | Nike | £150 |
| 3 | x | Reebok | £120 |
| 2 | x | New Balance | £125 |
| 2 | x | Gucci | £500 |
| 1 | x | B-Store | £125 |
| 1 | x | Helmut Lang | £150 |

## HATS / BELTS

| | | | |
|---|---|---|---|
| 1 | x | Vivienne Westwood hat | £120 |
| 1 | x | Aquascutum hat | £75 |
| 1 | x | Gucci visor | £150 |
| 1 | x | Lacoste visor | £50 |
| 1 | x | Gucci cap | £120 |
| 1 | x | Moschino cap | £80 |
| 2 | x | Kangol hat | £175 |
| 2 | x | Ralph Lauren belts | £90 |
| 1 | x | Louis Vuitton belt | £150 |

## UNDERWEAR

| | | | |
|---|---|---|---|
| 15 x | | Calvin Klein pants | £75 |
| 5 | x | Burlington socks | £25 |

| 2 | x | Ralph Lauren socks | £25 |
|---|---|---|---|
| 1 | x | Burberry socks | £10 |
| SUB-TOTAL | | | **£15,445** |

## JEWELLERY

| 1 | x | vintage Swatch watch | £40 |
|---|---|---|---|
| 1 | x | Vivienne Westwood chain | £80 |
| 1 | x | Karen Walker chain | £90 |
| 3 | x | Silas chains | £150 |
| 1 | x | Louis Vuitton money clip | £80 |
| 1 | x | Adidas keyring | (gift) |
| 1 | x | Vivienne Westwood cufflinks | £120 |
| SUB-TOTAL | | | **£560** |

## LUGGAGE

| 1 | x | Louis Vuitton wallet | £80 |
|---|---|---|---|
| 1 | x | Samsonite trolley bag | £70 |
| 1 | x | North Face rucksack | £60 |
| 1 | x | Louis Vuitton satchel | £380 |
| 1 | x | Louis Vuitton notepad | £180 |
| SUB-TOTAL | | | **£770** |

## ELECTRICALS

| 1 | x | Technics turntable | £350 |
|---|---|---|---|
| 1 | x | NAD amplifier | £200 |
| 1 | x | Mission speakers | £300 |
| 1 | x | Pioneer Mix CD | £300 |
| 1 | x | Roberts radio | £120 |
| 1 | x | Blackberry phone | (free) |
| 1 | x | Treo phone | (free) |
| 1 | x | Dyson vacuum | £150 |
| 1 | x | Sharp LCD | £900 |
| 1 | x | Pioneer DVD | £150 |
| 1 | x | Amstrad phone | £100 |
| 1 | x | Kenwood kettle | £40 |

| | | | |
|---|---|---|---|
| 1 | x | Olympus digital camera | £100 |
| 1 | x | Liebherr fridge (dispose of at tip) | £250 |
| SUB-TOTAL | | | **£2960** |

### FURNITURE

| | | | |
|---|---|---|---|
| 1 | x | Habitat sideboard | £300 |
| 1 | x | Anne Jacobson chair | £120 |
| 1 | x | Skandium chair | £100 |
| 2 | x | Muji storage boxes | £60 |
| SUB-TOTAL | | | **£580** |

### CROCKERY

| | | | |
|---|---|---|---|
| 4 | x | Bodum cups | £60 |
| 2 | x | Heal's vases | £150 |
| SUB-TOTAL | | | **£210** |

### COSMETICS (PERSONAL)

| | | | |
|---|---|---|---|
| 1 | x | Gillette Mach3 Turbo razor | £5.50 |
| 1 | x | Simple Soap | £1.00 |
| 1 | x | Dr Hauschka moisturiser 50ml | £9.00 |
| 1 | x | Simple deodorant | £2.00 |
| 1 | x | Colgate toothpaste 100ml | £2.00 |
| 1 | x | Colgate toothbrush | £3.50 |
| 1 | x | L'Oréal shampoo | £3.00 |
| 1 | x | L'Oréal conditioner | £2.00 |
| 1 | x | Dax hair wax | £3.50 |
| 4 | x | Waitrose recycled toilet roll | £1.50 |

### COSMETICS (HOUSEHOLD)

| | | | |
|---|---|---|---|
| 1 | x | Fairy washing-up liquid 5-litre | £9.50 |
| 1 | x | Mr Muscle bathroom cleaner | £1.50 |
| 1 | x | Mr Muscle kitchen cleaner | £2.50 |
| 1 | x | Mr Muscle sink unblocker | £3.50 |
| 1 | x | Flash floor cleaner | £1.00 |
| 1 | x | Cif bathroom cream | £1.50 |
| 1 | x | Domestos bleach | £1.00 |

| 1 | x | Fairy Automatic detergent 5-litre | £9.00 |
|---|---|---|---|
| 1 | x | Woolite laundry liquid | £1.50 |
| SUB-TOTAL | | | £64 |
| TOTAL | | | £21,345 |

## -96 days

I originally bought the brands on my TO BE DESTROYED list because I thought that they were the best ones for me. But how exactly had I come to decide that they were my kinds of brands? I wonder, had I chosen differently, would my life be any better or worse? I have come across a study conducted at Baylor University Medical Centre in the States that tests this very question.[13]

When students were asked to taste two unlabelled cola samples, which were actually Coke and Pepsi, an equal number preferred one over the other. However, when one sample was identified as Coke and the other left unidentified (both were actually Coke), there was a strong preference towards the labelled Coke, but no strong preference when the same was identified as Pepsi. Brand marketing has a direct physiological effect on the brain, and thus on the brain's capacity to make choices. When we drink from a can that is clearly marked Coca-Cola, our brains not only respond to the taste of the beverage, but associations we have learned about the brand.

A brand is a collection of perceptions in the mind of the consumer. Brands communicate messages so that we can attach positive associations to their product. With repeated exposure to advertising and marketing, we store these associations in the mind, the sum total of which combine to form a perception, the *brand image*. We then form an opinion around these perceptions relating to our wants, needs and aspirations.

When we browse over competing products in the store, we rely on these perceptions to help us make a choice. That choice is based upon the promises that the brand proposes to us. When we believe in those promises, the product becomes something of value to us.

Imagine a beer bottle with a sticker bearing the Carlsberg logo. The bottle will obviously contain beer and we can almost taste the product before it is opened. But imagine the same bottle with a sticker for Anadin attached. How, exactly, will that taste? Now imagine a bottle of pills with a Carlsberg label. Can we be sure of what the pills will do when we take them? Over time, we come to accept a brand's promises without question. The meaning of a brand can become so instinctive that we can anticipate what the product will do for us before we consume it.

BRAND PROMISES

| | |
|---|---|
| Promise of origin | *The product is authentic.* |
| Promise of performance | *The product is consistent, and will do what it is supposed to without causing harm or embarrassment.* |
| Promise of reassurance | *We will feel confident when consuming the product.* |
| Promise of transformation | *The experience will change our lives for the better.* |

Every aspect of branding exists to communicate positive messages about the product. The design of the packaging, the tone of the advertising, the environments in which we experience them; these things communicate layers of meaning that gradually build to form attitudes and feelings towards a product. These messages surround us in almost every aspect of our lives, which is why, when asked, we can recall information and form opinions about brands, many of which we have no real desire to consume.

## −93 days

Alarm bells ring again at my second meeting with Carol, when we spend ten minutes discussing the red Diadora shorts I have turned up in.

'What are you saying to me, Neil, by wearing those shorts?'

'Er, I dunno, what do you mean?'

'I really do like them a lot; they're such a vibrant bright red . . . you must have been in a good mood when you chose to wear them this morning.'

I'm beginning to think this is all a bit Mickey Mouse. I didn't come here to deconstruct my shorts. If I'd turned up in leather chaps or a diamanté-encrusted leotard, surely that would be a talking point? She senses my discomfort. 'Do you find it hard to accept compliments from people, Neil?'

'As a matter of fact, I do.'

'Funny . . . you spend so much time engineering an image of yourself to other people, yet you find it difficult to accept praise for all the effort you have made.'

She's right. For all the time and money I spend, making sure that my self-image is as perfect as it can be, I tend to deflect compliments with a throwaway, self-deprecatory remark, or, at best, an embarrassed blush of gratitude. Either way, the experience is uncomfortable.

'Did your father ever pay you compliments when you were younger?'

'I'm sure he did once in a while, but my only memories are of him being critical. I underachieved at school because I was lazy, and I had trouble concentrating in class. I fell into the "wrong" set at school and was promptly downgraded to the lowest stream, which was a disappointment to both my parents, but my father especially. Unfortunately, the more he pushed me to achieve, the more I rejected him.'

'Perhaps you don't know how to take compliments because you've never been taught how to, Neil?'

## –91 days

Brands. Everywhere. On my food, on my clothes, on my computer, on my phone. There is no escaping them. Each day I find new things to add to the bonfire list; each day I wonder how I will live without them, forget the emotional dependence; and how about the practicalities? Am I really going to cancel my Orange contract and bin the Blackberry? Go back to using phone boxes? Perhaps I'll just send letters: *Dear friend, fancy a drink down the pub tomorrow night? Do please write back ASAP and let me know. Yours sincerely, Neil.*

Credit and bank cards are controlled by some of the most powerful brands in the world; will I be cutting up the Visa? At the moment, I can see no choice. As for cigarettes, unless I can rent a field in South America, harvest my own tobacco and have it flown over, now is a good time to quit.

## -90 days

Perhaps this exercise will be easier if I stop looking and listening to brand messages (advertising to you and me). I make a firm promise to myself to ignore adverts as best I can in a city covered in billboards. When adverts appear on television, I will turn the sound off, or get up and make a cup of tea. Commercial-free BBC is the best option for radio.

In commercial print media, the lines between advertising and content are much more blurred. Having worked in this world, I know that half of a magazine's content may be paid-for advertorial, and the rest is largely influenced by somebody with something to sell. The concept of corruption in magazine journalism is difficult to define, because accepting 'gifts' in return for copy is standard practice. Brands lean on publishers to feature their products within the editorial pages in return for advertising. If the publishers refuse, the brands threaten to pull their ads, and no one wants that. In reality, most titles masquerading as 'lifestyle' magazines are nothing but shopping catalogues. So no post-bonfire magazines for me then.

A favourite weekend pastime for Juliet and me would be to buy all the papers, put our feet up in the front room and trawl through the supplements. The ritual would always be tinged with a feeling of guilty superficiality, as we would typically start glossy and end on newsprint; first, fashion, culture and a bit of celebrity gossip, then travel and lifestyle, ending in actual news (if at all). But from now on, I will only read the real news in the newspaper, and forego the gloss altogether.

## -88 days

Sunday. Newspaper day. Juliet sits contentedly flicking through the lifestyle supplements. I, however, am wading through the treacle of the obituaries pages. The urge to grab a glossy magazine is almost overwhelming. 'This summer's sexiest sunglasses', 'Minimalist house makeovers', 'Ten best iPod accessories' – garish coverlines pull at my rather weak constitution. No, they are evil, I tell myself. I'll only feel worse for reading them, like I always do. The images of beauty they project, the impossible aspirations they celebrate, might appear to offer an insight into a magical world of perfection and glamour, but in reality they only make you more miserable about your own lot in life. I have watched Juliet flick through a copy of *Vogue*, only to become increasingly anxious about her wardrobe, her weight and her lifestyle. Why do we put ourselves through it? Somehow we've been led to believe that it is important to look at things that remind us how imperfect we are. And we pay money to do this?

I occasionally rustle the papers to remind Juliet that I am reading THE NEWS and not some consumer fluff, but she ignores me. Finally, I snap.

'If we are anguished by the thought of failure, it is because success offers the only reliable incentive for the world to grant us its good-will!'

'What?' says Juliet, looking up from *Sunday Times Style*.

'Alain de Botton, *Status Anxiety*. You might want to think about it'.

Juliet stares blankly for a few seconds. 'You're just jealous. Get back to your obituaries.'

## –87 days

Back in therapy. Why am I so desperate to impress people with these brands, particularly when I find compliments hard to take? Why should I care what anybody thinks about me, least of all strangers? Can I not maintain some sense of self-esteem without the approval of others? Possible reason: I remember that the pretty girls at school never really paid much attention to me. I clearly remember one episode of rejection in the playground at junior school: a beautiful girl called Hannah with perfect long blonde hair (known as a Timotei girl), during a game of kiss chase, point-blank refused to kiss me, insisting that I was too ugly. In the playground you were either ugly or beautiful – the concept of ugly-beautiful hadn't arrived yet – and the moment galvanised my view of myself. I was fundamentally unattractive, the nice girls would never fancy me, and the best I could do in life would be to overcompensate in other ways. Which is where the brands come in.

'I think that conformity is a big issue with you, Neil,' says Carol.

'Really? I always liked to think of myself as a bit of a tearaway.'

'No. Throughout your childhood, you have been taught that you must conform to other people's expectations in order to be accepted and loved. As an adult, you are now anticipating their expectations by collecting these status symbols around you. I think part of your relationship with brands stems from you projecting unachievable expectations on yourself.'

She's right. If you asked me whether I cared what other people thought about me, my instant reaction would be no, I live life on my own terms and to hell with the rest. In reality though, I am completely ruled by status anxiety and the acceptance of others. My shoes might be slightly more special than the average man's, my mobile phone is probably more sophisticated than most, but that doesn't mean I am really any more confident in myself, any happier. Compared to the average man with boring shoes and a basic phone, I am the needier person. He obviously doesn't care too much about being accepted, or admired, or loved, otherwise he would try harder, like me.

## –86 days

During my time as a magazine editor, I often worked with brands that sponsored our parties and events. Some of the projects that I initiated would not have happened without the financial support of those companies. In this respect, you might say that our culture is all the richer for brands donating money to projects that would otherwise be financially unviable. Evian once saved a public lido in South London from closure by paying to renovate the pool with branded tiles. Microsoft's Xbox funded a skate park for underprivileged kids. The majority of art shows and music festivals would not exist were it not for brand partnerships. But, in my experience, the collusion often amounted to a sort of dance with the devil. During early negotiations, brand managers would agree that their involvement would remain unobtrusive or *below the line*. By the time of the project's fruition, the formerly agreed subtleties would make way for giant logos and bastardised content, having filtered through many levels of brand management. Often the sponsoring brand negotiated near-complete control of the proceedings.

I read in the paper today that the German World Cup is rife with bizarre demands from the sponsors. Budweiser, the official beer of the competition, ordered 1000 Dutch fans to remove their trousers before entering the stadium today. The offending orange trousers – the colour of the national team – were promotional giveaways from a rival brand, Bavaria, who had not paid FIFA any sponsorship money. And so the fans watched Holland's 2–1 victory in their underpants.

German fans have widely condemned FIFA for enforcing a ban on local beer brands at World Cup matches, forcing them to drink only Budweiser. The *Guardian* today notes: 'There is little doubt of the seemingly unlimited power that sponsors now wield over global sporting events.'[14]

## -85 days

It is fascinating to read about the ways that brands are manufactured in order to appeal to the senses. So much of the communication is instinctive, to the extent that even the managers at brands are probably unaware of the signals they are sending out.

Between 55 and 95 per cent of communication between humans is non-verbal. During a conversation, we are more likely to respond to gestures, tone of voice, physical appearance and context than to what is actually being said, although most of the time we are not conscious this is happening. We are more likely to believe what we *see* as opposed to what we are *told*. Brands communicate in much the same way.

The logos, symbols, typefaces and colours that combine to form a brand's identity trigger a range of emotions connected to the desirability of the brand. As consumers, we tend to be drawn to familiarity. If we are faced with a dilemma of choice, we will opt for the brand we know best first. Even when we try a product for the first time, we will tend to choose the famous brand because we equate fame with popularity; if a brand is popular, it must be good. This copycat effect is known in the business as *contagious demand*.

The colours that brands use have specific physical and psychological properties that can be linked to a product. Red is linked to masculinity, excitement, and can be 'felt' as friendly. Red also grabs our attention the quickest, raises our pulse rates and makes time appear to pass faster. Green evokes a sense of harmony, balance and refreshment. Unlike red, the eye doesn't need to make any adjustments to see green, and is therefore restful and reassuring. Of the other main colours, blue stimulates clear thought and is trustful. Yellow is optimistic, extroverted and creative.

Beyond the logo and colour, the brand name encapsulates all that is synonymous with the product and its values. To enhance *brand recall* the name is usually short, meaningful and easy to pronounce. Studies show that we will be positively inclined towards a brand if the name is pleasant-sounding. Names that start with harsh-sounding plosives, such as *b*, *d* and *k*, escape from the mouth quickly, and are associated with practical products (Black & Decker, Dewalt, Bostik). Softer letters such as *s* and *c* – sibilants – are associated with romantic and serene images and therefore luxury products (Chanel, Swarovski, Cacharel).

During a dinner party in the 1950s, a woman famously asked the industrial designer Raymond Loewy why he used two Xs when he designed the Exxon brand. 'Why do you ask?' enquired Loewy. 'Because I couldn't help noticing,' she replied. 'Well,' replied Loewy, 'that is the answer.' Brands often use repeated consonants (Coca-Cola) or vowels (AA), or onomatopoeic words that remind us of the product (Schweppes). Increasingly common is companies' use of basic words that trigger familiar images in the brain; when we see an advert for Apple, we already have preconceived associations with the word and are therefore more able to remember it. As we grow more familiar with the brand, the original meaning of the word becomes permanently linked with the product that has adopted it. While humble utility brands only claim to do what they say on the tin (Blu-Tack, Pritt Stick), names with more ambiguous associations (Liberty, *Cosmopolitan*) are capable of inspiring more grandiose aspirations.

Traditionally, brand logos portrayed the company name in an individual font, as in KitKat or Coca-Cola, often accompanied by a character or mascot such as the Michelin Man or the Jolly Green Giant. But more commonplace nowadays is the abstract logo, such as the Nike swoosh, or the Mercedes star. As a rule, linear logos and typefaces are more practical and dependable, while curvy logos are adaptable and creative.

The modern brand logo is visual shorthand for an array of mental associations and metaphors for identity, emotion and value; their presence on a product often demands greater worth than the basic value of the product itself.

## -84 days

A new magazine has been launched, devoted entirely to shopping. Fifty best winter coats. Spending habits of the stars. Jessica Simpson – style on a budget. Two hundred pages of the stuff. The magazine is called *Happy*. It's all becoming clear now. Where magazines and adverts were once essential tools for staying abreast of the Zeitgeist, I now see them for the devil's handiwork that they really are.

Careful, mustn't take this too far.

## -83 days

Sitting in a cinema yesterday, waiting for the film to start, I saw an advert for Lynx. During the advert, a man sprays himself with deodorant and, within minutes, he is besieged with beautiful women who are magnetically attracted to him. The message, taken literally, is that women will find you irresistible if you buy the deodorant. The last time that I bought Lynx, I noticed no improvement in my magnetic capabilities, unless the women were playing hard to get. Surely no man in the cinema really believes the promise that this is advert is making? Yet the advert must work. Otherwise the company would not spend the money producing it. A quick search on the web reveals that Lynx is indeed the biggest-selling deodorant brand in the world.

On a subconscious level, the branding *does* work, even though the product cannot possibly deliver on its promise.

Advertising has become so engaging, so fun to be around, that we tend to ignore the fact that it is there to sell us things. We treat adverts more like entertainment, which is why the cinema was full yesterday, 20 minutes before the film started. The ads have become part of the cinema experience. I know of very few people who would admit to being influenced, or even manipulated, by advertising. But I am starting to think that this is exactly how the brands want us to think. We approach advertising rather casually, believing that we are too savvy, too rational to be taken in by outlandish promises. In actual fact, we consumers are a lot less rational than we are prepared to believe. As Marshall McLuhan once noted: 'Ads are not meant for conscious consumption. They are intended as subliminal pills for the subconscious.'[15]

How many people, on seeing an inspirational advert for Nike, immediately sprint off in search of their goals? Not many. How many people secretly wish they were Serena Williams or Wayne Rooney? Lots. We are all given to daydreams of winning the lottery and becoming rich, winning *Pop Idol* and becoming famous, meeting Brad Pitt and falling madly in love. The emotions that we experience about a brand transform the moment when we use the product for the better. On an emotional level, a product does its job much better when there is a famous brand attached to it. Brand commentator Paul Feldwick believes that the transformational powers of the brand adds real value to a product:

> It is commonly asserted that paying more 'for the name' is a foolish delusion on the part of the customer, as little more than a confidence trick on the part of the seller. Yet the benefit to the customer is a real enhancement of his experience of consumption, whether it consists in peace of mind or as an imaginative experience.[16](Paul Feldwick, 2002)

To buy a Mercedes is not simply to purchase a quality-built German car, it is the purchase of confidence, glamour and sophistication.

The emotions that we expect to feel when we use a product, and thus the value of the product, are greatly enhanced by the brand that accompanies it. The branding seeks to make us feel passionate, excited and happy about ourselves. An advert on television makes us laugh, and we remember the positive feeling when we see the brand later on. On a billboard, a beautiful woman fellates an expensive ice cream; we then associate the ice cream with sensuous luxury. A brand of rum sponsors a tent at a music festival; we associate the brand with euphoric hedonism.

This branding may help manufacturers to sell more units, but it is surely at the emotional expense of the customer. Eating ice cream feels nothing like fellatio. A shot of rum does not guarantee instant euphoria. Being constantly let down on these outlandish promises must take its toll on our wellbeing.

## −82 days

When was the last time that a real person made me feel glamorous? Or told me that I was daring or intelligent or successful? Aside from the close relationships with Juliet and my immediate family, I cannot recall very many instances when I was paid a compliment that really made me feel good about myself. Brands, on the other hand, make me feel good about myself all the time. In building my self-esteem, brands give me the confidence to be myself, only better. They seem to understand my innermost desires, sometimes better than my friends do.

In 2005, the football team at Shevington Technical College in Wigan switched kit manufacturers from a little-known local brand to Nike. Parents were initially appalled at the high costs of the new kit, but the level of complaints soon receded when the team began showing a marked improvement in their performance. Player confidence shot 'sky high' when rival teams began complimenting them on their kit, and the overall level of participation in PE at the school rocketed as a result.[17] According to the Livingston Market Research Group in America, there are four emotional needs that we look for when we buy into the promise of a brand.[18]

1. **SELF ACTUALISATION** *OR* **I WANT TO BE IN CONTROL.**
   We derive self-esteem from setting and accomplishing goals, filling us with a sense of confidence and empowerment. We are in control over our destiny.

   *Example*: Microsoft 'Where do you want to go today?'

2. **INTERPERSONAL LOVE AND ROMANCE** *OR* **I WANT PEOPLE TO LOVE ME / TO BELONG.**
   Being loved by someone held in high regard gives us a sense of self-worth. The need to feel attractive, and to appear lovable.

   *Example*: Olay 'Olay, love the skin you're in.'

3. **NURTURANT AND PARENTAL ESTEEM** *OR* **I WANT TO BE RESPONSIBLE.**
   Taking responsibility for the wellbeing of offspring, or significant others we care about, makes us feel good about ourselves.

   *Example*: Scottish Widows 'Preparation is everything.'

4. **ALTRUISM AND SOCIETAL ESTEEM** *OR* **I WANT TO GIVE BACK TO SOCIETY, I CARE ABOUT THE WELFARE OF OTHERS.**
   Contributing to the broader wellbeing and welfare of society makes us feel better about ourselves.

   *Example*: Oxfam 'Helping people to help themselves.'

These emotional triggers do seem very familiar to me. One might argue that there is very little wrong with using products to make us feel better about ourselves. But there is an insidious side to emotional branding that the manuals often fail to outline, that is the triggering of negative emotions in order to sell a product. Surely brands are equally capable of eliciting greed, paranoia, inadequacy and competitiveness?

**1. SELF ACTUALISATION OR MY GOALS ARE SLIPPING AWAY WHILE EVERYONE ELSE IS ACHIEVING.**

Watching others enjoying better lifestyles than our own triggers feelings of envy and dismay. We worry that the course of life is out of our control.

*Example*: Moët & Chandon 'Be fabulous.'

**2. INTERPERSONAL LOVE AND ROMANCE OR EVERYONE IS YOUNGER / FITTER / PRETTIER THAN ME.**

Comparing ourselves to the standardised notions of beauty, we feel inferior, excluded, unlovable and lonely.

*Example*: Maybelline 'Maybe she's born with it – maybe it's Maybelline.'

**3. NURTURANT AND PARENTAL ESTEEM OR I CAN'T PROVIDE MY LOVED ONES WITH THE THINGS THAT THEY WANT.**

Failing to meet the expectations of others makes us feel anxious and depressed, and we feel obliged to overcompensate in some other way.

*Example*: Abbey 'Because life is complicated enough.'

**4. ALTRUISM AND SOCIETAL ESTEEM OR I DON'T CARE ENOUGH TO MAKE A REAL DIFFERENCE TO PEOPLE'S PROBLEMS.**

Seeing the suffering of those less fortunate than ourselves makes us feel selfish and guilty, compelling us to offset the shame in some way.

*Example*: NSPCC 'Cruelty to children must stop. Full stop.'

I know which type of emotional branding triggers me into buying; anxiety is the driver behind so many of my purchases. Rarely do I buy into brands so that people will love me more. Rather, I buy them in case people will love me *less* without them.

Spend a glorious day in the countryside to escape 'the buzz'. No shops, no billboards, the only logos to be found out in the fields are Hunter Wellington Boots on the feet of fellow walkers. Being surrounded by undeveloped countryside makes my brand neurosis redundant; people can and do live away from mindless consumerism – although I am sure they're all doing the weekly shop at the nearest out-of-town supermarket. For urbanised people such as myself, the country is a place where one comes to escape the frenzy of city life, but very few of us ever manage to stay beyond a weekend. We begin to miss the very thing we sought to escape. The silence of a rural field becomes deafening compared to the roar of traffic that streams past my bedroom window each day. With nothing to distract the eye, or indeed the mind, thoughts turn to 'the big picture', which is almost always an uncomfortable subject.

I am dependent on the city buzz for distraction, although I've always suspected that it wasn't entirely good for me. Rather like smoking, you know it is killing you slowly but you just can't seem to give it up. What is it exactly that causes this buzz? Certainly it is the hustle and bustle of people, lots of them, living in close confinement. But I now realise that advertising and branding contribute to the mental din; huge great billboards staring down at me from every angle of the eye, neon shop signs flashing furiously for my attention. Since birth, my brain has been continually stimulated by hundreds of images and sounds, the messages of which ring around my ears for days on end. Kalle Lasn, the founder of *Adbusters* magazine, describes this din as the *toxicity of the mind*.

Mr Muscle loves the jobs you hate. Burger King Flame-Grilled Whopper for only £2.99. Big Brother, tonight at nine on 4. New Elvive Anti-Breakage Shampoo from L'Oréal Paris. The KFC Family Feast for only £9.99, the perfect way to end your day. Oral B Pulsar, changing the way you brush . . . forever. Call 0800 50 50 50 for cheaper car insurance with the AA team, here to get you a better deal. Download official ringtones with jamster.co.uk. Disney Pixar's *Cars* in cinemas from July 28. Get yourself some hairapy with Sunsilk.

Always, keeps you shower fresh all day. Save double in the DFS summer sale. Big splash lashes and 50 per cent more length and curve with Rimmel London. Get closer to Robbie Williams with the W300i Walkman phone. Dentists recommend Sensodyne for sensitive teeth. Birds Eye: fishermen catch the salmon, freezing catches the freshness. O2, see what you can do.

It is impossible to avoid completely the glare of advertising while living in any city, particularly London. But since I resolved to stop looking and listening to so many adverts back in March, my head feels slightly clearer, the volume of the buzz turned down a notch or two. It is a relief to have fewer messages ricocheting around my mind throughout the day. As I head back into London, I wonder, will I be able to tolerate more than a weekend in the countryside next time I visit?

## –80 days

I come across a quote from the brand expert David Aacker, which would seem to prove that I am not entirely mad in thinking one can hold relationships with brands.

> Some people may never aspire to have the personality of a competent leader but would like to have a relationship with one, especially if they need a banker or a lawyer. A trustworthy, dependable, conservative personality might be boring but might nonetheless reflect characteristics valued in a financial advisor, a lawn service, or even a car.[19]

Studies in narcissism often prove that, as individuals, we are instinctively drawn to other people who display the same personality traits as ourselves, or indeed the traits we would *like* to see in ourselves. Thus we are drawn to brands in much the same way. In choosing one brand over another, we ask, 'If this product were a person, what would she be like?' And even more importantly, 'If it were a person, would I like, trust or admire her?' In making these decisions, we affirm self-worth to ourselves, and express our personalities to those around us. The down-to-earth, family-orientated Cola buyer will often choose Coke, while the young and up-to-date will reach for Pepsi. These are the unspoken consumer values that are the glue to brand loyalty; ultimately, brands help us validate our perceptions of ourselves. Product + personality = brand.

## −79 days

I have forgotten to add one very important 'to do' item on the list; give up smoking. I have been a casual smoker since the age of 16. The first brand that I smoked was Consulate, because I thought that the menthol would smell less strong and go undetected by the parents (I was wrong). As a staunch pro-smoker in my teens, I was attracted to the heritage brands that were popular during the 1950s when smoking was socially acceptable, so I smoked Dunhill. Finally, I changed to Marlboro, because all the cool people in London seemed to smoke them.

Taste in food being such an individual preference, I always found it rather curious that entire demographics of people would prefer the taste of one cigarette brand. But venture into any fashionable bar in London, and the cigarette vending machines are normally stocked with only one brand: Marlboro Lights. In the south west of England, Silk Cut and Benson & Hedges are the most popular brands among smokers. The market for cigarettes in northern England is dominated by Embassy and Royals. If all the smokers in a London pub were asked to name their preferred flavour of crisps, the response would be varied – as individuals, they would have different tastes from one another. So why would almost every smoker in that pub choose Marlboro Lights? I now realise that taste has little to do with the preference for cigarette brands. Cigarettes being such symbolic products, we choose the brand that encapsulates our identity best. Embassy Filters are smoked by working-class northerners. B&H are smoked by suburban housewives. Marlboro Lights are for southern posers. Rare is the smoker who changes loyalty to another brand of cigarettes. If he or she does, it is to another brand accepted by the same social class.

In 1899, the social theorist Thorstein Veblen attempted to show how everyday consumption had become a process of social distinction, coining the phrase *conspicuous consumption*. Veblen saw how the emerging class of wealthy industrialists in New England (the nouveau riche) had begun to dress, eat and behave generally in the same way as the upper-class Europeans did. Within the rigid class structure of the early 20th century, the landed gentry retained a higher social status than industrialists, but the newly affluent were keen to elevate their position, by purchasing and displaying expensive and tasteful commodities.

This wealthy new class mimicked the customs of their betters in order to raise themselves above the workers and artisans. The aristocracy looked down upon the new imposters with distaste. Veblen argued that this principle of social emulation – the poor always look to the wealthy for standards of taste – was the driving force behind ever-changing fashion and increasing levels of consumption. Those at the height of society were continually changing their tastes in order to distance themselves from the lower orders, who, in turn, were consuming more in order to catch up. Being the arbiters of good taste, the rich maintain their position in social hierarchy, creating a trickle-down effect, whereby the lower orders copy fashion and symbols of good taste, through the nouveau riche to the middle classes, and finally to the working classes.

Much has changed since Veblen assayed the silken top hats of Bradford millionaires. Yet this hierarchy of taste continues to affect different classes in our society. But, in our times, the orders have shifted, the trends are calculated, and commerce assists the process, for profit. The industrialists and their publicists are the taste-makers and the industry is called fashion.

Material objects take on social meaning, allowing us to express ourselves and communicate with each other. We want, buy and display things not simply because of what the things can do for us, but because of what things mean. The consumer choices that we make become part of our lifestyle. Our lifestyle becomes part of our identity. Even the most banal products, like bread, tell stories about our lifestyle. To choose white sliced Mother's Pride over Hovis Granary or

Tesco's Finest Ciabatta is to tell the story of our social standing, our upbringing and our aspirations in life. In so many instances, we are what we buy.

The plain white 'Value' brand is bought by someone who cannot or does not want to spend a lot of money on bread, or maybe they simply enjoy the taste of cheap bread; perhaps this is something they were brought up on. The more expensive and healthier 'Finest' brand reflects the choice of a consumer who is able or prepared to pay four times the price, is concerned with their long-term health over instant gratification, and enjoys the taste of 'something different'. By choosing 'Finest' over 'Value' we join a more refined, knowing group of consumers with a sensible and healthy lifestyle. *We* eat organic wholemeal bread; *they* make do with processed white.

In a time before mass consumption and urban living, we would use our family, jobs and personal achievements to define our identity. Today, most of us live in densely populated spaces, work for impersonal companies and are governed by seemingly anonymous organisations. Mass consumption offers us a bewildering array of choices in life and causes our identity to be less fixed. Engulfed in the crowd, we lose our individual identities and become one with the mass. The situation causes us to question our own self-image; we suffer from a crisis of identity. Brands allow us to become more like the person that would buy a certain loaf of bread. Our shopping list sets the style of our lives.

## -78 days

I need to start thinking seriously about my life after the bonfire. I'll need some clothes for starters. There is a vintage store – for vintage, read Oxfam at ten times the price – in town that sells non-branded plimsolls, very much like the ones my mother bought me for school before I seized control of my wardrobe, and the exact same shoes that I would later bully kids for wearing. They are plain white canvas with a thin sole, no branding or logos on them whatsoever, not even on the insole. And they are only £4.99. Previously, I would have thought nothing of spending £150 on a new pair of trainers, whether I could afford them or not. The circle is now complete. As the fashionably surly assistant bags my lo-fi footwear, I ask where the things come from.

'I've no idea where the manager got 'em,' she drawls, 'they just came in as a job lot. Probably China.'

Here lies the giant caveat in this no-logo crusade. With no brand to act as a guarantee of workmanship or origin, the quality and ethics of production is a gamble, with odds stacked heavily in favour of the sweatshop. Best not think about that for the time being, while I scoop up any unbranded item of clothing that I can find.

## -77 days

When I was young, my favourite TV shows all seemed to revolve around cars: *Knight Rider, Dukes of Hazzard, Magnum, Inspector Morse* (on a Sunday, as the least worst alternative to *Songs of Praise*). I always imagined that I would own a cool car when I grew up; something like a vintage Aston Martin or a 1980s Mercedes 350SL . . . sexy, but not too showy; a bit of class goes a long way. There was no question about the money to pay for it; I was one of Thatcher's children, after all.

I am unsure exactly what went wrong with the plan. At the age of 31, I am driving my partner's 1995 Citroën AX. Admittedly I prioritised my disposable income by taking on a crippling mortgage in Central London. But the plan was to be able to afford both. More even.

Never is this question more poignant when one is sitting at the lights in the AX, beside a sexy brand new open-top Audi with a teenage boy behind the wheel and a beautiful girl in the passenger seat. The anxiety is crushing. As I pull away from the lights, I try my best to keep up with the shiny new cars that cut in front from all sides. But it's no use. Who am I kidding? I'm driving an old banger made by a boring French company, and that's that.

To drive that Citroën is to experience a rollercoaster of emotions. I get into the car; the interior is cramped and flimsy. The Citroën logo greets me on the steering wheel. Ugh, Citroën, what a rubbish brand; the lukewarm also-ran to Peugeot, which isn't much good either. The kind of car driven by people who don't care about cars.

But this is okay. I remind myself that I'm not a 'car' person any more. I'm just getting from A to B in this thing and therefore it is not worth the worry. I pull away from the kerb, craning my neck to see round the Range Rover parked in front. Bloody SUV drivers, surely the dumbest car owners in the world. They should be taxed double, once for the car and once for the stupidity. Ah, suddenly I feel virtuous driving the AX. It is economical, reliable and, if anyone ever asks, I can tell them it's not mine, it's my girlfriend's. The next minute, I'm being cut up by an arrogant BMW driver. I speed after him and pull up alongside him at the lights in front. Ever keen to row with ill-mannered strangers, I begin to roll the window down, planning to give Mr BMW some choice road-rage patter. He looks over at me from his cocoon of air-conditioned, leather-trimmed luxury, waiting for me to explode. I stop short, however, suddenly feeling deflated. It doesn't matter what I say. It doesn't matter who was right or wrong. One of us is driving a beautiful car, and it's certainly not me. So who's the winner here?

For the rest of the journey, I drive like an 80-year-old vicar, allowing all and sundry to speed past as I wallow in my branded shame. I feel angry with myself; angry for not making enough money to afford a decent car; angry at how shallow I am for caring; angry with everyone else on the road for making me feel this way. I remember how, whenever I drove the car to my parents, I would imagine they felt embarrassed to have it parked by the house (neighbours' curtains twitching furiously – 'What a failure that Neil Boorman turned out to be'). If I ever drove to work, I made sure it was parked far from the view of my colleagues.

But, in fact, that Citroën has transformed me over time, in the same way the one careful lady owner has. When I first met Juliet, I consumed brands without question. I was adamant that the Gucci flip-flops, the Dunhill lighter, the LV wallet made me more sophisti-cated, more lovable, and more like the person I wanted to be. Infuriatingly, these status symbols failed to make much of an impact on her. Over time, I realised that she actually found the status brands distasteful, which secretly made me feel rather stupid. I carried on spending regardless, often hiding the stuff in the spare room where she wouldn't look. Always, I admired her for being relatively free of the anxious desire to shop, despite my showering her with fancy branded trinkets in an attempt to bring her over to my side of the fence.

Juliet doesn't go through this torment each time she drives the AX. It's a car. It gets you to where you need to go, end of story. In a few months from now, I'm going to drive, no, cruise that car around town for all to see. Yeah, that's me, behind the wheel of an AX; want to make something of it or what?

## -76 days

H&M has announced the appointment of Viktor & Rolf to design a new collection, which should spark another frenzy in the high street. Last year Stella McCartney launched a limited edition collection at Hennes and, on the morning of its launch, the world seemed to congregate outside the shops. Any woman with an ounce of fashion sense called in sick to work and queued for hours in the street for a once-in-a-lifetime bargain. Juliet was momentarily swept up in the hysteria and dragged me along at 9.30 a.m. for the store opening in Covent Garden. I found myself amidst an unsightly dash and grab, as hundreds of women – many of whom were old enough to know better – snatched fistfuls of clothes from the rails and ran towards the tills. No brand campaign has the power to manipulate consumers completely beyond their will, but there are plenty that can persuade people to skip work, queue in the cold, fight with fellow customers, and plunge further into debt buying new versions of things they already have.

Douglas Atkin, director of strategy for Mercedes, explains how brands can arouse this hysteria in his book *The Culting of Brands*. He compares techniques to those used by the Moonies:

> An individual with even the slightest sense of alienation from the world around them is often searching for a sense of community, most likely a group of people that will see his or her differences as a virtue. In exploiting this tendency in consumers, brands

promote openness and belonging to their cult, while demonising rival groups. They must mythologise the power of the individual connecting to each member through a system of belief.[20]

During the late 1990s, General Motors identified a segment in the car market that was yearning for a return to family values, previously filled by church and schools – America was looking for a caring car firm. And so the Saturn brand was created. Basing the brand identity around a wholesome set of values, Saturn owners were invited to visit the birthplace of the car – Spring Hill, Tennessee – over a weekend, to get to know the company, its employees and other likeminded owners. Hosted by Olympic athletes and rhythm 'n' blues stars, the weekend became a celebration of a newfound way of life. Members of the 'family' took plant tours; Disney hosted Camp Saturn for the kids; a couple even got married there, Saturn's president obligingly giving away the bride. Saturn provided an invitation to a lifestyle, a ready-made identity, and over 40,000 people responded.

In the words of Kevin Roberts, this is *loyalty beyond reason*. The mental health of the consumer is never questioned when these brand manuals evangelise how best to manufacture desire. And yet the consequences of this manipulation appear as news stories all the time. In 2001, a Chicago woman was spared jail after embezzling $250,000 from her former employer, after her defence team claimed that she used the money to fund buying binges – a type of self-medication in response to her depression. The judge accepted that theft of funds was beyond her control, believing as she did that shopping would bring happiness.[21]

## –74 days

I spend the day at the airport, waiting for a delayed flight to an overseas job. With countless luxury goods shops lining the corridors, Heathrow looks more like a high-end shopping mall. The seating area of the departure lounge is encircled by gleaming concessions for Gucci, Dior and Burberry. In fact there is very little else for travellers to do beyond shop while they wait for their flights. I take a token browse around the stores, but think better of purchasing – the gear would only be burnt in a matter of weeks.

It is no wonder that the luxury brands are congregated in spaces such as airports. International travel feels glamorous because we can escape the monotony of our imperfect lives, becoming whoever we want to be for two weeks. The aspirational goods on sale make the fantasy seem more real. Designer pens, diamond cufflinks and deluxe personal organisers are the essential affectations of the globetrotting businessman – directional bikinis and sun visors for the posh holiday-maker. Never mind that the gas bill, the mortgage and the overdraft need paying back home, an overpriced designer beach towel will make us feel that bit more the movie star on the beach.

In the luxury goods market, these branded trinkets are called 'entry point' products. They provide a sort of mass-market exclusivity that is expensively priced, but within the spending range of the average earner. The £200 sunglasses are really just pieces of moulded plastic. The perfumes are simply bottles of smelly water. We realise that the products are overpriced, but this only seems to make the things feel more valuable. To spend so much money on something that obviously costs so little to produce is to declare one's dedication to the aspirations of the brand. The logo on the side of the sunglasses is proof of purchase of that aspiration. With holiday money burning a hole in our pockets, it is little wonder that the airport insists that we arrive at least two hours before the flight; it gives us more time to shop.

Penned into this claustrophobic environment, the hoards of holidaymakers could surely benefit from a play area, even a crèche for kids. Perhaps an Internet café, a mini-cinema or a reading room would help to pass the time. In reality, the only non-consumer orien-tated space that I can find here is a dingy prayer room tucked behind the luxury stationers Smythson. But the departure lounge is not so very different from the wider urban environments in which most of us live. All social spaces in our towns and cities are dominated by consumption. Outside the home, the most comfortable place in which we can spend our time is the shopping mall. Besides the streets and parks, which are often rundown and dangerous to visit, the only spaces that remain free for people to roam are spaces of consumption.

The shopping mall is the place where we go to socialise, to promenade, to be entertained and, of course, to window-shop.

After three hours of people-watching, my plane finally boards. But the selling job doesn't end there. During the flight, the air stewards spend more time promoting their duty-free products than tending to basic passenger needs, parading gold watches down the aisle and announcing one-day discounts on Toblerone over the intercom. At one point, they add to the already stale air by spraying a new Gucci perfume around the cabin: 'If anyone should wish to take advantage of these low, low prices, please don't hesitate to contact one of the attendants, who are here for your complete comfort. Have a nice flight!'

## -71 days

Brand-free life after the bonfire is going to be challenging, to say the least. For two weeks now, I have been searching the Internet for a supplier of generic toothpaste. A company in Russia supplies hotel chains with blank tubes of paste that looks like little more than minty cottage cheese. I had a suspicion that cosmetics would be tough items to replace. So, I decide to turn instead to some homemade recipes; dental hygiene existed before Colgate, didn't it?

> **Toothpaste recipe for sensitive teeth**
> *Vegetable glycerin ½ cup (base)*
> *Cosmetic clay, white ½ cup (mild abrasive)*
> *Tincture of myrrh 35–40 drops (to prevent gum inflammation)*
> *Peppermint or spearmint or pudinhara 7–8 drops (fresh breath)*
> *Clove essential oil 7–8 drips (mild anaesthetic, for toothache)*
>
> Mix all the ingredients thoroughly. Adjust the quantity of glycerin to achieve the consistency of toothpaste. Store in a wide-mouthed bottle.

This should appeal to Juliet; she loves her organic vegetable box, and sometimes spends a fortune on expensive chemical-free cosmetics from Aveda and the like. She arrives home after my toothpaste discovery and I excitedly tell her that we are going homemade organic in the bathroom.

'Considering you hate cooking and preparing anything in the kitchen, I find it hard to believe that you'll be making your own toothpaste, Neil. Aren't you taking this a bit far?'

'A brand is a brand. The Colgate has to go. Anyhow, most of these brands use chemicals and additives, saccharin and sodium sulphate something. Toxic nasties, basically'.

'*Your* Colgate may have to go, mine's staying. Anyway, Colgate is not a status symbol, it's not a trendy brand. Why bother?'

'It's not as clear-cut as that.'

'Okay, well, they're your teeth you're risking.'

## -65 days

I limp into therapy, feet suffering considerable discomfort from the zero-cushioning of my non-branded plimsolls.

'Why do you think that you collect so many brands, Neil?' asks Carol. 'Do you ever feel satisfied that you have enough?'

'It feels like an addiction. I'll often find myself drifting into shops on my way to a meeting. I wake from a daze to find myself standing in a store, amongst things that I absolutely must have. I feel like I'm topping up my bank of happiness when I buy things for myself. Only the happiness never really lasts.'

'You compensate for anxiety by collecting as many things that will make you happy, yet you never stop to take stock of the happiness. The relentless pursuit of happiness is the quickest route to depression.'

'Don't we all crave happiness? Okay, I admit that I may have been looking in the wrong places for it, but surely there's nothing wrong with the pursuit of happiness?'

'The happiness that you're searching for is unsustainable. You've got to come to terms with the fact that we humans can never live in a permanent state of happiness. During our lives there are peaks of happiness and troughs of sadness, but it is the middle ground between the two that would best describe our day-to-day state. The best we can hope for, the best we can work towards, is some sort of contentment. You spend too much time concentrating on the icing, perhaps you should focus a little more on the bulk of the cake.'

## –62 days

After moaning about my foot pain on the blog, an anonymous reader takes sympathy and posts a pair of cushioned insoles to the office. I only wish they had included some toothpaste. My homemade effort is so gritty that my gums hurt, and I am positive my teeth aren't as bright as before.

## –57 days

I have perhaps been rather naïve in expecting my local markets to offer decent alternatives to the high street. I trawl around three places in Central London today – Leather Lane, Chapel Market and Strutton Ground – and none of them amounts to much good. The grocery stalls might offer an easy alternative to the supermarket, but it is obvious from the uniformly shaped apples and fluorescent red tomatoes that the produce is of the nuclear variety. When I ask one stallholder where the apples are from, he simply shrugs his shoulders and says 'from the depot'. This isn't quite the same shopping experience as Selfridges, or even Tesco for that matter.

There are lots of clothes for sale, but they are not quite the non-branded quality-made basics I had hoped for. Most of the stock is: a) genuine branded goods that have fallen from the back of a lorry; b) non-genuine brands produced by sweatshops with a poor eye for detail (Kalvin Cline boxers, Louise Vittone bags); or c) non-branded clothes fashioned from flimsy non-breathable and scratchy rayon/polyester cloth. No wonder these markets are dying. My hunter-gatherer instincts remain unsatisfied, the consumer kill amounting only to four vests, a sprig of broccoli and an organic deodorant salt stick from a healthy-living stall.

## -54 days

The plain plastic bags I'm given at the corner store seem to be the perfect anti-brand statement, and I ditch the North Face rucksack once and for all. But the bags are extremely flimsy and tend to split at the most inconvenient of times. I arrive for a therapy session only to realise that the bag has leaked a Dictaphone and notepad somewhere on the underground, along with half of my notes. John Lewis always made the strongest plastic bags. I miss them.

'Perhaps you should calm down with this de-branding thing, Neil,' Carol suggests. 'Take one step at a time.'

## -51 days

The more I think about it, the more I realise that brands help me to feel differently about myself. If I were going to a meeting and needed to impress, I would wear a completely different set of labels to those that I'd wear at a party or at the in-laws' house. Most people wear different clothes for different occasions. I could wear the same cut and colour of polo shirt to all three situations, but with a different logo embroidered on the chest each time. I'd be a different person. I wonder, when Jean René Lacoste first introduced a crocodile motif to his tennis outfit, did he ever imagine that a person's attitudes in life could be encapsulated by an inch of embroidery and graphic design?

LACOSTE

| Brand message | *the glamour of sport and leisure/European heritage* |
|---|---|
| Social meaning | *thirtysomething nod to the heyday of British football hooliganism* |
| Stereotype | *Northern scally/Southern trendy/Euro cheese ball* |

RALPH LAUREN

| Brand message | *American heritage/reverence for tradition/clean-cut lifestyle* |
|---|---|
| Social meaning | *aspiration or assertion towards high society* |
| Stereotype | *American jock/English chav/ironic chav* |

## BURBERRY

| Brand message | *English heritage/upper-class outdoor pursuits* |
|---|---|
| Social meaning | *same as Ralph Lauren mixed with a stale twist of cool Britannia* |
| Stereotype | *council estate hooligan/footballer's wife/middle-aged golfer* |

## YSL

| Brand message | *classic European glamour* |
|---|---|
| Social meaning | *reverence for the old-fashioned notions of beauty and glamour* |
| Stereotype | *rich old grannies/working-class parents who aspire to be rich* |

## NIKE

| Brand message | *physical excellence across cultures* |
|---|---|
| Social meaning | *belief in sport and leisure as (an American) way of life* |
| Stereotype | *wannabe gangsters/teenage hoodies/fitness junkies* |

## ADIDAS

| Brand message | *see Nike* |
|---|---|
| Social meaning | *see Nike, only more white and European* |
| Stereotype | *sports enthusiast/entry-level fashionista* |

## FRED PERRY

| Brand message | *updated English sporting heritage* |
|---|---|
| Social meaning | *not cool enough to wear Lacoste* |
| Stereotype | *aging mod/try-hard trendy* |

## CALVIN KLEIN

| Brand message | *spirit of 1990s American success* |
|---|---|
| Social meaning | *fashion for people who don't know about fashion* |
| Stereotype | *too random to quantify but predominantly unfashionable* |

## DIESEL

| Brand message | *the flamboyance of youth* |
|---|---|
| Social meaning | *not really as flamboyant as promised* |
| Stereotype | *Eurotrash teenagers/mums who want to feel young again* |

**HACKETT**

| Brand message | *bullish Anglo-Saxon spirit* |
|---|---|
| Social meaning | *borderline xenophobia and overt class-consciousness* |
| Stereotype | *lower- and upper-class lager louts* |

**HUGO BOSS**

| Brand message | *1980s European status symbol* |
|---|---|
| Social meaning | *terrible reminder of the worst of the 1980s* |
| Stereotype | *boardroom stallions/people who are ambivalent to brands and buy on price* |

Does the person reflect the brand or does the brand reflect the person? Carol keeps reminding me that alongside my personal de-branding, I must stop making snap judgements on the basis of other people's brands. This I think might be hardest task of all.

## -48 days

The sociologist Rachel Bowlby describes the act of window-shopping as 'the quintessential psychical drama of the 20th century, that starts with browsing and ends with buying'.[22] When we window shop, we whet our appetite for a more fulfilling, dynamic life; in browsing products we create new needs, to be sated the next time we purchase a consumer item. I certainly used to spend an incredible amount of my own time trawling the shops, especially department stores, in search of something, anything, to make me feel better about myself. Strolling around the ordered luxury of the shops, I would play out fantasies of ownership. Seeing a coat on display, I would ask the assistant if I might 'see it'. I would stand in front of the mirror, wearing the thing for the first time, and imagine what outfit would complement it, which social situations would suit it best, and how others might think of me with it on. But, window-shopping being quite different to *actual* shopping, I would postpone the purchase for another time. It is not the owning or wearing of the coat that excites me, more the *anticipation* of owning; a touchy-feely experience that bears little relation to necessity. It is wholeheartedly founded on desire and fantasy.

'Professional' window-shoppers tend to visit department stores such as Selfridges, where one can spend an entire day browsing in sumptuous surroundings, taking breaks in the store's restaurants and bars, indulging in a half-hour back rub or enjoying a facial treatment; it becomes a whole day out. Before the Industrial Revolution, the average shopping experience was a little different. Local stores were staffed by the owner and supplied by local tradesmen. Goods were usually stored behind the counter in boxes and cupboards, and the shopper would ask to see the goods before they bought them. More importantly, shoppers only visited stores according to necessity, when they needed to replenish stocks. Modern department stores filter out the noise and congestion of the outside world. There is order. Calm. As public spaces, they offer a sense of community; the store, the village hall and the social club all under one roof. Being a leisure pursuit, shopping is now legitimised as a healthy and moral activity, a thoroughly normal part of modern life.

There is no doubt that shopping, particularly for frivolous things, is enormous fun. On my way home from the library, I call into a shoe store and watch the delight sparkle over shoppers' faces as they slip on new heels and pose for themselves before full-length mirrors. Glamorous assistants float around the aisles with expressions of faint disapproval that change to acceptance the minute one makes a purchase. Technical-sounding dance music pumps from the sound system. The interior design and bright lighting dazzle the eye. These things combine to heighten the rush of hyper-reality – like a posh nightclub that has bent its strict dress code to let you, the ordinary punter, in, on the understanding that next time you'll try harder. No wonder people love to shop. Where else can one catch a glimpse of a more glamorous, more lovable version of oneself?

## −47 days

Army surplus stores might just save this project from complete failure. There I find shoes, running gear, basic clothing and athletic apparel, all non-branded, built to last, and at a fraction of the price of the branded versions. Ralph Lauren pea coat? £475. Army surplus pea coat?

£50 to you, sir. Fashion is so bankrupt of new ideas that army style is never out of style. God bless Her Majesty's Armed Forces. Full of newfound optimism, I spend the remainder of the day trawling the charity shops of London, where I fare much better than the market. A pair of nondescript jeans, several T-shirts, and a jacket that, with some alterations, a good wash at 70 degrees and a once over with the Remington Fuzz-Away, will be perfect additions to my new wardrobe. Where I once walked into Selfridges seeking transformation into a suave international jet-set type, I now amble into Oxfam with the aspirations of a self-taught stylist and dressmaker. I am clearly neither.

## -46 days

Stella Artois has announced that its draught beer is to be served in an ornate chalice from now on. The rather feminine-looking glass is seen in marketing circles as an attempt to dissuade lager louts from drinking the stuff. This would appear to be commercial suicide for Stella, whose core market in the UK is C2 or D (polite terms for lower-class, unskilled manual workers). This is a classic case of brand hijacking; the 'wrong' class of people consume a product, which lowers the perceived value of the brand.

Stella's marketing strategy has for many years centred on quality, famously describing its beer as 'Reassuringly Expensive'. They advertise via lavishly shot mini-films, illustrating the outlandish expense that common people will forego to taste their magical beer. The ads are primarily shown in cinemas, because people who go to the cinema are considered upwardly mobile. Throughout the rougher pubs of the UK, however, people commonly refer to the beer as 'Wife Beater'. It is in fact one of the cheapest lagers on the market, and, being one of the highest in strength, it is most popular among people who purchase according to price as opposed to quality (aka The Brawling Poor).

According to the press,[23] Burberry recently withdrew their checked baseball caps to prevent the brand being worn around the nation's council estates. So much for the new classless Britain.

Sitting outside a café, I see two women pass each other in the street, carrying the exact same Louis Vuitton handbag on their arms. One woman is in her late forties, dressed in an expensive-looking business suit and pearl necklace. She must be a professional woman who works in an office of some sort. The other woman is in her early twenties, dressed in a scruffy Nike tracksuit. She pushes a screaming child in a rather dilapidated pram. Both bags look authentic, but judging from the rest of the young mother's appearance, hers might well be a cheap copy bought from the market. For a split second, their eyes meet, and they seem to register their mutual taste in handbags.

Both women own the bag because they like the look of the thing, but I imagine that the motivations lying behind the purchase run deeper than aesthetics. The businesswoman appears to have made a success of her life, materially and professionally at least, and she wears the Vuitton brand to reflect both her social status and good taste. The young mum, who would appear to live further down the ladder of life, wears Vuitton because it sums up who she would *like* to become – elegant, glamorous, sophisticated.

Here is an example of Veblen's law of conspicuous consumption; the lower orders copy the lifestyle of their betters. No doubt the businesswoman will update her handbag collection when she sees too many working-class mothers carrying the same bag as hers. And so the cycle of fashion carries on. Some social theorists claim that branded consumption creates social mobility, that entry-point status symbols afford the owner a step up the ladder. A working-class person who buys an Apple computer on hire-purchase can chat in an online forum with an upper-class person who bought the same computer with the money from a trust fund. How the computer was paid for becomes irrelevant; the two people are united by the values of the brand.

It seems rather unlikely, however, that these two bag ladies would choose to spend any sort of time together, united only by their French designer handbag. I can't imagine the businesswoman taking tea round the young mum's council flat. The supposition that we consumers are free to buy whichever identity we choose is a fallacy. The working-class girl who buys into the designer dream may *feel* like a million dollars with the bag on her arm, but she doesn't *have* a million dollars, and she is not welcome within the society of people who do have a million dollars.

I've fallen foul of this trick countless times in the past. I remember feeling rather foolish standing in line at Gucci to buy a £50 keyring – all that I could afford – while the couple in front casually frittered several thousand pounds on footwear. To the upper classes, social climbers such as me are a joke. Working-class families that christen their babies with names like Chanel are a particularly good source of fun.

The overquoted Oscar Wilde once quipped that we are all in the gutter, but some of us are looking at the stars. In reality we are looking at a giant credit-card bill and a bunch of broken promises. Paying for acceptance from our betters. Seeking uniqueness in mass-produced goods. This isn't social mobility; this is a branded fantasy world.

## –42 days

The *Mail on Sunday* prints an article by revered *GQ* editor and style commentator Dylan Jones which, in a perverse sort of way, makes for a life-affirming read:

> . . . it's so easy now for everyone to buy into the world of style that those at the cutting edge have to try even harder to stay one step ahead . . . Aren't you getting tired of continually having to worry about whether your new suit is still 'new' or whether your leopardskin Cuban heels are still 'in' (they aren't by the way) . . . I have a suggestion . . . what say we have huge great labels on the outside (of our clothes) telling everyone how much everything costs? That way I could take off my jacket in the middle of a business meeting so everyone in the room could see the label on my sleeve – '£340', it would say, loud and proud. That way I could walk into a restaurant with

'£2400' plastered all over my jacket, or '£300' on my shoes
. . . Gauche? Perhaps. Crude? Quite possibly. Nouveau riche?
It's the only way to go baby.[24]

This type of status anxiety is all too familiar to me, although I never took to stitching price tags on my clothes – at least Dylan wears his intentions on his sleeves, so to speak. I imagine my new life without this constant anxiety, and it feels like an enormous relief.

## -38 days

The level to which advertising penetrates my life is astonishing, yet being part of the landscape of the city, it seems normal to be surrounded by billboards and TV screens throughout the day. So few people seem to question this reality that I often wonder if my increasing distaste for the things is a symptom of encroaching paranoia. The figures to be found in the library, however, do not lie:

Average number of ads we are exposed to each day: 3000[25]
Average number of ads exposed to by age of 65: 2 million[26]
Number of billboards lining the streets in America: 500,000[27]
Average number of brand names memorised by a 10-year-old: 400[28]
Worldwide advertising spend in 2006: $427 billion[29]

The social theorist Christopher Lasch describes adverts as mirrors, in which we are forced to compare ourselves with our potentially more successful selves: 'All of us, actors, and spectators alike, live surrounded by mirrors. In them we seek reassurance of our capacity to captivate or impress others, anxiously searching out blemishes that might detract from the appearance we intend to project.'[30] The trick to advertising is to offer the consumer a glimpse of himself that is only just out of reach, to encourage us to stretch ourselves just a little beyond our means. However, our real selves never catch up with our desired selves, remorselessly confronted as we are with ideals that are impossible to live up to.

If rumours on the Internet are to be believed, we shall soon have giant mirrors glaring down at us from space, as the US government considers the launch of a mile-wide ad-raft into low orbit. Interstellar advertising is not an entirely new phenomenon though – Pizza Hut placed their logo on the side of a rocket in 2001 that carried components to the International Space Station. Kodak had an advert placed on the side of the very same station.

## -37 days

'If we understand the mechanism and motives of the group mind, it is now possible to control and regiment the masses according to our will without their knowing it.'[31] Edward Bernays made this statement in 1928. Advertising and marketing techniques have become immeasurably more sophisticated since then.

## -36 days

Saturday afternoons are hell. Without the shopping, I feel nervous, twitchy, redundant; like a lad who returns from the army to Civvy Street, only the battle I crave is to consume as much as I can. There are only so many art galleries you can visit. Only so many walks you can plod around. Show me the lights and action, show me something that will catch my eye, raise my pulse, fill me with desire and hammer my wallet. Glamour. I want it, now.

*Ways of Seeing* is becoming a bible, the only thing to which I can turn to snap me out of the brand withdrawal. Pretty soon, I will be able to recite passages from that book like a puritanical Christian.

> The happiness of being envied is glamour. Being envied is a solitary form of reassurance. It depends precisely upon not sharing your experience with those who envy you. You are observed with interest but you do not observe with interest – if you do, you will become less enviable . . . The power of the glamorous resides in their supposed happiness: the power of the bureaucrat in his supposed authority. It is this which

explains the absent, unfocused look of so many glamour images. They look out over the looks of envy, which sustain them.[32]

## -27 days

I am walking along Bond Street, whiling away what is to be one of my last guilt-free afternoons of window-shopping, when a brand new Bentley, a tank-sized chrome monster, pulls over beside me and screeches to a halt. From the driver's side steps a dashing man, 40-ish, slick hair, deep suntan and bespoke suit. He strides over to open the passenger door, from which step two elegantly heeled feet and long flawless legs, followed by quite possibly the most beautiful woman that I have ever seen; immaculately groomed hair, subtle diamond jewellery twinkling all around her. The gentleman takes her hand and they dash into Louis Vuitton. I on the other hand am left standing, looking on in wonder.

A part of me wants to be that guy. A part of me thinks I *should* be that guy. I clearly remember my grammar school headmaster saying that I had the ability to be that guy; all I needed to do was work hard, and I could achieve any goal that I liked. I have worked hard since leaving school, harder than I really wanted to, and yet I am not the dashing guy who drives that Bentley. In a funny sort of way, I just expected wealth to come to me, in the same way some people quietly assume that they might find a way to live forever. Of course, I know that the car, the jewellery, the trophy wife would not be guarantees of a happy and fulfilled life, but I should like to have them anyway, just in case.

Later on at therapy, I confess to Carol that I often suffer from a sense of disappointment; disappointment with the world for failing to afford me this 'success' and disappointment with myself for harbouring such shallow goals. After all, my lot in life was by no means tawdry compared to most throughout the world.

'Have you stopped shopping for brands, or are you still buying?' asks Carol.

'It's coming to an end. I'm still buying branded food and toiletries, but there's no point buying expensive clothes, they'll be burnt in a month. I do still like to go and look though. I miss shopping a lot. It offers me visions of the person I'd like to be'

'But you're talking about empty shallow values. Who is the person you'd really like to be? That's what we've got to find. I don't think you *really* want to be this person who's into brands.'

'That's the reason why I feel so angry, so disillusioned. I've had these materialistic values drummed into me from an early age, and it takes a real effort to keep reminding myself that those values are false.'

'You've been brainwashed into believing something which part of you knows isn't necessarily true. Brainwash is a strong word, but I really do think that we are all brainwashed to a certain extent. I think you've got a lot going for you, but you have to convince yourself of that. I'd like the person you look up to, to be you. Start learning to love yourself.'

## -24 days

The power of the Internet is starting to work its magic, and the blog is starting to appear on all sorts of sites from advertising and branding websites to anti-corporate sites and blogs about other people's blogs. News of the project is feeding back into the minute pond that is London's media community. I visit an advertising agency to help on some consultancy for Ray-Ban sunglasses, and one of the managers there asks me, quite out of the blue, whether I consider Tesco's own-label hummus a brand, and, if not, will I be making my own? A long-forgotten friend from school contacts me to confirm that I am the same Neil Boorman who's planning to torch all his stuff. As is typical with most people's reactions, he expresses disbelief: 'You of all people!' I am becoming 'the guy who's burning all his gear'.

I have taken to pulling old branded favourites out from the back of the clothes closet and giving them one last spin as a pathetic kind of farewell gesture. Likewise, I have started indulging in brands of food that I might never taste again, visiting shops that I will no longer set foot in. Today I visited an Adidas store in a faithful old pair of Stan Smith trainers while munching Pringles. Watching television at a friend's house in the evening, an advert for McDonald's prompts me to leave early and make a final trip to the golden arches, even though, being a part-time vegetarian, I have not visited a franchise burger bar for the best part of five years. No matter, I must taste all available fruit before it becomes forbidden. My hosts look bewildered as I bolt for the door, mumbling something about all-beef patties in a sesame bun.

Half an hour later, I am munching my way through a Quarter Pounder Meal Deal. The 'restaurant' is full of drunken men in suits, skilfully negotiating their floppy Big Macs while fighting the urge to vomit. Several dishevelled black female cleaners fuel up before embarking on the nightshift at the local offices. The bright lights bounce off the yellow and red tiled walls; the roof of my mouth becomes coated in a film of grease. It's all coming back to me now, the misspent Saturday nights of my youth. My McDonald's was in Bexleyheath, south London, the only place teenagers could go to after the shopping malls and the parks were closed at night. In one booth alone, I'd broken up with two girlfriends and undertaken a large part of my GCSE revision. Some of the happiest moments of my pre-teen years were spent with my parents on a Saturday afternoon eating a plain hamburger and small fries – 'One day, son, you'll be old enough to eat a Big Mac!' I had my tenth birthday party at a McDonald's; they showed me round the fryers and the freezer and everything. It occurs to me that multinational brands such as these form many a building block in the memories of my life.

But no amount of nostalgia can dissolve the awful aftertaste of congealed fat and synthetic flavourings; this won't be something I'll miss in my new life. I make a break for the door, hoping I won't be spotted leaving the place, not through any sort of status anxiety, but through an encroaching sense of paranoia that has been developing for some time now. Ninety-nine per cent of the population neither knows nor cares about my project, yet I am starting to feel nervous being around these large brands, in case someone catches me.

I happen upon a study[33] which would seem to prove that, far from being uniquely obsessed with brands, young people, especially teenagers, are capable of 'reading' other people's brands with incredible sophistication. Forty people in Liverpool were asked to photograph a selection of the personal possessions that best reflected their personality. According to the study, 'teenagers not only selected a larger number of branded goods than adults did, but were also much more articulate, knowledgeable and involved when talking about brands'. Teenagers use the symbolism of their favourite brands during the construction of their identity, gaining a sense of belonging when they use the same brands as those in their peer group. Mobile phones in particular are an important mark of acceptance within social groups, each using different covers, ringtones and glue-on jewellery to express their individuality.

Am I part of a generation that has been targeted as never before, or have I simply failed to mature beyond the mentality of an 18-year-old? I have a feeling that it is a combination of the two.

In the second part of the study, participants were shown photographs of each other's possessions and were asked to comment on the type of person they thought owned the brands. One photograph included a pair of Adidas Gazelle trainers, Shockwaves hair gel, Lynx deodorant and a Reebok sweatshirt. The group typically described the owner as 'outgoing, flirty, energetic, active, young, single, image-conscious'.

I remember taking comfort in the 1980s strapline for VW cars, 'If only everything in life was as reliable as a Volkswagen'. If only every person in my life was as dependable as my Adidas trainers. Brands certainly seem to provide comfort from the insecurities of modern life. No matter where you are in the world, a can of Coke will look the same, taste the same and perform the same functions. It might be fashionable to bemoan the homogenisation of popular culture, but brands offer consistency in an ever-changing world, and this reassurance is a vital element in their value, to both the brand owners and to us as the consumer.

But the uniformity of the brand is only the bedrock of its meaning. Once we interact with them, they become part of the storyboard of our lives. When I smell Piz Buin suntan lotion, I remember sizzling hot days spent by the pool at my parents' package-deal holiday in Spain. The taste of Marmite returns me to my best friend's house, where we would gorge on endless rounds of toast after school. The advertising industry refers to these types of products as *family brands*; things that we buy throughout our lives to return us to the happier times. These deep connections tend to occur during our formative years, helping to maintain brand loyalty for the rest of our lives. Little wonder then, that the brand, with its consistent and reassuring message can sometimes replace the less reliable relationships that we have with people.

Not only did my personal collection of brands give me comfort, it came to symbolise my autonomy. I felt confident in the knowledge that I had sought out and obtained these things, concrete evidence of the goals that I had set myself and later achieved. We are defined by our actions, mine being the ticking-off of items from my continually updated shopping list. Overregulated and legislated as we are, consumer choice would seem to be one of the last acts of autonomy available to us. Is this why groups of people are so commonly referred to as consumers these days? In 'Consuming Goods', Rosalind Minsky comments that 'Shopping offers a form of power which many may feel they lack in other areas of their life and for some, may act as a defence against feelings of culturally or psychically induced emptiness and meaninglessness'.[34] The consumer is king.

With the right brand of tool at my disposal, I feel more confident in my ability to achieve goals. A good workman never blames his tools, but said workman is rarely seen without the tools of 'the professionals'. Thus the professional brand of product, the pro-tool becomes indispensable to the task in hand by way of an age-old confidence trick. My own DIY skills became slightly less shambolic when I purchased the most expensive power drill on the market. Or so it would seem.

## -20 days

The vultures are beginning to circle. Opportunistic friends who know how much treasure is buried in my wardrobe have begun to ask if they can save some items from the bonfire, give them a good home, if you catch my drift. Rana, a friend in PR, throws me some last-minute work for Sony PlayStation, to which I offer my customary gush of 'If there's anything I can do to repay the favour, please say.'

'Actually there is . . .' he replies to my surprise. 'Can I have your Helmut Lang jacket? You'd be burning it anyway? As a thankyou for all the work I've given you.'

The jacket in question is perhaps one of my favourite pieces; a pale blue silk bomber jacket, it never fails to draw compliments, and it has obviously caught the eye of Rana. I stare blankly into space for a good few seconds, playing the scenario over in my head. It has to be burnt, so why not give it a good home? But it's a £400 jacket; I almost bankrupted myself buying that thing.

'Fair enough,' I gulp, 'I'll drop it by the office tomorrow.'

## −19 days

This is the litmus test. I stuff my bomber jacket into a Sainsbury's shopping bag and stride down to Rana's office. He greets me in a meeting room with a long table and chairs, a room designed for meetings of far greater importance than this one. From the sweat on my palms and all down my back, one would think this was the most important meeting of my life. I shove the bag into his hands, and he looks a little bemused at the stifled angst obviously written across my face.

'I won't try it on here, Neil, but thanks a million. That's really generous of you.'

He spared me the pain of watching him wear it, at least. I stumble from the office feeling reckless, then stupid, then cheated, then relieved. Yes, I loved that jacket. Yes, I felt a million dollars when I had it on. But it's gone now. Soon, all of it will be gone. The sooner I come to terms with it, the better.

## −18 days

Under three weeks to go. Dear God, the time is now. De-branding my life is becoming a Herculean task; everything I own, everything I use day-to-day is branded. Moreover, I love surrounding myself with this stuff. It gives me confidence, meaning, happiness. What on earth have I let myself in for? I can feel a double knot of anxiety growing in my stomach as the days count down. It is currently the size of an apple.

TO DO LIST
**Buy unbranded**
food (market, farmer's delivery service)
clothes (market, Internet, vintage stores)
bag (army surplus)
fridge (caterers' supplier)
oven (caterers' supplier)
kettle (army surplus)
landline phone (vintage store)
crockery (charity shop)
deodorant/soap/shampoo/toothbrush/razors
    (wholefood market/independent health stores)
washing-up liquid/detergent/bleach/toilet roll
    (wholefood market/independent health stores)

**Cancel contracts**
Orange mobile
Holmes Place Gym
British Telecom
British Gas
London Energy
Churchill Insurance

**Arrange new contracts**
phone
energy

**Essential de-brand**
Apple Mac computer

The current upheaval in my life is such that I can no longer concentrate on my research and I abandon the British Library, which is a shame because it is one of the few public spaces in London that is free of advertising. Such is my evaporating attention span that I cannot focus on my Mac for more than five minutes at a time. However, I have elected my Apple laptop as the one essential item to be saved from the fire. I use it for work, for entertainment, as an electronic back-up for my brain. It has transformed my life and is very rarely out of my sight. I toyed with the idea of using the computers at the public library, but that would surely take me beyond all reach of my senses.

I once heard a story about the writer Will Self, a committed believer in inconspicuous consumption, who paid a mechanic to remove all traces of branding on his Volvo 760 Estate. Tired of driving around in cars that could be taken as statements of his lifestyle, Will chose the Volvo for its unique drabness and capability of blending into the boring fabric of the road. The mechanic then removed any visible badges from the bodywork, the windows and the interior for complete anonymity. Since Apple Mac laptops are anything but drab and anonymous, I decide to have the thing de-branded.

## -17 days

By pure fluke, this month's *Macworld* magazine runs a feature on kerr-aaazy people that modify their computers with new body shells and go-faster stripes. I contact them all, pleading with them to remove all traces of the Apple logo from the case, the keyboard and the desktop. As I type the emails, I am aware of the extreme futility of my request. By the day's end, however, three 'Mac mod specialists' accept the challenge in exchange for cash. It will doubtless cost more than the computer's worth, but rational thought having long since been abandoned, I agree on a price and the de-branding is under way.

## -16 days

The first piece of mainstream press appears in the *Sunday Times Style* magazine, a two-page feature with an image of myself lying atop a pile of soon-to-be-burnt branded items, with a huge cheesy grin on my face. The piece is sandwiched between adverts for Burberry, Gap, L'Oréal and a limited edition gold Motorola RAZR phone, designed by Dolce & Gabbana, the high priests of gaudy fashion. Considering the revenue that newspapers make from these adverts, I am amazed that the senior editor didn't quash my lone cry for anti-consumerism before printing. Perhaps he was away on holiday.

The next day, my blog is flooded with emails from readers of the *Sunday Times*:

> Pathetic self-promotion in itself rather than giving the items to charity says all we need to know about you really.

> If you're so anti-label, then why sign a book deal? Or did you find a crap publisher to go ahead with the book?

> I wish you all the worst, this really shows us just how shallow the world is when something like this is branded as newsworthy. Then again, we can't all be middle-class journos masquerading as social revolutionaries.

> Anyone with two brain cells would have sold them or given them away, given the money to a charity of their choice and simply been fulfilled themselves without feeling the need to publish any of this.
> Paulie B

> Please please please please please, read the comments on your blog. It is a great idea, and while the bonfire idea is very symbolic and impressive, could you not sell the

items and give the proceeds to charity? And save the
ozone in the meantime.
Tom Fennell

It's a kind of interesting conceit, although the
'burning' bit is only logical from a self-promotional
perspective. Symbolic, maybe; pretentious, definitely.
Having read your posts, you do sound like a bit of a
tosser.
Anonymous

Pathetic. Please throw your conceited self onto the fire
along with your possessions.
Anonymous

What are you going to buy with the book profits? What a
dreadfully superficial and jejeune stunt this is. And
yes indeed, the bonfire is an act of immature idiocy;
not donating/freecycling good clothes or property runs
directly counter to the positive aspects of withdrawing
from consumerism. It's an act of look-at-me selfish
individualism, which is the challenge you actually need
to work on both for yourself and society. That's what matters, not whether there is a label on your shoes or not.
Anonymous

I have become used to the one-line character assassinations and casual
death threats by now, but the intelligent criticisms are beginning to
score body blows. My 'selfish individualism' is indeed a challenge that
awaits me – I just happen to be stumbling upon these things in the
glare of the public eye. Which is a situation entirely of my own
construction.

Adding to my anxiety is the small matter of the bonfire's venue –
or lack thereof. I had originally planned to stage the fire outside some
iconic monument to consumerism such as Selfridges. The police, the
local council, the anti-terrorism unit and the Oxford Street retailers'

association soon crushed that idea. Legitimately staging a fire anywhere in Central London starts to look almost impossible, successive sites falling foul of strict health and safety laws on air pollution. Most local councils tend to shy away from the symbolical violence of 12-foot anti-consumerist bonfires on their doorstep. Which is fair enough.

## -15 days

The BBC homepage runs a long article on the upcoming bonfire, which triggers another flood of emails, only this time they are from around the world and they are by far nastier than anything I have received before. In the overused words of Malcolm Gladwell, we have reached a tipping point. The BBC calls to book an interview on breakfast television. The *Guardian* asks me to write a response to the barrage of criticism and I am lined up to talk on no fewer than 21 different radio stations in the coming days. There is no time to digest the hostile comments that continue to flood my inbox, although the really nasty ones are starting to penetrate my thick skin. I have often wondered how it must feel to be sucked into the eye of a media storm, especially when there is so much public hostility involved. This is it.

## -14 days

07:40 Picked up by a cab (nice Audi) and taken to the Television Centre to be interviewed on BBC1's breakfast show. I'm plonked in a waiting room on my own with half an hour to spare before I go on . . . half an hour to try to control my anxiety level, which is already sky high, having never appeared on live TV before. Gulping down some water I start to relax a little, only for the TV in the room to spring to life, playing the show I'm about to go on: 'Coming up, former Eastender Michelle Collins, REM's Michael Stipe and a journalist who is about to burn *all* his brands.' Jesus Christ.

08:30 With ten minutes to go, I am pacing outside the studio trying to hold down my breakfast. Michelle Collins is stuck in traffic apparently, so I might have to go on for longer. Or they'll rush the REM guy on early.

08:40 I am sitting on the studio sofa, waiting to go on. This is my last chance to make a run for it. What would they do? Go straight to news and travel? I might never work on television again, but what price dignity? Suddenly my gormless picture flashes up on a big screen behind me, the cameras turn to face me and we are away.

08:45 The interview is over. Didn't corpse or stutter thankfully, and the questions were fluffy, as they say in the game. Completely buzzing with adrenaline, I cross the studio floor and bump into Michael Stipe, who is waiting to go on. 'Hey, dude, good piece. I read your blog yesterday. I think it's a cool thing that you're doing.' I am lost for words. He continues: 'I bought these shoes from Prada yesterday, but only because they're the most comfortable I can find.' I'm still frozen. 'Er, thanks very much, Michael. Er, nice jacket, where did you get that from?' 'You don't wanna know.' He shakes my hand and walks onto the set.

11:30 Juliet, my mother and a close friend call to say well done on the television.

12:00 Radio interview with an Irish station. Thankfully, they don't ask any tough questions as the adrenaline is starting to impair my faculties. As long as they don't ask me for a viable alternative to capitalism, I'm okay.

13:00 Radio interview for a station in New Zealand. It is difficult to comprehend how this project has spread from my front room in London across the world to New Zealand.

14:00 I speak to the fire officers/health and safety people who are working with me on a site; they are concerned that I have asked the general public to throw their gear onto the fire alongside me on TV this morning. That was a big mistake. Must not do that again.

15:00 Interview with the *Independent on Sunday*, which is far more demanding. Plus, I am tiring of the sound of my own voice.

17:00 Meet with some BBC producers who are interested in filming a documentary on the bonfire. I am running on vapour now, a disorientating feeling of exhaustion and adrenaline that I can imagine can become quite addictive if you keep it up for long. So far, the BBC is the only broadcaster to pick up on my story. Is that because they are the only broadcasters in the UK that are ad-free, and the others cannot afford to upset the paymasters? Probably not, but it makes for a nice conspiracy theory.

18:00 I stumble onto the street after the meeting, feeling a bit faint, and spark up a Marlboro Light. The smoke stings my eyes and I stand hunched in the street, rubbing them better. The adrenaline is giving way and I am finally crashing. Seemingly out of nowhere, a complete stranger on a bike stops and yells, 'Oi, I saw you on telly this morning. When are you going to burn your stuff?' 'September 17th.' This day cannot get any more bizarre. 'I don't buy any brands if I can help it. Have you heard of the Greenfutures website? They do loads of stuff that would be good for you.' 'Oh, okay, cool.' I'm so taken aback that anyone would recognise me in the street that, for the second time today, I'm left stuttering for words.

20:00 Go to bed. Stare at the ceiling and begin to panic that I have created a monster I cannot properly handle. Then fall asleep.

## -13 days

The torrent of online abuse shows no signs of abating and my blog eventually crashes under the volume. Close friends who have read the comments call to say 'don't let the bastards get you down'. New blogs and chatrooms are joining the call for my head on a branded stick, and the best thing I can do, bar calling the bonfire off, is to stay away from the Internet and focus on the task ahead. The production of said task is also the cause of great anxiety, on account of there not being a London council prepared to green-light the event. Very few boroughs of the city permit large public fires in this age of strict environmental protection, even on Guy Fawkes Night. New environmental laws dictate that I could not burn most of the things on my list if it were to go ahead; only organic fibres may be burnt. The book might have to be renamed *Campfire of the Three Organic Shirts*. That my event appears to be a pseudo-anarchistic publicity stunt calling for the immediate ending of capitalism and life as we know it may be working against my favour. Thirteen days to go and no venue. I have lost half a stone and begun to chain smoke. Each night I fall asleep worrying, and each morning I awake in a panic. A dreadful nightmare looms ever closer and I cannot wait to get on with my new life, brands or no brands.

## -9 days

The solution to the bonfire's venue problem comes riding in on a Harley Davidson; I manage to find a motorcycle-riding council official who subscribes to the spirit of the project and okays a square that is slap-bang in the middle of the city, facing the offices of Bloomberg, no less. It is decided that I will burn most of my clothes and take a sledgehammer to the rest to placate the air pollution officials. In smashing up my television, I will be fulfilling a childhood dream.

Where can I find a non-branded sledgehammer?

The *Guardian* invites me to respond to the now-deafening levels of criticism online and in print with an article in the main paper. Doubtless the piece will only spark further hostility, but I need to defend my corner. I feel rather disingenuous writing the piece on my Apple laptop, which is yet to be de-branded. Its logo blinks at me infuriatingly from the screen.

**Bonfire of the Vanities**

Six months ago, I began writing a blog entitled bonfireofthebrands.com. I announced on the site that I was going to destroy every branded item in my possession, having concluded that I was suffering from an addiction to the status and aspirations surrounding brands. As a former editor of youth lifestyle magazines, I had caught a glimpse of the inner workings of advertising and marketing, and found some practices distasteful. Further more, I felt rather cheap that I had used my position to champion these brands, almost as if they were gods. So, in order to cleanse this addiction and highlight some concerns surrounding advertising and consumerism, I vowed to burn all my stuff and start again, brand free.

I imagined [Bonfire of the Brands] would find favour with any number of social groups who face the daily pressure to consume beyond their basic needs: parents beleaguered by the pester power of their kids, teenagers under pressure to conform to peers, and any adult whose credit card contributes to the £200 billion of consumer debt that we must repay in the UK. How very wrong I was.

Here was another middle-class London journalist moaning on about the luxuries that many around the world cannot afford. Instead of burning these things, why not give the lot away to charity, or, better still, just count my blessings and keep quiet? An anonymous blogger suggested 'If you truly, really want to live without brands, bugger off to the Highlands of Scotland, burn your stuff by yourself, come home when you've come to terms with life without an Alessi arse-flosser and carry on with your new unmarked life. Quietly.'

I think this reaction has less to do with charity than the overall value that we have come to place on branded things; nowadays, to willingly destroy an expensive bag amounts to the same moral and cultural neglect as burning a book. However, when we strip away the marketing spin surrounding modern brands, our devotion to the things is nothing short of irrational. Take two white T-shirts. They are identical in size, shape and quality, but one has a logo on the breast. The plain shirt costs £5 from a market stall, the branded version costs £50 from a department store. Considering they perform the same basic function, the rational choice would be the market option. Yet the majority of us would choose the branded option whenever we could afford it. We would somehow be letting ourselves down otherwise.

A comment on the BBC homepage asked, 'Why not enjoy the finer things in life if you can afford them? What's wrong with appreciating the exclusivity of a designer suit? It may not be worth the asking price you paid but how good do you feel walking down the street? Can you put a value on that?'

Of course there is another function that the branded shirt performs; the logo on the breast transforms the experience of wearing the thing. To display the brand is to prove to yourself (and anyone that cares to look) that you are of a certain standing, that you are worth something in life. In this respect, the brand transforms the product from something of utilitarian function into an object of meaning and desire. That is why we buy overpriced products, from iPods to Heinz baked beans, over cheaper but lesser branded alternatives. I wonder, if my bonfire contained only non-branded items, would the outrage be quite so great?

The brand, then, is both a badge of identity and a means of personal fulfilment; no wonder people feel defensive when they're told it's all an expensive con. But that's what these brands really are. The extra £45 paid on that branded T-shirt pays for a fantasy that does not exist, a quick fix of happiness that does not last. I would suggest that most rational people understand that consumption provides little sustainable contentment (for all our affluence, *New Scientist* places us 24th in the happiness league, behind Nigeria and El Salvador). They would also concede that the price we pay for these branded things is far too high and is crippling to our budgets. And the ethics of production? The environmental impact? None of this is news to the average consumer. Yet we continue to consume according to want, not need, each day of our lives. I simply state that this 'want' is manufactured and manipulated by the emotional advertising of brands, and, at some point in the future, it has got to stop.[35]

## -5 days

Friends call early on the morning of publication to say well done for getting the piece printed, and not to worry about the moaning lefties who've slandered my name on the *Guardian* comment site. I cannot bear to look, but the criticism must be seriously harsh, because Dana, a regular visitor to the blog whom I have never actually met, finds my email address and writes:

> I'm just sorry that people are getting you down.
> Fame brings out the best in humanity, and sadly, the worst as well.
> Just know that there are people out there that support you 100 per cent, and are rooting you on.
> Feel free to email me if you need someone to talk to.
> xxx Dana.

I almost cry. Both friends and now perfect strangers are rallying around me, doing their best to stave off the criticism, which I have invited upon myself.

In between the organisation of the bonfire, the grind of press interviews, an ongoing public debate on my character and the impending
destruction of my beloved brands, I am starting to crumble under the
pressure. Public criticism is a curious thing. Nothing is said directly to
my face, it's all done on message boards and comment pages in print.
Daily life goes on as normal, but all the while you are aware that
thousands of people are discussing your character behind your back.
I pass people in the street and catch their glance. Have they read the
story in a paper or seen me on TV? Are they forming a negative opinion as we pass each other by? Of course not. They don't even know
who I am. This is starting to develop into paranoia.

A close friend, Daniel, senses my imminent collapse, and takes
me out for a cup of tea in a quiet square in the city, a rare oasis of
calm for office people seeking respite from the relentless grind, and a
place for bosses to carry out illicit relationships with their secretaries.
Although Daniel tries to create a sense of calm, he has the opposite
effect. 'Boy, have you seen the comments on the *Guardian's* site
today?'

'No, I can't bear to look at them. It's probably the same stuff
though . . . middle-class moaner, give it all to charity, be thankful for
what you've got. I should be getting used to it by now.'

'Well, it's best that you don't look, mate. Have you thought about
taking their advice? Why not appease them all at the last minute
and make a grand gesture . . . have someone there from Oxfam and
surprise them all by giving it all away.'

By this time, I am confused and emotional.

'But it's not a charity event, it's an act of protest. Why should
I give in?'

'Because otherwise you'll be public enemy number one. If you
don't believe me, click on the *Guardian* comments page.'

Perhaps I should back out? I make frantic calls to all involved.
'I'm not wobbling,' I tell them, 'just reacting to the public hostility.'
While I await their responses, I go home to read the *Guardian* com-
ment pages. It is awful; ten negative comments to every positive one.

The topic has moved from the validity of the event, to the nature of my character.

My agent calls, 'For God's sake, ignore all this bullshit and stand firm, Neil. It's going to be great.' She promises to call me every day until the bonfire to check in on my metal health. Bless her.

## -3 days

My last therapy session before the bonfire is today. I try desperately to compose myself before the meeting, but the pressure has become too much. I am convinced the bonfire will be disrupted by a lynch mob, or that photographers will be trying to catch me out with a brand of something in the street; the dread and anxiety is awful.

'You've knowingly set yourself this impossible task,' says Carol. 'I'm not surprised you feel anxious. You mustn't be too harsh on yourself.'

'I simply can't wait for the eighteenth of September.'

'Fine, but just be aware that you're not going to be transformed into this new brand-free person overnight.'

'I haven't really had time to think about the stuff I'm burning. My thoughts are mostly with all the criticism I've been receiving. People are writing long rants about the thing, as if they were possessed.'

'You're putting yourself on the line, and that carries the risk of criticism. But the best you can do is to stay strong. You know, somebody who takes the time to write a long hurtful essay on a website has got a mental problem. If they haven't got anything better to do than attack a complete stranger, then they have some personal issues that they need to deal with. These people are paranoid and envious; they're obsessive people, who write anonymous letters. It's like frustrated masturbation . . . they're having a wank all over you. You need to build a protective umbrella so it doesn't fall on you.'

I stare blankly into space for some minutes.

'Aside from the criticism, how do you feel this de-branding has gone?'

'I certainly feel like I am disconnecting from my personal possessions; I'll miss them terribly when they're gone, but in a funny way I'm looking forward to a new life without the status anxiety. I sometimes worry that I might be developing some sort of paranoid grudge against these companies, a sort of resentment that I have been manipulated into becoming this obsessive brand junkie.'

'Don't make the mistake of thinking that these brands have implanted these desires to consume inside you alone; they're inside all of us. The advertising only exasperates those feelings. Think of kids who wear school uniform; they'll always customise their kit, because, like us, they want to be individuals, to be unique. It's just a way of turning a bland uniform into something personal. You got seduced somewhere down the line by advertising. You believed that if you adopted these brands, then you'd be special and different and stand out from the crowd of anonymous people. You can be unique and special without these things. But that doesn't mean you have to give up brushing your teeth with Colgate, or drinking a bottle of water when you're thirsty.'

'Well, I'm trying to prove a point, so I've got to see that through.'

'Tell me, do you honestly believe that people are going to judge you on the basis of what make your shoes are?'

'I would. Perhaps not so much now, but I used to. When I got dressed, I'd think about who I was going to be meeting that day, and I would often wear stuff according to what I thought would impress them.'

'Is this about personal taste, or the value of the brand?'

'I think it's a bit of both.'

'If your partner came home with something she had bought and it was the wrong brand, would you think less of her?'

'I wouldn't love her any less, but I'd tell her that she'd let herself down by buying the wrong thing.'

'Suppose you told her you didn't like the product, but then she told you it was made by a brand that you liked; what would you think then?'

'I suppose I would dislike it less. I know, it's tragic.'

'We need to move you on from this, Neil. Perhaps you're projecting anxieties about yourself onto other people. Burn your stuff first, and then we'll deal with this afterwards. It's a vicious circle; you're anxious about yourself, so you think you've got to look good to compensate. But then you feel anxious about whether you actually look good. It's a long-term habit that you have to break. But we're getting there.'

## -2 days

The production company that I have hired to stage the event has looked at their insurance cover, realised that they would be liable if the bonfire raged uncontrollably and burnt the City of London alive, and has therefore decided to abandon the project. I am now frantically organising transportation, seeing in shipments of non-branded bottled water, and sourcing gazebos, sledgehammers and a megaphone by myself. Thankfully the pyrotechnics company handling the actual fire are still happy to work. This extra responsibility means that I have no time to come to terms with the fact that, in three days' time, I will have destroyed most of my worldly possessions. Thinking about it now, I don't really care any more. In this sense, the catharsis of the project seems to be working; while only months ago, I was emotionally attached to my favourite brands and frequently craved shopping trips to acquire more, now I feel as though I have managed to detach myself from the things. It is just stuff, after all. I can live without it.

Having said that, the afternoon spent bagging up all my brands does not pass without fleeting moments of panic, regret and nostalgia. I come across bags of clothes that I had clean forgotten I owned, some of them unworn with their price tags still attached (the classic symptom of a shopaholic). The temptation to hide some items away 'for safe keeping' is huge. Several people have joked that I might keep a few outfits from the fire for personal use in the privacy of my own home, and right now that doesn't seem like a bad idea. As Juliet and I stuff black bin liners with dusty clothes and gadgets, I catch myself burrowing a cashmere Ralph Lauren jumper and a super-rare 1980s

Lacoste jacket into a drawer, just for safe keeping. Juliet later finds the stash and returns them to their rightful place in the 'to burn' bags. Rumbled.

## −1 day

My flat looks as if it has been burgled, only the thieves were disturbed mid-snatch and fled the scene without the swag. Bin liners cover all available floor space, bulging with my beloved branded things. Cupboards and shelves look bare and dusty, where trophy items were once displayed. There seems little point in keeping the table on which my stereo once proudly sat, a guaranteed conversation piece at dinner parties on account of the sleek design and expensive gold-plated wires. It is so tempting to rummage around the bags for one last touch and feel of some prized possessions, but Juliet busies herself tying them up to prevent any wrongdoing. Throughout these past few months, she has not once questioned the method in my madness (although I am sure that she has serious reservations). Rather, she has been the supportive rock to my neurotic histrionics. I couldn't ask for anything more in a partner.

One outfit, indeed my favourite outfit, has a 24-hour reprieve from the bin bags, for I need something to wear out on my last night on the tiles as a person of branded persuasion. For the last time, I pull on my Lee jeans, Helmut Lang shoes, polo top and Christian Dior mac (all black for maximum Johnny Cash-style intimidation). The weather is poor with a high wind and light drizzle, but I decide to walk the journey to the bar in Soho, a chance to enjoy the clothes for one last time. I certainly feel better for wearing this stuff; the shoes make a manly clatter as they hit the ground, and I'm sure they make me walk with a touch more confidence. No one would know that they were Helmut Lang unless they asked, but that's not the point; I know and that's enough. The Dior mac occasionally billows in a gust of wind like some sort of superhero cape, but, with the collar turned up against my neck, I am shielded from the elements by a layer of luxury. It reminds me of a 1980s advert for the breakfast cereal Ready Brek. Children who ate the warm porridge in the morning would set off to

141

school with a nuclear glow around their bodies; that's how these brands make me feel now. Both my body and my spirit are bathed in a protective glow of luxury, somehow shielding me from the harsh cold rigours of reality that lie beyond my force field. In Tom Wolfe's *Bonfire of the Vanities*, Sherman McCoy insulates himself from the horrors of the outside world within his accumulated luxuries. Inside this cocoon, he was master of the universe.

I arrive at the bar feeling quite confident, with these designer crutches propping me up. A friend introduces me to his new partner.

'You're that guy who's burning all his stuff?'

'Yes, that's right.'

'You don't look very non-branded to me.'

'I haven't burnt it all yet. It happens tomorrow.'

'Why don't you just give it all to charity?'

'Uh, em, excuse me, I must get to the bar.'

This scenario is repeated several times over the course of the next two hours. I stand at the bar, head-to-toe in designer gear, drinking a bottle of Coke, sucking on a Marlboro Light, waiting for something magical to happen. I run through my usual conversational routine of complimenting people's outfits and asking where they got them from. One girl has a Cacharel scarf. Another has a Marc Jacobs handbag. In my previous life, I would have been genuinely interested, making judgements about these people as I went. Now I am simply going through the motions, because I can't think of anything else to say. Someone returns the compliment and asks me where I bought my mac from. Six months ago, I would have given the answer with some thinly disguised pride. Now I just feel embarrassed. What does it matter where it's from?

This is boring. I cut the evening short and walk home alone, conscious that the anxiety knot in my stomach has grown to the size of a melon. By the journey's end I am groggy, hungover almost, as if I were having withdrawal symptoms from medication. Perhaps these brands have become alternative reality pills to me, and I am now finally coming to terms with the real world that surrounds me. In the film *THX118*, the subservient communities pop a strict course of pills each day to maintain their sense of wellbeing. If their happiness dips and they begin to question their lot in life, a computerised voice urges them to take more: 'TAKE TWO PILLS NOW, AND FOUR MORE IN TEN MINUTES' TIME. DON'T WORRY, HELP IS ON THE WAY.'

# BONFIRE DAY

# 17 september 2006

The day of reckoning. I wake at 6 a.m., sitting bolt upright with what I'm sure is a crazed look in my eye. A BBC Radio car is waiting downstairs to interview me for the World Service. This is the twentieth time in two weeks, and I am now utterly bored of the sound of my own voice. I rattle off the usual sound bites . . . addicted to brands . . . they bolster my self-esteem . . . lost without them . . . must make amends . . . cathartic experience etcetera. Let's just get it over and done with.

I have an hour to write the pre-bonfire speech that I'm going to give through a suitably militant-looking megaphone (the Adastra 952, possibly the last branded thing that I will buy). There remain endless piles of stuff to be bagged up before the van is due to arrive at midday. For some reason, I left my expensive clothes until last, and, now as I come to the task, I don't feel much like throwing these beautiful things away. A lovely silk bomber jacket by Raf Simons, a Vivienne Westwood suit, some shirts made in Savile Row by Kilgore. The temptation to hide them away is strong, and I catch myself looking for some sort of a stronghold. But there would be no point, I could only wear them disguised on the other side of the world.

By midday, the flat's contents sit in bags throughout the place. A marketing friend of mine once produced an edition of fake Louis Vuitton bin liners as an ironic joke. It would seem rather apt to cart my possessions off in the things today, had I kept some. Disconnecting the Sharp LCD TV, digital receiver and Sony DVD player (with 5.1 surround sound that I never properly set up) the awful truth is beginning to dawn. Juliet looks slightly panicked. As much as we both moaned about the quality of television and forever vowed to watch less overall, we will miss the thing terribly, and the room looks horribly bare without it.

There follows undoubtedly the most surreal six hours of my life. My friend Tim arrives, sweating and drunk from the night before, to help load my possessions into a van. I am amazed that a lifetime's worth of spending fits neatly into one transit van. We arrive at the venue, Finsbury Square, and unload the stuff – 'Gently!' I say to Tim as he tosses the TV from the van, and he looks at me as if to say 'What's the point?' The heavy work done, Tim shoots back home to nurse his hangover. For half an hour I am left standing on my own, in the middle of a city square with my entire branded life scattered around me. A lone dog walker strolls past with an expression of bewilderment. I light up a cigarette from a fresh box of 20 Marlboro Lights and savour every drag; this will be the last day of smoking for me, and I'm determined to enjoy every last one of these before the day is out.

The team from Fantastic Fireworks, the pyrotechnics company, arrives and starts to build the fire sculpture. Ros, the lady in charge, has an incredibly calming influence on the entire proceedings, which I envisaged would be fraught with tension, coming mostly from me. 'There's no point getting stressed about these things, Neil . . . it doesn't make them happen any easier.' I later find out that Ros is a bona fide hippy from Cornwall. Juliet and my friend Daniel arrive to help and we begin to unpack the gear. The plan was to recreate the set-up of my front room on the lawn. But it looks more like a stall at a car boot sale. Not for the last time today, I wonder if my stuff is *good enough* to burn.

Time elapses with dizzying speed, only to be halted by passers-by who stop to ask what on earth we are doing. 'I'm burning all my stuff in a protest against branded consumerism.' 'Why would you wanna do that? What a waste.' By six o'clock, the fire sculpture has been built, a 12-foot cone of wire with thick paraffin-soaked rope wrapped around it. We tack on some choice branded ephemera for effect. A crowd of people starts to gather around the perimeter of the site. God, this is really going to happen. It is unnerving to have the material contents of one's life displayed in public, and the old status anxieties come flooding back, as I wonder what these strangers must think of my consumer life's work. Amid the crowd, I can pick out close friends and family, all looking on and wishing me well; Carol is waiting in the wings in case of an emergency breakdown, and even strangers that have regularly posted comments on the blog make themselves known to me.

Somebody in the crowd points to the pile of goods and shouts, 'Is that it?'

'What do you mean?'

'Well, I thought there'd be more stuff.'

'Well, I'm sorry to disappoint you. I'll try harder next time.'

By 6.45 p.m., everything is in place. The security arrives, looking suitably beefy and belligerent. My assistant arsonist Alan drags himself out of bed and makes it down just in time to pull on his boiler suit. The pyrotechnics guys stand by with gigantic flamethrowers. The angry lynch mob I feared has stayed away. They probably decided to go shopping instead. A crowd of around 300 has gathered and there is a real sense of tension in the air. All eyes are on me, chain-smoking in the wings, and the attention is becoming uncomfortable. It's time.

I stride over to the display and pick up my megaphone to give the speech. Adrenaline floods my body, drowning any last doubts or fear with pure energy, and, from this moment on, the proceedings are a complete blur.

'Thanks for coming . . . I'd like to take a minute to explain why I'm doing this today. I am a member of a generation that has been sold to from the day it was born. And what you see today is the result . . . a person that is addicted to brands. Every one of the 3000 adverts I am exposed to each day promises that my life will be richer if I spend my money on their products.

'O2 – "See what you can do". Nike – "Just do it". L'Oréal "Because you're worth it".

'I've been buying these things, believing they would make me more successful, more likeable, more sexy . . . as you can see, it didn't work.

'When we pay for a branded product we pay for a daydream, and, boy, do we pay for it through the nose. You see this polo shirt from Ralph Lauren? This cost me £65. I bought this non-branded one from a market yesterday for £3.

'These brands are nothing but an expensive con. In the UK, we are £200 billion in debt over this stuff. We may be one of the richest countries in the world, but, emotionally, we're one of the poorest. In the league tables of happiness, we come 24th, behind El Salvador.

'From tomorrow, I am going to try and find happiness somewhere other than in a department store. And today, I'm going to rid myself of an addiction to these brands once and for all. *Good riddance!*'

The crowd cheers and I feel a massive rush of energy. The flamethrowers burst into life, and the bonfire catches light with a ferocity that takes everyone, including me, by surprise. The technician walks methodically around the sculpture shooting flames at the base of the cone. It is fully ablaze within seconds. A baby in the crowd begins to cry and there is a collective gasp at the intensity of the heat. I grab some clothes and run towards the fire, recoiling slightly at the incredible temperature. Without hesitation, Alan and I grab fistfuls of luxury clothes and lob them into the flames, where they seem to evaporate on contact. The crowd cheers every time a new armful of clothes is thrown. After several minutes, I am exhausted and the flames begin to die down.

I return to the megaphone.

'Due to health and safety laws, I cannot burn all the stuff you see here today. So, I'm going to take a sledgehammer to the rest of it . . . here we go!'

I pick up a sledgehammer and swing it at the LCD television. Alan is straight in there with a devastating blow to the Technics turntable. The crowd gasp again, but this time in a sense of horror. The flames were dazzling, but the sledgehammers are more violent. We pummel furniture and electrical equipment into smithereens. A BBC presenter

150

and cameraman appear amidst the carnage to ask how I'm feeling right now. 'Er, I dunno, pretty good, I suppose.' 'Go for the Dyson!' shouts someone from the crowd. I turn away from the camera crew and swing the hammer wildly at the hoover. It feels good.

The majority of durable goods are smashed, but there are still lots of clothes and shoes left over. Returning again to the megaphone, I thank people for coming and say that anyone who wants the rest of the gear can come and get it. The crowd stampedes the barricades and we have the beginnings of a bun fight. I look on, weary and dazed, as people barge their way past to grab my stuff. A father says to his boy, 'Focus, son, focus . . . go for the bike!' Newspaper reporters appear from the wings to ask questions and I do my best to give coherent answers. A cloud of designer ash from the extinguished fire fills the air as children forage wildly through the wreckage for something to take home. 'I wonder if any of this'll be worth something on eBay?' says one stranger.

The free entertainment having drawn to a close, the crowd soon disperses and I am left literally picking up the pieces. Familiar faces emerge from the throng to congratulate me, all bearing the same look of bemusement and concern. I wonder if this is the reaction one might receive when performing as a clown; the crowd appreciates your effort but feels a deep sense of sympathy too.

The ash begins to settle and the hired help shovel the charred and smashed remains of my branded life into bins. I change into my first officially non-branded outfit and head off to a nearby pub, where some of the spectators are drinking. Walking inside The Griffin, I see half the clientele are holding or, worse still, wearing items from my formerly branded wardrobe, scavenged from the remains of the fire. One guy seems only to have recovered one shoe from my collection but is wearing it none the less. Another has my Ralph Lauren cashmere jumper draped over his shoulders, the wrists only slightly burnt by the fire. He raises a glass to me, 'Cheers for the jumper, mate!'

Glasses of lime and soda – the only non-branded drink in the pub – line up at the bar as well-wishers buy me drinks and offer congratulations. But I have long since lost the capacity for conversation. I can feel an almighty crash coming on, made far worse by the ferocious desire to smoke a Marlboro Light, so Juliet and I slip away and head for home, eager to watch the proceedings on BBC news.

We return to the flat, all forlorn with half-bare shelves and cupboards, the doors of which lie open. The spare room, previously stuffed with clothes and kit, now strewn with empty boxes and redundant coat hangers. Disconnected black cables are all that remains of the television. No watching the news coverage, then. Juliet, faithful to the end, simply smiles, 'Not to worry, darling.'

It's all gone. For good. Throughout this project, a part of me has been in denial about the effect it would have on my life. Up to the very last minute, I had the opportunity to pull out, shame-faced perhaps, but with my collection of brands, my symbolic self, intact. That moment passed two hours ago, and I am left with only a handful of press clippings and charred eyebrows to show for it. A box of receipts stretching back a decade is the only evidence of my meticulously branded former life. It is all too much to bear, and I leave the flat alone to smoke what has to be my last ever Marlboro. Pacing up and down the street with tunnel-vision eyes, I drag deeply on the cigarette, savouring every last gasp. Its embers reach the butt and I flick the thing into the road, marking the moment in my head as the last of being a smoker. I reach into my pocket for the door keys, but instead find my money clip, bought at Louis Vuitton by Juliet for Christmas one year. I unclip it from the money, give it one last loving glance and gingerly toss it into the road next to the cigarette. The final grandiose gesture of the day.

# POST-BONFIRE

# day 1

I wake up in a half-empty flat, littered with boxes, bags and bits of branded gear abandoned in the rush to stage the fire. The din of the Monday morning rush hour is in full swing outside as the world goes about its normal business. I on the other hand am languishing in a darkened bedroom, feeling exhausted from the climax of six months' planning and completely numb from its effects. I would normally medicate such misery by slumping in front of the television – but I don't have one any more. I stumble to the shower to freshen up, only to realise that I haven't yet made any soap. Ethically produced non-branded shampoo I have, 90 per cent non-effective deodorant salt stick and uncomfortably abrasive homemade toothpaste I have. But no soap.

By midday I manage to drag myself out of bed for an interview at Radio 4. I have always wanted to appear on Radio 4, just once, but I'd hoped I'd be in better spirits. In the studio, the presenter makes a comment that I later realise will become a recurring refrain from people I meet: 'I'm surprised, Mr Boorman, you don't look very different from the rest of us.' She expected me to walk around Central London in a sackcloth and sandals, obviously. 'You look like a cross between Tom Cruise and Joe 90.' I'd not yet found unbranded contact lenses and had resorted to wearing my old charity-shop glasses. I take it as a compliment, mumble through the interview and bumble back to the flat feeling completely deflated. Such was my one and only turn on BBC Radio 4.

On the walk home, I pass a woman munching a bag of crisps; I've not eaten properly for days, what with all the anxiety, and I am struck down with an insatiable urge to binge through a family-sized bag of salt and vinegar crisps, Kettle Chips or perhaps a tube of Pringles. My heart sinks as the daily reality of a non-branded life kicks in. I have to anticipate and prepare for everything before I leave the house, otherwise the experiment will fail. Later on in therapy, I tell Carol how empty and depressed I feel, that I'm paranoid somebody from the newspapers will catch me out if I slip up, and that all I really want in life right now is a packet of Walkers Salt & Lineker crisps. Not for the first time, she warns me not to take this project too far.

By the end of the day, the press storm dies down to nothing, the phone and email becoming ghostly quiet; my grandiose effort has joined the rest of the day's news as wrapping for fish and chips. My parents call – on the semi-non-branded ethically run Phone Co-Op landline – to check on my mental health. They have been surprisingly supportive of me these past few months, considering their son has just destroyed thousands of pounds' worth of perfectly good possessions. 'I think I understand what you're doing, son, and I say go for it, if this is something you really believe in,' says my mother. Other people are less supportive, especially people in publishing and advertising. Steve, an editor at a 'quality' men's magazine, calls to taunt me with tales of his new purchases.

'Guess what I'm wearing right now?'

'I don't know, but I'm sure you want to tell me.'

'Brand new pair of John Lobb shoes, bespoke from Jermyn Street. And a nice bit of cashmere from Pringle. Feels great, I can tell you. So how's the crusade against capitalism going?'

'Well, it's early days, but I'm expecting a revolution some point soon.'

'Good luck, mate, because you're virtually unemployable otherwise.'

# day 4

I have spent three days hiding under my bedclothes, and Juliet is becoming concerned. I have to restart my life at some point, I suppose, but there seems little to get up for right now. The daily habits of my previous life are so entrenched that I am still flitting around the flat on autopilot. Watch TV. But I don't have one. No TV? I'll listen to the radio. No radio? I'll call a friend. No phone? I'll smoke a cigarette. No. Bloody. Cigarettes. I imagine Juliet is pleased to leave this nuthouse for work each day. I myself have no work to go to; essentially, this no-frills, no-fun, no-brand life *is* my job.

I have to leave the flat and try to gain some perspective on the situation. What if someone spots me from the television, a reporter even? As long as I am completely brand-free, they can't touch me. What to wear? I can choose from a dozen plain T-shirts, a couple of pairs of jeans and some rather uncomfortable school plimsolls. Previously I would step out with confidence, head held aloft, waiting to meet the gaze of any passers-by that might connect with mine. Now I amble from my front door with shoulders hunched forward, head and eyes darting nervously to avoid the stare of both pedestrians and the surrounding billboards.

There are, of course, no photographers waiting, and no one, as far as I can see remembers me.

What to do with the day? I could buy a cup of tea – but the sandwich stores nearby are all branded chains. If I did manage to find an old family-run café, they would probably serve me Tetley's or PG Tips with a carton of St Ivel milk substitute. I could walk to the park, but it looks very much like rain. Perhaps take a stroll down the high street – only there is nothing there for me now. Cinema – my local branches are run by the Odeon chain. I could buy a book – but the small stores gave way to Borders and Waterstone's many years ago. Perhaps I should concentrate on leisure activities that *don't* involve consumption. What exactly do people do when they're not shopping? Visit relatives? Go sightseeing? Go to art galleries? I'm sure my brand disorder stems partly from the fact that, beyond visiting the high street, there is very little else to do in this country. I walk the hour-long journey to the Serpentine Gallery in Hyde Park to kill time. Not a bad lifestyle really, I keep reminding myself.

According to the blurb on the wall at the Serpentine, the exhibition surveys 'practices spanning appropriation, Pop and socio-political critique'. Being a newly appointed anti-consumer warrior, this work should appeal to me. But my legendarily short attention span finds difficulty settling on any of the work. After 20 minutes of looking studious but not actually looking at anything, I break for the gift shop, hoping there'll be something to buy, whereupon I bump into Sarah, an old friend who used to be a designer at *Wallpaper* magazine. She is a minimal APC blouse and clever shoes from Camper kind of girl – a classic graphic designer – not that I was interested any more.

'I saw you on the news. I must say, you don't look any different from before!'

'Yes, people keep saying that. What did you expect to see me wearing?'

'I don't know, shabby charity-shop clothes, I suppose. I don't believe all this stuff is non-branded. Let me see inside your jacket.'

She checks for labels on every item of clothing I am wearing, save for the underpants, which I solemnly promise are army surplus finest. A gallery attendant looks on in wonder. Is Sarah frisking me because my outfit looks too normal to be true? Or because she suspects the whole exercise is a charade? Perhaps the new, serious Neil is rather unapproachable and she's clutching at conversation points before the customary five-minutes window of polite conversation draws to a close. Having passed the non-branded test, she runs out of conversation and we part company; both rather hoping, I imagine, that we don't meet again for some time.

## day 5

Tom Hodgkinson, editor of the *Idler* magazine, has written a rallying speech for the book, which arrives today. I became friends with Tom after a copy of the *Idler* arrived on my desk during a typical 15-hour day at the magazine I was editing. The *Idler* manifesto – to reject the work ethic and pursue a simpler life – seemed to be completely at odds with my own plan for self-betterment; working and consuming as I was with a kind of masochistic zeal. The philosophy seemed like a joke to me, but subsequent meetings with Tom would prove to me that a person could define himself beyond the status of working and shopping. Tom seems to have reached the same conclusion that I am working towards, only without the accompanying histrionics. And the piece has a temporarily uplifting effect on my otherwise morose state of mind.

### Why I Can't Be Bothered With Brands

Branded goods are a kind of consolation prize for the wage slave. While we may be downtrodden in one way or another during the day, humiliated by bosses and bored by co-workers, the brand gives us the opportunity to wield some power once we are released from the factory gates. In today's vernacular, brands 'big us up'. So, however small and useless we have been made to feel, we are suddenly courted and flattered by advertising, and all we have to do to feel like a king again is buy something from Gucci. From pauper to prince. I know: I've done it. But the boost is temporary. The next day we are slaves once more. Chronic disappointment is built into the brand system. Just as consumer goods are created with planned obsolescence in order to make us keep buying, so brands leave us wanting more. One purchase fails to deliver its promise of making us feel free and attractive. So we buy something else. Again we are disappointed and so it goes on: trapped in a vicious cycle of work–spend–work.

In this sense brands are the evil twin of slave-work and therefore are an enemy to idleness and an enemy to freedom.

This is not to say that the idler rejects spending of all kinds. Ten years ago I bought a coat from the Soho tailor John Pearse for £300, a tweed number with velvet collar. Last year I spent £70 having it repaired and it looks as good as new. This is money well spent: John Pearse is an independent tailor who greets you when you enter his shop. Scoffers out there will argue, 'Yes, but he's a brand.' Well, he may be, but the scale of his operation is miniscule compared to a Nike or a Hugo Boss. In the world of clothes, small is beautiful. Brands are evil partly because of their enormous scale. And it is worth paying for quality rather than quantity. Quality lasts. Style never goes out of fashion.

It's surely also the mark of an individual to refuse to be branded. It's daft to spend money on Nike clothes. The mark of a moron. Anyone who does so has been merely duped by the million-dollar marketing campaigns. To buy Nike shows a sheep-like nature and a lack of imagination and style. And I would make the same argument for Tesco, Argos and Loans Direct. They are shops for fools.

Anyway, who in their right mind would want to be branded, like a cow? A brand identifies you as someone else's property. It is the mark of a tamed and exploited animal.

Brands promise freedom but they deliver the opposite: the worst kind of slavish conformity. So that's why I can't be bothered with brands. They are too much like hard work. Spend less, work less. Abandon quantity; embrace quality.

## day 6

Saturday. Most people, I imagine, are out shopping for a new top to wear at tonight's social engagement, perhaps a CD that they heard on the radio during the week. Maybe stopping in to Pret a Manger or Carluccio's for a bite to eat. Lovely. I am shopping for food and detergent at the local market. I must gather all the week's supplies, because the market only opens today.

I don't remember food costing this much at the supermarket. Trusting the local Sainsbury's to be generally fair priced, I would normally throw items into the basket without paying much attention to the price. I am quite sure, however, that milk didn't cost £2 a pint. The market version *is* organic, but still. The foodstuff on display here is small in portion, misshapen and often caked in dirt, all at great cost. The experience is undeniably more enjoyable and virtuous-feeling than the supermarket equivalent though.

By the time I have called round to the fishmongers, the bakers and the hardware store, the day is nearly spent. As a 'treat' to myself, I pay a trip to the local army store, where I am now becoming quite familiar to the staff. What can I be tempted by today? Jackboots? Russian cossack hats? Perhaps a six-foot wide camouflage net? I feel the need to make just one non-essential purchase, so I buy an ill-fitting black cable-knit jumper (a snip at £5). The wool is so scratchy it might well double as a kitchen scourer. It's not like Harvey Nichols in here.

Juliet forces me to meet friends at the local pub in the evening. I have barely spoken to a soul since the bonfire, and it seems important that I do not wholly withdraw from my previous life. The friends that we meet are regular London people, most of them struggling to make ends meet in average jobs that pay just enough to get by. But even here, the unspoken game of brand top trumps is underway, with the chips of the game – mobile phones, car keys and wallets – lying among the beer glasses and ashtrays on the tabletops. I know every item's owner. James, the BMW keys, the Blackberry is Daniel's and the B&H cigarettes are Steve's (always keen to assert his working-class heritage). I know none of these people is so shallow as to leave their trinkets on display simply to impress, but they are displayed none the less. When my friend Justin pulls a Prada wallet from his pocket, I wonder what thought processes led him to buying the thing. He most likely spent a day looking around the shops, choosing which wallet was to his taste, or perhaps afforded him the most taste. Undoubtedly, the thing cost him a day's wages, and at that price, a lot of thought must have gone into the purchase. However discreetly these items might appear on a person, they do not appear from thin air. The wallet's owner catches me staring at the thing and snatches it back into his coat pocket.

'Sorry, Boorman, didn't mean to flash my brands at you. I know it must hurt.'

'You don't have to hide it from me. I won't sprout hairs and start howling at the moon.'

'So, what have you got on there?' says Justin, pointing to my jeans. 'I reckon you've been to Levi's and just torn the label off. Let me have a look.'

161

This is run-of-the-mill banter but I'm in no mood for jokes. Unwilling to be frisked twice in one week, I push Justin away as he reaches for the back of my jeans, shouting expletives for effect. Juliet steps in to avoid further confrontation. I was never the argumentative type among friends. I quietly nurse my now-trademark lime and soda and do my level best to engage with the situation.

## day 7

If I bought a bar of Snickers from a corner shop, unwrapped it before I left and shoved the whole thing into my mouth as quickly as possible, surely nobody would be the wiser? The withdrawal from nicotine is beginning to transform into hunger pangs and, today, only mass-produced artificially tasty chocolate bars with big flashy logos on the wrapper will do.

Somehow finding myself in a sweet shop, I stare gormlessly at the racks of chocolate until the shopkeeper breaks me from my trance.

'Anything I can get you, mate?'

'Er, do you have any bananas or apples?'

'No, mate, only sweets and crisps.'

## day 9

The deadly phone silence at home is broken by Rana, my former colleague and proud owner of my Helmut Lang jacket, who calls to offer me some work. Grateful for the distraction, I duly walk over to the office, taking in some autumnal sun. Pre-bonfire, I would normally have pulled together a combination of brands to help me feel business-like but edgy, an offensive of top-level labels to match those of Rana, whose zeal for purchasing brands, and understanding their language, equals, if not outstretches mine. This being the new me, I must rely on old-fashioned charm, dressed as I am in terribly plain clothes. I pass an advert for Nokia, and the strap line asks, 'Which side of you do you want to be today?' There is only one side of me now.

It can't be more than 70 degrees today, but as I reach Rana's office I seem to be perspiring far more than normal. Unlike Sure, which 'never lets you down', my non-branded anti-perspirant salt stick has failed miserably and large damp patches begin to form around my armpits. Luckily there is no smell as yet, only moisture.

'I've got some work for you, Neil, on the new PlayStation 3. We've converted a warehouse into a bar for two months, and I want you to host a night. All the gear's laid on, loads of exclusive games to play and free drinks. I'm basically paying you to bring a good crowd down.'

'Well, I'd love to. I'm sure the bar is really, er, cool, and I really could do with the money' – I'm beginning to become flustered here; you don't turn down work like this as you may never be asked again – 'but I can't really get involved with any brands.'

'Huh? I thought that was just your clothes. What, you're not doing any brand work again? Seriously, you'd be crazy to turn this down, it's good money.'

'I'm sorry, I appreciate the offer but . . .'

'I understand. Listen, I'll keep you on file for after your book comes out. You'll be back to work after that, right? This is just a social experiment. You shouldn't keep it up for too long. Anyway, you can't, it's in your blood.'

How many people are lucky enough to be offered work as easy and profitable as this? Curiously, I don't feel as disillusioned as I might have; a moral victory in my admittedly futile private war.

'You might want to think about some branded deodorant, Neil,' quips Rana as I shuffle out of the office. 'Whatever you're using isn't really doing the job.'

## day 11

The remodelled computer casing arrives from Mac Mods, together with a CD containing de-branded software. Thus begins the most pointless modification ever undertaken on a computer.

# day 13

I simply could not be bothered to pack a day's supplies in my bag this morning. It is such a bore making sandwiches each day, lugging fruit and bottles of tap water around with me. What a luxury it must be to go and buy a packet of crisps when one feels hungry, to nip out of the office and get a can of Coke when the mood takes hold. By mid-afternoon, I am caught short in the street with a sudden pang of thirst, the kind where you can feel your body starting to dehydrate. Any sane person would call into a newsagent and pick up a bottle of Evian. I am dashing into the rather grim toilets of a local pub, to drink from the washbasin tap. Now this *is* madness.

Didn't there used to be drinking-water fountains in British parks and on high streets? I wonder why they were removed. Vandalism? Or perhaps, as a service, there was no money in it for the local council. Why would any business provide something if no profit could be gained?

The tap water tastes of chlorine. At least with bottled water, you can be sure of what you are drinking. When I pick up a bottle manufactured by a brand that I trust, I don't have to look at the label or check the quality before I buy. You know exactly what you are buying into. In surrounding myself with labels, I suppose I had attempted to package myself in the same way; appealing to the senses, consistent in character, easily identifiable and dependable in content. People could look at me and see what they were buying into.

# day 14

I peer down from the bedroom window, watching people stroll to work, in and out of shops, talking, laughing happily with their friends, enjoying daily life. Two guys drive by slowly in an open-top Saab, and a few women turn round and look in admiration. Another woman strides confidently down the road with a Dior bag swinging from her arm, her eyes shielded by a huge pair of Gucci sunglasses like a St Tropez film star. An outdoorsy couple walk past with North Face backpacks and Saracen walking boots (must be professional tourists).

People everywhere are getting on with their lives, aided by their chosen brands, which do not seem to be causing them any trouble whatsoever. Has the general public been brainwashed in a giant consumer conspiracy, or have I completely lost touch with reality?

## day 16

I have not lost touch with reality. There is a growing body of evidence to suggest that this branded lifestyle is psychologically harmful. I am back in the library, and what I read seems to back up my decision. For decades, psychologists have been employed by industrialists to study the consumer mind for the purposes of increased sales. The harmful effects are only now being recognised by a small number of specialists throughout the West. During my research, I came across an incredible doctor of consumer psychology, Helga Dittmar, whose work would seem to validate many of the anxieties that I have suffered throughout so much of my life.

### Consumer Culture Ideals

Consumer culture is best seen as 'the sociocultural, experiential, symbolic, and ideological aspects of consumption' now characterised in mass consumer societies by an obsession with 'to have is to be' and a cult of perfect beauty, however exacting. Through the advertising and fashion industries, consumer culture presents individuals with images that contain 'lifestyle and identity instructions that convey unadulterated marketplace ideologies (look like this, act like this, want these things, aspire to this kind of lifestyle)'. The symbolism inherent in consumer goods can be defined as the images of 'idealised people associated with [the good]' (Wright, Claiborne, & Sirgy, 1992), and the message is that buyers do not only consume the actual good advertised, but also its symbolic meanings (successful, happy, attractive, glamorous), thus moving closer to the ideal identity portrayed by media models. Idealised media models not only communicate that affluence and beauty should be central life goals for

165

everybody, they define the parameters of what it means to be beautiful, successful and happy. Of course, consumers do not simply take these messages at face value, but it is very hard – if not impossible – to remain untouched by the continuous exposure to these normative sociocultural ideals portrayed in the mass media as 'normal', desirable and achievable. The sheer exposure to advertising – on TV, radio, the Internet, billboards, products, in cinemas, magazines and shops – is staggering, with estimates that individuals see as many as 3000 advertisements a day. Although there is diversity in the nuances of idealised imagery, they seem variations around prominent themes, with the material 'good life' centrestage.

## The Material 'Good Life'

The central idealised identity refers to the 'good life', where an affluent lifestyle, studded with expensive consumer goods and activities, is heralded as a material. Profiled now more than ever by idealised models who are celebrities, a super-affluent ideal is made to appear possible for 'ordinary' people. A typical example is the footballer David Beckham, known globally and an advertising model par excellence, who promotes diverse products, including Police sunglasses, Vodafone, Gillette and Pepsi. Similar to the 'body perfect', there is a halo effect around the material 'good life', where affluence is associated not only with success, control and autonomy, but also an interesting personal life, happiness and successful intimate relationships. Thus, advertising creates a 'reality' that is not real. Furthermore, it not only presents idealised, unrealistic images which pose a problem for many people, producing self-doubt, identity deficits and negative emotions, but it also presents the supposed solution: to buy the consumer products promoted, which will get them closer to these ideals. Buy and this will enhance your sense of self-worth; indeed, buy 'because you are worth it'!

**Consumer Culture as a 'Cage Within'**

The process through which advertising influences people is subtle: nobody believes that adverts are real in a literal sense, and nobody believes that they will transform into a supermodel or a celebrity if they buy product X. Rather, consumer ideals have indirect, but powerful, effects on individuals' thoughts, feelings and behaviours, which take effect over time. For instance, TV plays a prominent role in constructing what individuals see as consumer reality. TV life differs dramatically from social reality because expensive possessions, costly consumer behaviours and wealth are heavily overrepresented. A US study found that the more television people watched, the more they overestimated the percentage of Americans who are millionaires and own expensive possessions, such as tennis courts (O'Guinn & Shrum, 1997). Moreover, responses to advertising are not always thoughtful and deliberate, but can be quite automatic. For example, exposure to advertisements featuring thin female models makes certain groups of women feel more anxious about their own bodies, even when they see these images only fleetingly and do not pay much attention to them (Brown & Dittmar, 2005). Therefore, the mass media plays a significant role in how individuals construct their own versions of material and bodily norms. This, in turn, impacts people's sense of self-worth through psychological mechanisms, such as discrepancy creation and upward social comparison.

Consumer culture is curtailing vulnerable people from within through value internalisation and construction of a negative identity, where people feel far away from their ideal, and bad about this gap. Yet its pernicious effects go further because of the supposed, but illusory, solutions advertising dangles in front of people for managing and repairing identity deficits and negative emotions. They are encouraged to strive for unhealthy and unrealistic ideals, the material 'good life' and the 'body perfect', pursuits likely to increase identity deficits and negative emotions still further. In short, consumer culture is analysed as a 'cage within' because the internalisation of these two ideals as personal value systems cannot but lead to negative identities and negative emotions which, in turn, people then seek to remedy through consumer goods. The resulting appetite for consumption is, of course, considered vital for a thriving economy, and fuelling such an appetite is the purpose of advertising. This suggests that immense profits are to be made of people's misguided search for identity and happiness through consumption. In turn, this makes it highly unlikely that the idealised imagery in consumer culture will change any time soon. After all, if product sales failed to continue to rise, or even started to drop significantly, because a large enough number of people chose simpler, less consumer-oriented lifestyles, corporate interests would be seriously jeopardised. Indeed, the functioning of capitalism itself could be called into question.[36]

It seems clear to me now that I have spent my life compensating for the 'negative identity' that I suffer from, comparing myself to the idealised images that confront me each day. Thinking of the countless times that I spent money with companies that promised self-betterment, it is difficult not to feel cheated, manipulated. I am not entirely sure that the advertising industry deliberately sets out to undermine the confidence of the consumer, but the by-product of this relentless drive to purchase contentment undoubtedly damages vulnerable people such as me as a result. I am not sure if this damage is a fair price to pay for a thriving economy.

## day 17

My material consumption is virtually nil. Food is delivered from the local farmers' market. I have bought enough non-branded clothes to last for a week before washing the whole lot, in generic industrial detergent. I reckon the only two branded products that I have consumed so far are Thames Water and British Gas. Now, I realise I can do something about this. I can switch my energy supplies to a renewable-sourced company. I call British Gas to cancel my contract. I have been looking forward to this day for some time and my voice is full of glee. But the professionally deadpan call operator ignores my enthusiasm for termination of the contract.

Call operators and sales assistants, often the first point of contact with the customer, are essential to the delivery of the *brand experience*. The ethos of the company must be projected through its workers, who are trained to act in accordance with behavioural manuals. Which is why this call operator will never rise to my triumphalism. Arlie Russell Hochschild, professor of sociology at the University of California, describes this phenomenon as *emotional labour* – the emotional style of the service that one delivers being part of the job. Observing air steward training at Delta Airways, Hochschild noted that the girls are taught to wear concrete smiles, suppressing their real emotions throughout the time they are on duty:

> The pilot spoke of the smile as the flight attendant's asset. But the value of a personal smile is groomed to reflect the company's disposition – its confidence that its planes will not crash, its reassurance that departures and arrivals will be on time, its welcome and its invitation to return. Trainers take it as their job to attach to the trainee's smile an attitude, a viewpoint, a rhythm of feeling that is, as they often say 'professional'.[37]

The branding of emotions may be exhausting to the employee. But it can also be rather draining for the customer. Purchasing is transformed into a sterile experience by the insincere greeting, the stylised language and the formulaic dialogue. I truly believe that these disingenuous interactions only add to our greater anxiety. It causes me to feel suspicious towards anybody that extends me a smile. Having withdrawn my business from many of these companies, I might possibly regain a little faith in human nature once more.

Am I imagining things when I detect a hint of sympathy from the operator at British Gas when the contract is finally cancelled? Perhaps their brand manual instructs them to play the wounded soldier at the point of termination? Having spent 50 minutes waiting on hold to speak to an operator, this tactic, if it indeed exists, is lost on me.

## day 18

In my previous life, I would sit around at dinner parties, moaning about the disappearing independent shops on the high street, how the supermarkets and chains were enforcing standardised culture upon us, and that the banks and utility companies relied on us being too lazy to switch when they hiked up their charges. But I never did anything about it myself (too busy shopping). Now I am being forced to come good on fashionable consumer warfare rhetoric with an ethical audit, and although it is a tedious process having dozens of standing orders shifted from one company to another, I must say I do feel virtuous.

## day 20

As the days and now weeks drag on, I come to understand that, in practical terms, this project is simply an exercise in dropping one set of consumer habits for another. It had become a habit of mine to rely on the convenience of the high street to fulfil even the slightest whim. Rarely would I have actually planned a day's food consumption. Why would I? There was always a shop or café nearby that would cater for that need. Hungry? Buy a packet of something to eat. Thirsty? Buy a bottle of water. Bored? Buy something for the distraction. For almost every need or desire that pops into my head, there is a product waiting to fulfil it, and a shop ready to sell it to me. Truly, a consumer paradise. But, there being mainly branded chain stores selling branded goods on London's high streets, very few of these options remain open to me any longer. Therefore, to exist outside the comfort zone of the flat, I must plan the day ahead, anticipating my basic needs and sourcing a supply.

The system begins with the weekly shop at the markets; enough food for seven breakfasts, packed lunches, dinners and snacks, plus ingredients for the homemade cosmetics, non-branded versions of which I've not been able to find. One afternoon spent mixing glycerine, baking soda and base oils provides enough toothpaste and cleaning agents for a week. Lunchboxes and snacks have to be prepared religiously each morning to avoid a potential Snickers or Pringles ambush. Similarly, I pack a two-litre flask of water each day. Eating a packed lunch at the desk draws looks of sympathy from colleagues and sipping from flasks in the street gives off the image of a traveller or worse, a tramp. But why should I have to hand over £5 a day to a coffee chain in order to legitimise my place in life?

At the beginning of this project, friends would often ask me which branded goods I expected to miss the most. Adidas perhaps, Ralph Lauren? I never imagined it would be a decent make of toilet roll – Andrex, Bounty, Double Velvet – anything but the thin plastic-coated stuff that I must now buy in bulk from the local janitorial suppliers. Heaven forbid I forget to buy the stuff in advance; Juliet has begun to stockpile her own supply of luxury branded paper for herself, and I occasionally creep into the bathroom to feel the stuff between my forefinger and thumb; so soft, so velvety.

Finding brand-free entertainment is problematic, but far more rewarding. No eating at chain restaurants or bars (no great loss really), no Hollywood films at branded cinemas (again, no great loss) and of course no shopping as leisure. In fact, most of the branded entertainment on offer in London is as plastic and malnourishing as the majority of packaged rubbish passing as food in the supermarkets. Walks, galleries and museums, food and parties at the houses of friends – these fill the gaping hole in my daily schedule that was once occupied by clothes shopping. The frantic bulk purchases of no-brand clothing from markets and the Internet are now standing me in good stead, although I am no longer leading the pack in directional men's leisurewear. Instead, I rely on the old-fashioned warhorse that is the colour black. With simple black clothes, and the odd alteration at a backstreet tailor, you have a wardrobe fit for any social engagement, particularly funerals. I am of course quietly dying inside as the new season's clothes and accessories flood the shops. But this is something best left to denial for the time being.

## day 30

I have survived without brands for almost one month. Reducing one's life on paper to a set of consumer routines is a humbling experience, to say the least; when products are bought almost entirely for their function, they cease to be symbols of lifestyle, becoming products that facilitate the eternal cycle of eating, sleeping, shitting, washing and keeping warm; a caveman's existence in 21st-century London. Some might say that non-branded, homemade bathroom cleaner is a lifestyle statement in itself, but furiously scrubbing at the bath-scum for half an hour with little more than baking soda and vinegar could surely never be considered a stylish life, by anyone's standards.

More than ever though, I have come to see these brands simply as bad habits that I picked up through a considerable amount of laziness on my part. I would go about my day, blindly consuming packaged goods at will, unquestioningly feeding every desire like a zombie. The convenience of consuming on the go afforded me more time to think about the more important things in life, like earning money, so I could afford to go out and do more shopping.

Another convenience I relied upon with brands was their magical powers to inspire confidence. Wearing expensive logos on your chest can make you feel good, but so too can the small things in life, like tooth-paste. I would clean my teeth with Colgate to freshen my breath before most social interactions, from business meetings to nights down the pub; knowing that my teeth were clean, that my breath smelt fresh gave me that little bit of extra confidence, a sort of insurance policy against, heaven forbid, somebody spotting a bit of food in my teeth or recoiling from bad breath. Social suicide. It occurs to me that companies such as Colgate and Wrigley's play on some of our deepest insecurities. When you buy a tube of toothpaste or a pack of gum, you're not simply buying mint, fluoride and any number of breath-freshening agents, you are buying security and confidence; the confidence to be yourself, only without the nasty smell.

Beside the unpleasant natural smells of the pits and orifices, this project is having a detoxifying effect on my body. My diet is far healthier, having given up junk like Coke, Mars bars and Pringles. Having quit the Marlboro Lights, I'll most likely live longer. I am also richer for it; all this home cooking, cheap clothing and free entertainment leaves my monthly income in the black for a change. There is really nothing of great cost available for me to spend it on.

| BRANDED ITEMS DESTROYED | | | NON-BRANDED REPLACEMENTS | | |
|---|---|---|---|---|---|
| **CLOTHES** | | | **CLOTHES** | | |
| **TOPS** | | | **TOPS** | | |
| 14 x | Ralph Lauren shirts | £910 | 6 x | polo shirts | |
| 2 x | YSL T-shirts | £150 | | (www.indigoclothing.com) | £30 |
| 2 x | Judy Blame T-shirts | £200 | 6 x | plain T-shirts | |
| 3 x | Lacoste polo shirts | £150 | | (www.europeanwear.com) | £25 |
| 2 x | Vivienne Westwood shirts | £200 | 4 x | T-shirts (local market) | £20 |
| 3 x | Siv Stoldal | £210 | 2 x | T-shirts (army surplus) | £20 |
| 3 x | Nike T-shirts | £150 | | | |
| 1 x | Kappa T-shirt | £40 | | | |
| 1 x | Diadora tracktop | £40 | | | |
| 2 x | Kilgore shirts | £240 | | | |
| 2 x | Bernhard Willhelm sweatshirts | £300 | | | |
| 1 x | Gucci T-shirt | £80 | | | |
| 1 x | Sergio Tacchini tracktop | £80 | | | |
| 1 x | Sergio Tacchini polo shirt | £70 | | | |
| 1 x | Kim Jones T-shirt | £50 | | | |
| 1 x | Gucci polo shirt | £60 | | | |
| 2 x | vintage Gucci sweat tops | £120 | | | |
| 1 x | Gucci shirt | £120 | | | |
| 1 x | Raf Simons T-shirt | £50 | | | |
| **JEANS / TROUSERS** | | | **JEANS / TROUSERS** | | |
| 1 x | Lee jeans | £60 | 2 x | trousers (army surplus) | £30 |
| 3 x | Levi's jeans | £180 | 3 x | running shorts | £15 |
| 2 x | Adidas tracksuits | £200 | 1 x | jeans (charity shop) | £5 |
| 1 x | Lacoste tracksuit | £50 | 2 x | jeans (vintage market) | £30 |
| 2 x | Ralph Lauren shorts | £100 | 2 x | trackpants | |
| 1 x | Diadora shorts | £20 | | (www.europeanwear.com) | £15 |
| 4 x | Adidas shorts | £80 | 1 x | tailoring/alterations | £45 |
| 1 x | Sergio Tacchini bottoms | £50 | | | |
| 3 x | Helmut Lang jeans | £600 | | | |
| 1 x | Ellesse trackpants | £30 | | | |
| 2 x | Siv Stoldal cords | £200 | | | |
| 1 x | YSL jeans | £180 | | | |

## JUMPERS

| | | Left | | | | Right | |
|---|---|---|---|---|---|---|---|
| 3 | x | Vivienne Westwood | £450 | 2 | x | charity store | £15 |
| 2 | x | John Smedley | £200 | 2 | x | vintage market | £20 |
| 2 | x | Lacoste | £120 | | | | |
| 3 | x | Clements Ribeiro | £500 | | | | |
| 4 | x | Ralph Lauren | £500 | | | | |
| 1 | x | Bernhard Willhelm | £300 | | | | |

## COATS

| | | Left | | | | Right | |
|---|---|---|---|---|---|---|---|
| 2 | x | YSL jackets | £400 | 1 | x | pea coat (army surplus) | £65 |
| 4 | x | Lacoste jackets | £350 | 1 | x | trench coat (vintage store) | £20 |
| 1 | x | Raf Simons bomber | £200 | 1 | x | bomber jacket (vintage store) | £35 |
| 1 | x | Burberry overcoat | £300 | 1 | x | leather jacket (vintage store) | £45 |
| 1 | x | Bernhard Willhelm bomber | £120 | | | | |
| 1 | x | vintage Pierre Cardin bomber | £70 | | | | |
| 1 | x | Dolce & Gabbana blazer | £150 | | | | |
| 1 | x | vintage Christian Dior mac | £80 | | | | |

## SUITS / TIES

| | | Left | | Right |
|---|---|---|---|---|
| 1 | x | Vivienne Westwood suit | £400 | None |
| 1 | x | Joe Casely-Hayford suit | £400 | |
| 1 | x | Vivienne Westwood tie | £50 | |
| 1 | x | Daks tie | £40 | |

## SHOES

| | | Left | | | | Right | |
|---|---|---|---|---|---|---|---|
| 11 | x | Adidas | £770 | 3 | x | plimsolls (www.thecostumestore.co.uk) | £15 |
| 2 | x | Nike | £150 | | | | |
| 3 | x | Reebok | £120 | 1 | x | high-top plimsolls (vintage market) | £20 |
| 2 | x | New Balance | £125 | | | | |
| 1 | x | Helmut Lang | £150 | 1 | x | smart shoes (vintage store) | £25 |
| 2 | x | Gucci | £500 | | | | |
| 1 | x | B-Store | £125 | | | | |

## HATS / BELTS

| | | Left | | Right |
|---|---|---|---|---|
| 1 | x | Vivienne Westwood hat | £120 | None |

| | | | |
|---|---|---|---|
| 1 | x | Aquascutum hat | £75 |
| 1 | x | Gucci visor | £150 |
| 1 | x | Lacoste visor | £50 |
| 1 | x | Gucci cap | £120 |
| 1 | x | Moschino cap | £80 |
| 2 | x | Kangol hats | £175 |
| 2 | x | Ralph Lauren belts | £90 |
| 1 | x | Louis Vuitton belt | £150 |

UNDERWEAR

| | | | |
|---|---|---|---|
| 15 x | Calvin Klein pants | £75 |
| 5 x | Burlington socks | £25 |
| 2 x | Ralph Lauren socks | £25 |
| 1 x | Burberry socks | £10 |

**SUB-TOTAL** — **£15,445**

UNDERWEAR

| | | |
|---|---|---|
| 10 x | trunks (www.europeanwear.com) | £35 |
| 5 x | Y-fronts (local market) | £10 |
| 20 x | socks (local market) | £25 |
| 4 x | vests (local market) | £15 |

**SUB-TOTAL** — **£580**

JEWELLERY

| | | | |
|---|---|---|---|
| 1 | x | vintage Swatch watch | £40 |
| 1 | x | Vivienne Westwood chain | £80 |
| 1 | x | Karen Walker chain | £90 |
| 3 | x | Silas chains | £150 |
| 1 | x | Louis Vuitton money clip | £80 |
| 1 | x | Adidas keyring | (gift) |
| 1 | x | Vivienne Westwood cufflinks | £120 |

**SUB-TOTAL** — **£560**

JEWELLERY

| | | |
|---|---|---|
| 1 x | Money clip (secondhand market) | £20 |

**SUB-TOTAL** — **£20**

LUGGAGE

| | | | |
|---|---|---|---|
| 1 | x | Louis Vuitton wallet | £80 |
| 1 | x | Samsonite trolley bag | £70 |
| 1 | x | North Face Rucksack | £60 |
| 1 | x | Louis Vuitton satchel | £380 |
| 1 | x | Louis Vuitton notepad | £180 |

**SUB-TOTAL** — **£770**

LUGGAGE

| | | |
|---|---|---|
| 1 x | rucksack (army surplus) | £30 |

**SUB-TOTAL** — **£30**

| ELECTRICALS | | | | ELECTRICALS | | |
|---|---|---|---|---|---|---|
| 1 | x | Technics turntable | £350 | 1 | x Recycled phone | |
| 1 | x | NAD amplifier | £200 | | (recyclemyphone.com) | £25 |
| 1 | x | Mission speakers | £300 | 1 | x Kettle (army surplus) £20 | |
| 1 | x | Pioneer Mix CD | £300 | 1 | x Fridge (industrial suppliers) £100 | |
| 1 | x | Roberts radio | £120 | | | |
| 1 | x | Blackberry phone | (free) | | | |
| 1 | x | Treo phone | (free) | | | |
| 1 | x | Dyson vacuum | £150 | | | |
| 1 | x | Sharp LCD | £900 | | | |
| 1 | x | Pioneer DVD | £150 | | | |
| 1 | x | Amstrad phone | £100 | | | |
| 1 | x | Kenwood kettle | £40 | | | |
| 1 | x | Olympus digital camera | £100 | | | |
| 1 | x | Liebherr fridge (discarded at tip) | £250 | | | |
| SUB-TOTAL | | | £2960 | SUB-TOTAL | | £145 |

| FURNITURE | | | | FURNITURE | |
|---|---|---|---|---|---|
| 1 | x | Habitat sideboard | £300 | 1 x sideboard (vintage store) £150 | |
| 1 | x | Arne Jacobson chair | £120 | 2 x chairs (vintage store) | £100 |
| 1 | x | Skandium chair | £100 | 4 x boxes (janitorial supplies) £40 | |
| 2 | x | Muji storage boxes | £60 | | |
| SUB-TOTAL | | | £580 | SUB-TOTAL | £290 |

| CROCKERY | | CROCKERY | |
|---|---|---|---|
| 4 x Bodum cups | £60 | 4 x cups (vintage store) | £15 |
| 2 x Heal's vases | £150 | | |
| SUB-TOTAL | £210 | SUB-TOTAL | £15 |

| COSMETICS (PERSONAL AND HOUSEHOLD) | | | COSMETICS (PERSONAL AND HOUSEHOLD) | | |
|---|---|---|---|---|---|
| 1 | x Gillette Mach3 Turbo razor | £5.50 | 1 | x Disposable razors (market) | £5.00 |
| 1 | x Simple Soap | £1.00 | 1 | x Organic soap (wholefood market) | £4.00 |
| 1 | x Dr. Hauschka Moisturiser | £9.00 | | | |

| | | | |
|---|---|---|---|
| 1 | x | Simple deodorant | £2.00 |
| 1 | x | Colgate toothpaste 100ml | £2.00 |
| 1 | x | Colgate toothbrush | £3.50 |
| 1 | x | L'Oréal shampoo | £3.00 |
| 1 | x | L'Oréal conditioner | £2.00 |
| 1 | x | Dax hair wax | £3.50 |
| 4 | x | Waitrose recycled toilet roll | £1.50 |
| 1 | x | Fairy washing-up liquid 5 litres | £9.50 |
| 1 | x | Mr Muscle bathroom cleaner | £1.50 |
| 1 | x | Mr Muscle kitchen cleaner | £2.50 |
| 1 | x | Mr Muscle sink unblocker | £3.50 |
| 1 | x | Flash floor cleaner | £1.00 |
| 1 | x | Cif bathroom cream | £1.50 |
| 1 | x | Domestos bleach | £1.00 |
| 1 | x | Fairy Automatic detergent 5 litres | £9.00 |
| 1 | x | Woolite laundry liquid | £1.50 |

| | | | |
|---|---|---|---|
| 1 | x | Homemade moisturiser 1-litre: (cocoa butter £4) (almond oil £1.50) (orange peel oil £2.50) (www.meltandpour-supplies.com) | £8.00 |
| 1 | x | Deodorant salt stick (whole food market) | £6.00 |
| 1 | x | Homemade toothpaste 400ml: (glycerin £5) (baking soda £3) (peppermint oil £1.75) (www.herbsofgrace.com) | £9.75 |
| 1 | x | Toothbrush (local market) | £2.00 |
| 1 | x | Shampoo (wholefood market) | £6.00 |
| 1 | x | Conditioner (wholefood market) | £7.00 |
| 1 | x | Beeswax hair wax (www.honeyshop.co.uk) | £1.00 |
| 20 | x | industrial toilet roll (janitorial suppliers) | £8.00 |
| 1 | x | Washing-up liquid (janitorial suppliers) | £3.50 |
| 1 | x | Bathroom/kitchen cleaner: (baking soda £4) (2 litres vinegar £5) (catering suppliers) | £9.00 |
| 1 | x | Bleach 5 litres (janitorial suppliers) | £9.00 |
| 1 | x | Detergent 5 litres (janitorial suppliers) | £7.00 |

| | | | |
|---|---|---|---|
| SUB-TOTAL | | | £64 |
| TOTAL | | | £21,345 |

| | | | |
|---|---|---|---|
| SUB-TOTAL | | | £85.25 |
| TOTAL | | | £1,165.25 |

| WEEKLY OUTGOINGS | | SERVICE (PER MONTH) | |
| --- | --- | --- | --- |
| British Gas | £5.00 | Good Energy | £10 |
| London Energy | £5.00 | | |
| British Telecom | £10 | The Phone Co-operative Landline | £20 |
| Orange mobile | £27 | | |
| Churchill home insurance | £5.00 | No insurance (nothing of great value to insure) | |
| Holmes Place Gym | £17 | No gym membership fee (run round the park instead for free) | |

| GROCERIES | | GROCERIES | |
| --- | --- | --- | --- |
| Sainsbury's/Waitrose | £120 | Farmer's veggie box (delivered) | £35 |
| | | Meat from butchers | £15 |
| | | Fish from fishmongers | £25 |
| | | Carbs/dairy/condiments (wholefood market) | £45 |
| Evian bottled water | £7.00 | Water flask (no charge) | |
| Marlboro Lights | £21 | No cigarettes | |
| TOTAL | £227 | TOTAL | £150 |

# day 35

Important, exciting news and events are going on right now, events that, had I chosen not to destroy my Blackberry with a sledgehammer, I could be party to. Several weeks of disconnection from the world of mobile telecommunications, combined with a withdrawal from nicotine, television, shopping and other perfectly normal aspects of modern life is, according to Carol, fuelling my anxiety and paranoia. In a bid to reclaim my sanity, I give up and contact The Phone Co-Operative to order a mobile. Being a small business, there is one phone line to the office, and I initially leave a message on what sounds like a domestic answering machine; not the most encouraging sign of an efficient service provider for international satellite communication. But, as I have begun to learn, sprawling size does not necessarily equate to good service. My whole life, I have been so used to dealing with businesses via call centres, being treated as a number in a queue, that I have never really known what it is like to do business with a small company. To speak to a human being and receive personal service seems antiquated and doomed to failure; if they were a successful company, they shouldn't have time to deal with me personally. What is this network made up of exactly? Tin cans and string?

Against all expectations, I have a new number, a new SIM card and a recycled, de-branded, unlocked handset within five days. The handset costs £20 from www.recyclemymobile.com (complete with the previous owner's address book). To avoid any potential statements of aspirational lifestyle, I choose the cheapest, nastiest, most basic phone on the website; as a status symbol, this phone says I have the hopes and dreams of a nomadic goat farmer. The buttons are so primitive they hurt my fingers when I dial a long number. An object of pure utility, this is not something that draws admiring comments when left on the table of a pub, and when I use it walking past gangs of young hooded phone robbers on the street, they pay me no attention whatsoever.

Modern celebrities are the foot soldiers of capitalism; PR men to the industrialists, they endorse any product as long as the price is right, accepting any sort of publicity so long as it boosts their own personal brand. 'Selling out' used to be an insult, but celebrities have turned it into an aspiration. Having achieved so much of the success that we ourselves desire, having become the idealised image that we see in the adverts, one would assume that these people would be satisfied with their lot. And yet, for all the fulfilled brand promises, so many of them seem to unravel emotionally before our eyes in the news each day.

Phillip Hodson, a media psychotherapist, well read in the culture of celebrity, has written me a profile of possibly the most branded celebrity on the planet:

### Brand Beckham

It is impossible to live in this environment and completely resist the beguiling blandishments of market myths but how should we analyse those who appear overly seducible? The dilemma is complicated because we also inhabit a celebrity culture consisting of famous individuals who themselves represent brands – e.g. 'Brand Beckham' – that mainly consist of an addiction to pushing other brands, e.g. Brand Rolex or Brand Versace, and the public ends up trying to compete.

As a psychotherapist, what most strikes me about – say – the female half of the Beckham brand is the apparent fragility of her persona. This is of course a paradox in itself because she represents a universally recognised 'persona'. But drawing on reports of her alleged behaviour, and in no spirit whatsoever of an attack, there appears to be a tragic insecurity at the heart of her self-image. It gives off this sad message: 'I am *nothing* unless every aspect of my appearance is exclusive, of the most costly, perfectly arrayed and leads me to command the envy of other women and the admiration of all men across hectares of newsprint.'

At its most serious, a person in such a position is sufficiently a slave to their appearance that the idea of an inner life is altogether denied, as is the life of the mind (Posh, we famously recall, does not read books). It is as if by making her body some type of universal idiom she were able to defeat all personal criticism. Yet for Mrs Beckham, alas, in her desire to command approval, she also provokes disdain. For instance, it is widely hinted that her obsessional consumerism no longer includes much in the way of consuming calories. How, it's asked, can such a person age? How can such a person die? How can such a person feel comfortable in their skin? As the Romans said, nothing human can be perfected: Posh must fail. But then by her own criteria, she will fall. Branding has an older meaning – wearing a scar of servitude to a tyrant master. These modern tyrants go by names such as Vuitton, Conran, Gucci and Lagerfeld.

I am forced to conclude that only somebody who felt a bit like nobody could possibly expend all this anxious energy on external appearances. If the aim is to avoid cosmic feelings of inferiority, then it achieves the opposite effect. Clearly, only someone who has strongly felt inferior, as child or young woman, could generate the motivation to become so fussy. Only someone who feels so haunted and hunted by demons from the past could continue to act out on the public stage the notion that one is, sadly, one's hair extensions. And the tragedy is that we make branded idols of individuals who practically cease to exist when the camera is absent.

During bouts of depression, I would often spend days slumped in front of the television – MTV in particular – gawping at celebrities that were visibly dripping with success. They seemed to offer living proof that the material lifestyle, and the emotional stability that I yearned for, was indeed possible to achieve. And yet the recurring stories of the rich and famous, the champions of the material lifestyle, are littered with misery – a glaring truth that I somehow managed to ignore back then. If the winners that partake in the materialistic race of life cannot reap any sort of contentment, there can be little hope for the aspiring middle ranks such as me. Better to opt out of the race altogether then.

## day 41

Each day, I step out onto the street as a blank canvas. Nothing about my person has much to say about the person that I am, or would like to be. I feel largely invisible. In reality, very few people probably noticed me before the de-branding but the odd knowing glance from another label victim would be enough to validate the money I'd dedicated to the image. I do, however, feel the constant glare of advertising. I walk onto a tube platform, to find that the entire tunnel's advertising space has been bought out by one company, dominating the eye-line as it curves along the wall. I try desperately not to look, but my eyes make an involuntary dart to the images; some spray-stencil text, some images of a footballer (I think it's Thierry Henri) and a slogan 'I am what I am'. It has to be a campaign for Reebok. In fact I know it is. Looking away is hard; the colours, the graphics, the messages in the text are so much more alluring than the humdrum life going on around it. I turn to see what the other waiting passengers are doing; each and every one stands staring blankly at the ads. Eventually, I manage to pull away from the glare and focus on the ground for the whole ten minutes before the train comes.

As I board the train, my eyes flick across three different ads in the carriage before I sit down. I avert my gaze and instead focus on the passengers. The woman opposite me, wearing Sketchers sneakers, Levi's jeans and a DKNY jacket, is reading a newspaper, the back cover of which carries a full-page ad for Samsung mobile phones: 'IMAGINE THE ENVY . . . THE NEW D520. GET IT TODAY'. I can feel an opinion forming around the girl's brands, the message of the advert is starting to sink in. There's nothing I can do but close my eyes and wait for the journey to end.

While I am conscious that this diary is starting to sound like the rantings of a madman, I remain convinced that I should be able to go about my daily business without having, quite literally, to close my eyes to avoid being sold to. But for anyone living in an urban environment, there is no choice in the matter. The adverts are everywhere and beyond junking the TV and cancelling the subscription to magazines, there is no getting away from it. The messages will always somehow penetrate the mind. Perhaps this is where the consumer battleground lies, if it does indeed exist; in the mind.

## day 44

In therapy, Carol presses me on my relationship with advertising.

'When I look at advertising, it makes me feel sure that everyone else is having a better time than me. It tells me that other people are more beautiful, popular and successful than I am, and I need to keep up to stay in the game. Like sex, if you believe everything you see in the adverts, everyone's having regular, incredible sex, and if you're normal, you should be too. I know it's rubbish, most people I know suffer bed-death in relationships and the single ones are pretty lonely, but it's difficult to have to remember this every time I see an advert.'

'No one's going to make an advert showing how ordinary life is,' says Carol. 'Have you ever been in a country where they don't have any adverts?'

'Maybe parts of India.'

'I was in communist Yugoslavia in the 1960s, and there were no billboards or advertisements there. I did feel like there was something missing. Although the idea of advertising is rather intrusive, there's something very familiar to the ones that work or click. We know them very well, and they are comforting in some way. What would you miss if there were no ads?'

'It's a love/hate thing. I've often found that adverts are more entertaining than the programmes on TV. Parts of my life have been defined by ad campaigns and when I look back on periods of my life, some brands and their campaigns spring to mind alongside the memories of my personal life. The BT ads with Maureen Lipman; the Smash ads with the robots; Honey Monster; Ronald McDonald . . . I sometimes feel nostalgic for certain brands, and even feel sad for ones that disappear.'

'How do you feel when you look at adverts?'

'They transform me. I travel into a fantasy world. I look at an advert for Jaguar cars, with the handsome guy driving and the beautiful woman sitting beside him, and I think, boy, if I drove to therapy today in a new open-top Jag, I'd be much happier. It's nonsense, I know, but I slip into the fantasy all the time; it's like a daydream. It reminds me of the monologue in the film *Fight Club* – "We've been brought up to believe that one day we'll be millionaires and movie stars and rock gods. But we won't. We're slowly waking up to this fact, and we're very, very pissed off." I identify with that.'

This is the penultimate therapy session with Carol, and, while we've come a long way, I think we're both worried that my materialism has deeper roots than a love of brands. Honestly though, who wouldn't be happier driving to therapy in a Jag? I once witnessed a friend of mine turn from a short, fat and hairy loser in love to certified stallion by a machine with four wheels. Joe was one of the first people in London to have a BMW Z3 sports car, an incredibly desirable motor at the time, having been featured in a James Bond movie. His sex life, he would often tell me, had improved beyond all recognition since he bought it. That the car was flash was undeniable, but I had trouble believing that women would be so shallow as to date a man simply for the car he drives. To prove the point he took me for a drive one Saturday afternoon to a busy high street with the roof pulled down. To my amazement, we quickly became the focus of attention as we cruised beside the crowded pavement. Men became transfixed, eyes wide and mouth gaping with a naïve, almost joyful admiration, until they caught sight of the driver, at which point the eyes would narrow and mouth purse in a sort of begrudging respect or barely concealed jealousy. But the women; the women's glances passed from the car and onto the driver much more quickly than the men. They recognised the beauty of the car, but the person driving the car seemed to be much more important. Stopping at the lights, a couple of girls giggled and waved at us as they crossed the road. Joe casually ignored the girls, and glanced instead at me, overflowing with smug satisfaction. Incredible. I now recall my mother telling me that she originally accepted a blind date with my father in the late 1960s because he had an E-Type Jaguar. They've been married for over 30 years now, and I wouldn't say either of them are as shallow as the people gawping at Joe's BMW. Ten years on from that drive, however, Joe is still very much single.

## day 50

If all our possessions tell stories about the people we are (or would like to be), few things shout so loudly as the coffee-table book. We occasionally flick through them to remind us of our own good taste, and leave them on display as status-driven conversation pieces for visiting guests.

Predictably, my coffee-table book collection focused on product design and advertising.

Juliet finds a few books that have escaped the bonfire, and I find myself thumbing through them with an altogether different perspective than before. It seems incredible that in these books we should celebrate campaigns that have worked best in manipulating us to buy. Not only do we look upon adverts as entertainment, they have become a sort of art form. I remember sitting through a three-hour television programme that counted down the 100 greatest ads of all time. Each year, the *Sunday Times* produces a supplement entitled *Superbrands*, which celebrates iconic brands that 'set the pace'. In one of my glossy books, *Advertising Today*, the author Warren Berger describes advertising as 'the most powerful art form on earth . . . shaping the popular culture . . . endlessly entertaining and incisive . . . it is a mirror that reflects our values, our hopes, our dreams, our fears.[38] It feels rather satisfying to dump these books into the bin, where they belong.

## day 56

Eight weeks have passed and I remain relatively unscathed, give or take two packets of Extra and a value pack of Huggies toilet roll, which were all emergencies, I promise. The main thing is that I have not bought one piece of branded clothing, not so much as looked at a magazine or a television, and not stepped foot inside a chain store. However, the mood swings are still in full swing. I remain safe cooped inside my brand-free utopia of a flat, but the minute I walk out the door, I feel temptation lurking behind every billboard and shop front. Imagine being a man visiting London from a country where all women are forced to take the veil, to find half of the city's female population running around in mini-skirts and stilettos? That's how it feels; irresistibly seductive, yet terrible and forbidden at the same time.

Still, I feel lighter, unburdened physically by the lack of clutter in my new life. Gradually, the values of my beloved brands are beginning to matter less. Yes, I would like to be driving an open-top Saab dressed head-to-toe in Ralph Lauren, swigging a Coke and smoking a Marlboro Light, but the urge is less powerful than before.

The online war as to my legitimacy in life rages on, with an average of 70 per cent in favour of my public hanging. I decide to stop reading them once and for all after I receive this gem from a Mr Foley:

PLEASE TAKE MY EMAIL OFF UR SYSTEM COS I'M NOT INTER-
ESTED IN UR PROPAGANDA.

NIKE TILL I DIE, DOUBLE CHEESEBURGER EVERYDAY.

YOURS AXEL FOLEY.

## day 57

Having established some sort of routine over the past 50 days, I can now reveal the following rules of thumb for anyone with a foolhardy or bloody mind to do the same:

**1.** There is next to nothing on the high street for the non-branded consumer. Buying non-branded invariably means buying local from markets and the occasional back-street store. A total week's shopping requires a well-planned day travelling around town, which, depending on your outlook on life, is either a wholesome back-to-basics way of filling time, or an inefficient bourgeois fantasy which ends in the car park of the out-of-town supermarket. Basically, Saturday is still shopping day, but not shopping as leisure ('Can you charge me as much as you can for those shoes as I want them to make me feel like a superstar?'). Rather it is shopping as necessity ('Can you go any lower on that bag of turnips?').

2. It is easy to fall into the habit of paying *more* for certain products without brands attached because a sub-culture of middle-class centre-left thirtysomethings has managed to commodify honest small-scale produce into an expensive lifestyle. Aspirational non-branded produce like organic farmers' food and clothes cost a fortune. Rather than paying a premium to have a brand attached, you pay even higher to have none. My record for the most overpriced non-branded fair trade organic loaf of bread stands at £7. These people like to call the lifestyle 'living off-grid', which all sounds fine, except one needs an extremely well-paid job on-grid to afford a small block of cheese.

Away from the organic market, however, less sexy products can come at a fraction of the price of famous brand names; generic Ibuprofen retails at £1.20 for a bottle of 20 in the chemist whereas Nurofen sells at £2.36 for a packet of 12 pills. A regulation army rucksack cost me £30 compared to an identical version from North Face at £60. In these cases, one really is paying a premium for the brand attached. Being of no discernible origin, one does wonder how and where the things were made; surely five pairs of pants for £10 can only have been manufactured at a profit in a sweatshop in India or China.

3. The independent shopkeeper has died a death for a very good reason; generally they don't serve the customer as well as the chain stores do. They open and close at inconvenient times. They don't carry extensive stocks of anything and they all carry a faint smell of slow death about them. This is due in part to economies of scale, but also because some shopkeepers simply cannot be bothered to compete with efficiently run chain stores. No matter what, my local butcher closes at 4.30 p.m. on the dot, despite customers queuing or browsing, and despite the fact that 90 per cent of the local population works until 5.30 p.m. Rules are rules, see.

However, a little patience is well rewarded. After the initial shock of inefficiency and unfamiliarity, these 'quirks' start to become attractive. You partake in actual conversations with the shopkeeper, which over time can develop into a shared sense of community; something which I have heard of but never actually experienced. My hatred of service providers has subsided since switching to ethical companies, and now I actually pay my bills on time, as opposed to stringing them out until the final demand, just to cause minor inconvenience to 'the bastards' at the so-called megacorps – a fruitless and unsatisfying endeavour.

4. Life goes on without television. There are times when I would like nothing more than to flop in front of the box and be spoon-fed visual junk after a hard day's work. But even so, I am forced to entertain myself in ways which are ultimately more satisfying – like talking to my partner beyond the standard 'How was work?', 'Terrible, I'm snowed under', 'Yeah, me too' routine. There is time for real conversation, for reading, playing games or just thinking. My mother was right when she used to yell at me to turn the damn thing off and do something less boring instead. At work, I can be excused from mundane water-cooler conversations about last night's telly. Killing painful chitchat dead with a solemn 'I wouldn't know, I don't have a TV' becomes more satisfying every time. I once read an Italian report claiming that couples with no TV in their bedrooms enjoyed 60 per cent more sex than those who watched television in bed. I can happily confirm that this is indeed the case.

5. By looking at fewer adverts I feel less inclined to shop. By staying away from the shops, I am both cash- and time-rich. The less I am exposed to adverts, the more my self-esteem climbs; I feel less browbeaten by the adverts, which once served as a constant reminder of how unsexy, unpopular and unsuccessful I was (the remedy to which would be to buy more products).

6. The only people who *really* care about the logos on your breast aren't worth knowing in the first place. Another classic from the Maternal Truism Hall of Fame, but more relevant now than ever before. I have become invisible to other brand-orientated people. I am paid less attention in shops and bars. I am generally paid far fewer compliments

on my appearance than before. But any potential relationships I might have had with these people would most likely have been transient and shallow. At least this is what I tell myself when old colleagues fail to return my calls. While I mourn the loss of status that accompanies conspicuous consumption, it is a liberation to go about my business without the underlying anxiety of brand top trumps. What do my logos say about me? What do people think about my logos? What do I think about their logos? Are my logos better than theirs?

## day 58

My ability to converse on the subject of popular culture is on the wane. At a party tonight, I failed miserably to make a contribution to a discussion about Apple's impending entry to the mobile phone market, and whether the new Bugaboo pushchair – the one in which all the cool celebrities are carrying their kids – is worth the £300 price tag. Oh, and whether the debut solo album from Fergie, lead singer of the non-threatening commercial hip hop group The Black Eyed Peas, is any good. Given there is a giant hoarding over London Bridge plugging the album, I know it exists – it's entitled *London Bridge*, some connection here? – but as to the contents, the cultural validity of the thing, I am blissfully ignorant. Some people might consider this evidence of my falling behind the Zeitgeist, a fear that I was indeed once plagued by. In fact, it's bliss to be unaware of such things. I remember the name of Fergie's album, even though I cannot remember the date of my mother's birthday, and that is more than enough knowledge on the subject. With no MTV blaring from the gym, no radio seeping from the high-street shops, no gossip columns chattering in the magazines, my brain has only negligible data stored on Fergie, leaving more space for something infinitely more satisfying, of my own choosing. This is surely the benefit of disconnection from 'the grid'.

## day 60

The next step in my journey, as Carol frequently reminds me, is to stop judging other people by the same standards I used to set for myself. While I have managed to control my own shopping habits, the call for inconspicuous consumption has fallen upon deaf ears among the general population of London, and it is extremely hard not to notice, and therefore judge, people by the things they surround themselves with – invariably covered in logos – even in the un-commercialised sanctity of the British Library, where I work each day. The area in which I sit is commonly known to staff and regulars as 'laptop alley', a long hallway lined with sofas and 'workstations' crammed with people and their laptops. A good few people visit on a daily basis, sitting in the same space on each occasion. Too British to say hello, I have no idea what their names are or what they do. But I do know which brand of laptop they have, and I have thus begun to know them by these labels.

During my psychographic test at ESP all those months ago, I learnt that people who buy PCs such as IBM or Dell do so because they are practical people. You buy an IBM for what's inside the box (Pentium processors et al). In contrast, those who buy Macs are 'big picture' consumers, people with creative imaginations who buy for meaning as opposed to practicalities. With this in mind the laptop's brand values, coupled with the rest of a person's gear, give me a clear impression of who they are, without ever having to do something rash, like, talk to them or something.

**WOMAN 1**
*14-inch Apple iBook: creative/independent thinker*
*Solomon hiking shoes: outdoorsy/asexual*
*Indigo Levi's 501 jeans: entry-level fashion*
*Casio G-Shock watch: transient teenage fashion*

Mid-twenties student, possibly from Europe on account of outdated watch, aspires to be someone different/special but aspirations are so far confined to the high street.

*Verdict:* nice girl next door with hopes for something bigger

**WOMAN 2**

*Black IBM ThinkPad: utilitarian/business-minded*
*Reissued vintage Asics running shoes: bland, non-fashion*
*Two-litre bottle Tesco water: practical*
*Marks & Spencer plastic bag: sensible produce at sensible prices*

No one walks into a store and asks for an IBM laptop by name; as with the rest of her brands, the purchase was made according to value for money (although not simply the cheapest price), ease of use and non-showy mass-market appeal.

*Verdict:* self-confident but risk-averse and boring as hell

**MAN**

*White Toshiba Notebook: fake Apple*
*Four-stripe trainers (unidentifiable): fake Adidas*
*Stonewashed jeans (unidentifiable): mass-market conformity*
*Tight-fitting Oakley T-shirt: ostentatiously athletic*

If ever there was a non-brand of laptop, it has to be Toshiba. What exactly are you buying into with Toshiba? At first glance the computer looks like a Mac but it's not. At first glance the shoes look like Adidas but they're not. One glance is all you need for the Lycra top that says look at my muscles ladies/boys, aren't I a stallion?

*Verdict:* narcissistic fraudster

**WOMAN 3**

*17-inch G4 PowerBook: if you're gonna spend, spend big*
*Vodafone Blackberry: businessperson on the go*
*Mulberry handbag: discreet money*
*Badoit water bottle: cultured affluence*

Incredibly successful at what she does and enjoys the fruits of her labour, or independently wealthy with nothing more to do than shop. If it's the latter, she's justifying her lot in life by dipping her toe in the sea of knowledge, but just for fun.

*Verdict:* scarily successful or wealthy professional shopper

### ME

*Nondescript white laptop: generic product with nothing to say*
*Plain clear plastic water bottle: generic product with nothing*
    *to say*
*Plain white plimsolls: generic product with nothing to say*
*Non-branded black rucksack: generic product with nothing*
    *to say*

Nothing to say, except that I lost my marbles after one too many trips to the shops and developed a pathological hatred/allergic reaction to branding, and now prefer flimsy, uncomfortable, unappealing products as opposed to stuff that is well made.

*Verdict:* paranoid puritan with depleted self-esteem or just boring guy in plain clothes

It occurs to me that no matter which products I surround myself with, they will always make a statement of some sort. Each person has their own brand, their own collection of values, and they automatically project this through the things they buy. Mine is a non-branded brand. The only consolation is that I constructed the image of my own accord, rather than buying it pre-packaged off the shelf.

# day 75

It is the first day of December and Christmas has been under way for two months, in the shops at least. Perhaps unusually for someone so enamoured with shopping, I have grown to loathe Christmas over the years. I cannot recall the exact point when Christmas degenerated from a family-meeting, present-giving, face-stuffing time of wonderment to what has for many years been a season of cruel torture. As a teenager I would fill with a warm sense of festive cheer whenever I heard the generic Christmas tape (Wham! The Pogues, Elton John etc.) drifting out of heaving stores, or saw snow falling in the adverts on television. However, at some point during my twenties, the sleigh bells of 'Last Christmas' and the endless ho-ho-ho-ing of the adverts began to induce spasms of dread; the list of presents to buy, the office parties to endure, the over-crowding of Central London as hoards of out-of-towners swarmed to the stores, the big tourists. I would attempt to spend my way out the misery by purchasing ever more extravagant gifts for the missus and surrounding family. This present-giving technique was akin to the military tactic of Shock and Awe; small presents lavishly packaged from luxury stores that would blow away any possible competition from rivals in the family. Mini-hampers from Harrods always did the trick. My gifts famously enjoyed the biggest wow factor on the day, but, frustratingly, the compliment was rarely returned. The gifts I received would almost certainly find their home at the charity shop on December 29.

At the beginning of this project, I feared Christmas would be the toughest test of both my constitution and my sense of wellbeing. But, against all odds, I feel the least depressed of any festive season. Perhaps being out of the game has relieved me from the usual anxieties. Certainly, being shielded from the barrage of TV and magazine advertising has helped.

Christmas is normally the time of year when my life-long dedication to free spending is rewarded with invitations to in-store parties for 'special customers'. Such is the twilight world of the serial shopper. These invitations used to make me feel rather special, some recognition that my custom was valued, that I wasn't your normal shopping tourist. They are of course nothing more than effective data capture and direct marketing. Nevertheless, a personal invite from the head of the Bond Street retail traders' association to a mince pie and mulled wine hoedown (with a one-night-only 20 per cent discount on all stock) did sound like fun. Despite my absence from the stores post-bonfire, my name has not been wiped from their memory banks, and a number of invites land on the mat. It is with a mixture of maudlin nostalgia, faint self-disgust and absurd triumphalism that I tear the lot up and toss them into the recycling bin.

'Don't tear them up!' says Juliet, grabbing the ripped cards from the pile. 'Don't you want to see your friends? You've not spoken to any of them since your burning.'

Through years of compulsive shopping, I had made several good friends amongst the store owners and managers. I often joke to several of my closest friends that I bought my way into their affections.

'Well, I don't know if I should really go. It's not like I can actually buy anything. It feels rather fraudulent.'

'They'd be pleased to see you, I'm sure. You can have a conversation with them without spending money.'

## day 80

Having taped up the party invitations, we decide to visit one store, a small one that sells shoes and clothes made by young designers on Savile Row. I spent a good few quid down there in my time, so I would hope that the owners, Matthew and Kurt, would be nice. The event is held on a Thursday, late-night shopping in Central London, and it is my first taste of Christmas hell. Wading through the crowd on Oxford Street, I notice several buildings covered in spinning projected logos for a new Nintendo games console called Wii. I heard on the news that these things had completely sold out in advance. Crowds seem to be gathering outside the HMV Megastore, where they must be doing some sort of promotion. I love the shoppers' dedication and loathe the rampant consumerism in equal measures.

Breaking free from the scrum, we make it to the store party, and, to my relief, the owners give me a warm welcome. Why wouldn't they? It's not like my bonfire is single-handedly bringing down capitalism, branded consumerism, or even mid-market contemporary menswear, for that matter.

'We've missed you,' says Matthew. 'I know you're out of the market for a while, but you can still come in and say hello. You don't have to buy anything.'

I have discussed this in therapy; I assume people's love is conditional. But this is simply not the case. I can stand in a shop, converse with friends and not spend any money.

'Anyhow, you can look around next season's stock. Your experiment will be over by then and you can buy as much as you like, right?'

'I'm still finding unopened bags from your store which Neil hid from me and forgot to burn,' jokes Juliet. 'I dread to think how much he was spending here.'

'Yes, we certainly do miss Neil,' says Matthew.

As this banter ensues, my brand radar detects at least three items sitting on shelves across the room.

'I like the look of those shoes against the wall.'

'Yes, mate, they've got your name written all over them.'

The old consumer thought processes come flooding back to me. How fine the shoes would look on my feet, the outfits I would pair with them, the glances of approval they might elicit from people who would care. Life would almost certainly be better for owning them. I give the party five more minutes and we leave.

Back along Oxford Street on the way home, the bridge and tunnel shoppers have scurried off home – or to a bar to coo over the day's catch – leaving only one great queue of people snaking from a computer game store. There must be at least 500 people stretching off to infinity. Several girl-next-door-type PR girls, dressed in Wii-branded uniforms are flitting up and down the line, keeping the boys amused (the queue is composed of 99 per cent teenage boys plus long-suffering girlfriends/parents). It is bitterly cold, but the crowd seem as though they are in it for the long haul, with fold-out chairs, thermos flasks and performance fleeces to keep the elements at bay. Amazed at the dedication on display, I stop to speak to one boy in the queue.

'I thought these consoles had all sold out.'

'They did. I reserved mine three months ago. I'm waiting to pick it up.'

'But it's half 11.'

'They don't release them until midnight.'

'Oh, I see.'

The queue goes on for what seems like miles. People have their iPods linked up to speakers, kids dressed head-to-toe in Nike are rapping to each other. Waiting for a store to open on a cold winter night isn't an ordeal for them; it's a social event. Further along the line, we spot a group of boys, dressed in identical Wii T-shirts holding a giant hand-drawn sign: I SMELL FRESH Wii!!!!!

## day 100

> Die-hard shoppers are out in force today, snapping up bargains of up to 70 per cent on the high street. Thousands were seen queuing at 9 a.m. when the shops were due to open. One couple from Wales had left their home at 2 a.m. to be among the first in line at London's Selfridges department store. In other news, it's been a day of terrible violence in Baghdad and Saddam Hussein has been sentenced to hang.
>
> *Capital Radio news report, Boxing Day*

A whole 24 hours after Christmas Day, and the shops are flinging their doors open to the general public's stampede. The media can talk of little else. Sitting at the in-laws' house, watching TV and sifting through the papers (a rare treat for me in my non-branded life) the festive blues finally catch up with me, as news of this buying frenzy splashes across the entire British media. Christmas Day itself had gone well – I'd got away with buying food-based presents from the local market (artisan chutneys and other overpriced jars of nonsense), while the relatives all tastefully observed my brand-ban by giving small sums of money (that'll do nicely) – and the result had been a largely uncommercial Christmas. However, this sales fever now engulfing the country gives rise to an empty feeling of dread in my stomach, not least because, exactly one year ago, I was standing in line at the stores myself. Seeing things from a new perspective, sales fever looks more like sales lunacy, which two-thirds of the nation has contracted.

'Sales hit fever pitch as stores are mobbed!' splashes a newspaper headline. A shopping consultant on the *GMTV* breakfast show warns shoppers to be careful; although we might be saving up to 70 per cent on purchases we still have to pay the 30 per cent and this can all add up. The message is not to get too carried away, because you might end up buying stuff that you don't really need. The front pages of some newspapers tell tales of more consumer heroism, as dedicated bargain hunters go to superhuman lengths to snap up previously overpriced but now ludicrously underpriced stuff. The gap between advert breaks on TV seems to be a lot shorter than I remember, with a dozen discount sofa superstores competing for business. Boxing Day, it seems, is the traditional day to buy leather sofas.

Who in their right mind would get up at the crack of dawn on the second day of Christmas to go shopping? The Next sale in Brent Cross opened at 4.30 a.m. and was apparently 'besieged' by 5000 shoppers within the hour. In an interview for the *Evening Standard*, a spokesman for the Oxford Street retailers' association answers the question: ' Shopping is a leisure pursuit and, besides, what else is there to do? It's a chance for people to spend money on themselves after buying for other people.' 'The Christmas spirit has finally come to the high street' says a store manager on a radio interview. This is the second time I have heard that phrase today, and both times 'Christmas spirit' has been used to describe the general public's willingness to spend money in shops. Not content with fleecing us pre-Christmas for gifts, the poor old retailers are in desperate need for us to spend wildly in the sales too.

## day 101

The car journey home from the in-laws to Central London is hijacked by ongoing sales fever. As we approach the city and attempt to pass the turn-off for an out-of-town shopping centre, the motorway becomes gridlocked with irate shoppers jostling for lane space, becoming visibly more angry as every second of spending opportunity ticks by. I am surrounded by 4x4s, luxury saloons and People Carriers, all crammed with families eager to shop. In situations such as these, the brand of one's car is of no relevance whatsoever; they are all equally useless as we sit bumper-to-bumper sucking in each others' exhaust fumes, throttles roaring wildly in expectation of the jam moving another inch or so. On the car radio, the relentless sale adverts raise the fever pitch even further. There are no subtleties of salesmanship in the messages, which rely solely on basic greed and panic . . .

> REMEMBER, THESE PRICES CAN'T LAST!
> HURRY, YOU'D BE MAD TO MISS OUT.
> WITH PRICES THIS LOW, YOU CANNOT LOSE!

By the time we finally make it into Central London, the first day's trading figures are announced on the news; Britain's plucky bargain hunters spent at a rate of £800 million per minute yesterday. Worryingly, the government has warned that millions of adults will struggle to make the best of the sales because they do not have the mathematical skills to work out the value of the bargains. The Department for Education says that 14.9 million adults in England lack the numeracy skills of an 11-year-old needed to work out the value of 'buy one, get one half-price'. In other news, an actress from *Desperate Housewives* arrived in a horse-drawn cart to open the sale at Harrods.

Juliet and I start to rationalise; we could do with a few things for the home, a new duvet and pillows, say. We *are* passing a department store on the journey home. I couldn't possibly buy the goods myself, but she could. I'd just stand outside the store, or maybe observe from a safe distance in-store. Would that be cheating? What the hell, it's 70 per cent off! Within minutes, the car is parked – free parking and no congestion charge for shoppers! – and we are walking into John Lewis, the first time I have entered a major brand of store for some time. The ensuing frenzy resembles a smash-and-grab for supplies in the minutes before a nuclear strike; men, women and children rummage bins of products with a possessed look in their eyes. That used to be my old trick: grab first, try and buy later. Considering how many people are crammed into the store, the air is hushed, save for the jostling of busy feet. There is no time to talk.

The bedding section on the third floor is no less manic. In fact, the generally older demographic of duvet buyers appears to be more gritty and dogged in determination than the younger fashionistas on the first floor. We arrive at a wall of almost bare shelves that might once have groaned under the weight of boxed duvets. Today there are only three. Juliet picks up the cheapest box to study the price, when a battle-worn lady in her late fifties appears from nowhere and lays two bony hands firmly on the box.

'Excuse me!' says Juliet, turning scarlet in shock and amazement.

'I'm taking this,' the old lady snaps back, any notion of dignity long since abandoned.

'But I'm holding the box. Surely that makes it mine?'

'You were just looking. I saw you from across the room. I've travelled 50-odd miles, specifically to get this duvet. I'm sorry, but it's mine.'

'Well, let's ask an assistant. There may be some more in stock.'

'There aren't, I've already asked.'

This is now a matter of principle. Both Juliet and the old lady tug at the box, and we have the beginnings of a scuffle. They both look to me for mediation, but I have long since left the building, mentally. This is civilised society? Savvy, rational, autonomous consumers, living amidst the splendour of late capitalism? All I see here are grown adults, fighting like rabid dogs over new versions of things they already have, simply because 20 per cent of the overvalued price has been knocked off. If the store can afford to sell the duvet at the discounted price, why was the pre-sale price so high? Why do we consumers fall for this charade each year? Why do we need a new duvet in any case? Why am I standing in this store at all?

I grab the box from them and march to the till. I pay. I unpack the duvet from the box, rip off the branded label from its corner, bundle it into my arms and stride out of the store, till receipt dangling from my clenched teeth, leaving both Juliet and the old woman for dead.

Carol warned me not to take this project too seriously, to be careful not to feel alienated from society. At this moment in time, I am not entirely sure who is crazy and who is not.

## day 106

New Year's Day. According to the news, authorities in São Paulo have banned all street advertising throughout the city as of today. No billboards or TV screens or fly posters. Even shop signs must conform to new restrictive sizes. London would surely feel like a ghost town if advertisements were outlawed here.

## day 120

The environmental consequences of consumption seem to be moving up the agenda in the media, with the release of the government-commissioned study, the *Stern Review on the Economics of Climate Change*. Sir Nicholas Stern warns that climate change will eventually disrupt economic and social activity on a scale similar to that of the great wars and economic depression of the first half of the 20th century. Politicians from all parties are talking about our individual carbon footprint, and how best we can reduce our impact on the environment. So far, the rhetoric is limited to air travel and energy consumption in the home. It seems odd to me that the debate excludes the management of demand for consumer products, which, according to the Carbon Trust, accounts for 42 per cent of our footprint. The accepted solution to climate change from the main political parties seems to be not to curb consumption but to offset it; carry on as normal, but plant a few trees to make it all better. Tony Juniper, spokesman for Friends of the Earth, seems to be the only major figure in the debate that sees this strategy as a giant fudge.

> Carbon offsetting schemes are being used as a smokescreen to divert attention from the tough choices that we have to make, which is about demand management. Buying offsets is not, as some would like us to believe, a 'magic bullet' to prevent further climate change or a solution to the growth in emissions. We no longer have the luxury of living energy-wasteful lifestyles in wealthy countries while using our money to reduce emissions overseas.[39]

It seems madness to me that we should tackle environmental destruction by turning off the odd lightbulb, but continue to consume needlessly on the high street. Are there any politicians on the national stage that are prepared to stand up and argue that, for all the economic difficulties it might create, we simply need to start consuming less? Clare Short MP, the former minister for international development, is one of the lone voices calling for a moratorium on the hyper-consumer culture that we have in the UK. It has taken me several months to make contact with her, but she has finally agreed to comment on the issue for the book.

If we compare the levels of wealth and consumption that we enjoy across our society, even among the poorest, to that of our grandparents, we are all very rich. And yet the quality of our lives is quite poor; everyone is stressed out, everyone is disgruntled; shopping, shopping, shopping, we are sliding into debt; we have no time for the people we love. There is something really unhealthy in our society, a perpetual greed that can never be satisfied which has become the culture, and it makes people miserable.

As a student from the 1960s, I remember it being cool to buy clothes from jumble sales, wear things that we made ourselves, and it was really cool to not buy expensive stuff. It was by far a more creative and fun-loving generation. We now have fallen into a trap, of buying everything and creating nothing. Brands have created new versions of things we've always enjoyed, but at a greater cost, and invented new things for us to need, to keep us all on the treadmill of greed and unhappiness. Take packaged food, for example. It's generally crap food, and it makes people unhappy. You can see it on the faces of the growing number of people who are obese.

We could break out of this cycle. We are reaching the point in human history where all our basic needs are catered for, and we could start enjoying the freedom that gives us. It means we don't need to work so many hours, we can have more time for the people that we love, music, poetry, cooking, whatever turns us on. Wouldn't it be brilliant if we all said sod it, we don't need any of that? Yes, we need some clothes to wear, but what difference does it make if we have 80 pairs of trainers or two?

Our current levels of consumption contradict the environmental challenges that lie ahead of us, but politicians are too scared to ask us to simply consume less. The environment has moved up the political agenda, but the political elite is adamant that we must retain economic growth. They are too scared to point the finger at the greed of consumerism because they fear unpopularity. And yet, politicians' public popularity is already at an all-time low.

I think people are becoming sick of the old order, and we are reaching a turning point. But the change isn't going to come out of politics. Rather, there's going to be a social movement. The 1960s movement came from the people, not politicians. It was a symbolic casting-off of old rigidities. It was tolerance and change in social attitudes that spanned all generations. I think about the great temperance movement that spread across the world, or the womens' franchise movement, which were both worldwide phenomena. Historically, these big sweeps of change never come from the political elite; they are movements that bubble up from beneath. We are going to have, we have to have and it would make us happy to have a change, coming from ordinary human beings who say 'I don't want to be trapped, I want more time, less stress.'

Developing-country governments aspire to the consumer culture of the West as a model for their own expansion. In his book *Plan B 2:0*, the environmental analyst Lester R Brown points out that if China carries on growing at the current rate, by 2032 their GDP will be equal to that of America's today, adding 1.1 billion cars to the current total of 800 million. The amount of petrol needed to run the things just doesn't exist. If they consume as much paper per head as we do currently, we won't have enough forests to cope. Our way of life is not compatible with living sustainably on this planet and it is no model for developing countries to aspire to. If we don't shift to a less consumerist and throwaway society, we'll hit crisis after crisis, and it's coming soon.

Although there is horrendous inequality and poverty in Africa, and we should never romanticise poverty, there is much we can learn and you find something in the villages that is enormously dignified and fine. There are communities that build their own houses, give love to their children, communities where they give respect to their elders, and behave with enormous dignity, which is something that we have lost in the UK. There is no need for us to become less comfortable or go starving, but some of the changes that are necessary will make us more dignified and happier as human beings.

Perhaps Clare is right. With the political climate being adverse to consumption management, change can only come from within society. But it is difficult to imagine the iGeneration abstaining from hyper-consumerism without an immediate reason for doing so. Adam Curtis once asserted to me that a correction in consumer culture will only come about with the demise of surplus leisure – when there are more matters of immediate importance, socially and economically, to fill our time than browsing for new shoes.

## day 123

In 2000's *No Logo*, Naomi Klein argued that 'as more people discover the brand-name secrets of the global logo web, their outrage will fuel the next big political movement, a vast wave of opposition squarely targeting transnational corporations, particularly those with very high name-brand recognition'.[40] Seven years after publication, Klein's hugely popular polemic has undoubtedly raised awareness around corporate social responsibility (CSR). But this doesn't seem to have translated into action on the high street. Nike, one of Klein's major targets for allegations of malpractice in the workplace, has seen revenue rise from $9.5 billion to $13.5 billion since the book's publication.[41]

According to *Media Week*, brand loyalty towards the company is perceived to be 'stronger than ever'. Indeed, none of the companies mentioned in *No Logo* – Wal-Mart, Ralph Lauren, J C Penny – have been particularly troubled by the forecasted wave of ethical consumerism. The flaw in Klein's theory is an underestimation of the power of emotional branding and the apathy it creates with the consumer. Ethics are no match for feelings, which is what companies such as Nike deal with. I would argue that, although the general public may express a concern for CSR, it is not strong enough to break the emotional attachments towards their favourite brands.

I decide to put my theory to the test by polling opinion outside Nike Town, the trainer megastore on Oxford Street. I stand outside the entrance for an entire day's trading, and attempt to interview customers leaving the store with a Nike shopping bag. Are Nike's customers aware of the allegations levelled at the company? If so, why are they still shopping there?

Oxford Street is saturated with charity fundraisers, sandwich-chain flyers and Christian activists who compete for shoppers' attention and the endless human traffic flows at an ill-tempered hurry – not ideal conditions to conduct a survey. After several fruitless attempts, I bag my first catch of the day, a fashionable-looking teenager called Joe. He wears a bright green T-shirt with a giant statement printed on the front – 'Just Say No' – presumably a copy of the famous protest T-shirts that Katharine Hamnett produced in the 1980s. Joe has just spent over £100 in the store.

'Is Nike your favorite sportswear brand?'

'Definitely.'

'Any idea why?'

'No, not really. It's just the coolest.'

'Okay. Do you keep an eye on the papers for things like corporate social responsibility – sweatshops and pollution – that sort of thing?'

'Yes, I have to. I'm doing business studies at university.'

'Is it something that you care about?'

'Yes, I certainly do.'

'In the past, some people have criticised Nike for allegedly using sweatshop labour. Were you aware of that?'

'I suppose I do know about that. I haven't really thought about it that much. Oh dear, I'm looking a bit hypocritical, aren't I?'

I am starting to feel a little self-righteous and ashamed about embarrassing this lad. The situation becomes more uncomfortable with the final question.

'I want you to guess how much Nike's factory workers in Vietnam get paid. Is it £25 a day, £25 a week or £25 a month?'

'I'd say £25 a week.'

The poor guy looks rather sheepish as he shakes my hand and returns to the slipstream of passing trade. My questions might be loaded, but my intention is not to embarrass; I simply want to prove that ordinary, decent people might care about ethical consumption, but not enough to stop buying their most desired brands.

I stand outside the store for the best part of seven hours, pestering customers as inconspicuously as one can under the gaze of the store's security staff. Groups of Nike-clad kids congregate on the pavement, endlessly playing with their mobile phones, the girls preening each others' hair, the boys sizing up rival gangs. Young parents drift in and out with their aspiring child athletes. Gym-fit career women while away their lunch hour here, presumably browsing for Lycra. Overseas tourists stop for picture opportunities outside the giant window displays. It would seem entirely natural to spend time and money with this supposed corporate pariah – as if *No Logo* had never happened.

Some interviewees are surprisingly bullish about their apathy towards CSR, being somehow proud of their right to indifference. 'This is the First World. Vietnam is the Third World. Of course they get paid less than us,' says a Polish man in his late thirties. Most people seem to be aware of questions about Nike's reputation on human rights, but admit to a laziness that prevents them from switching loyalty to an apparently more ethical brand, if such an option did indeed exist. By the day's end, I have completed a total of 48 questionnaires. These are the results:

| Age | 16–35 yrs (66%) | 35–65 yrs (34%) | |
| --- | --- | --- | --- |
| Average spend on a pair of trainers | Up to £50 (19%) | Over £50 (81%) | |
| Do you think that factory workers should be treated humanely and paid fairly? | Yes (95%) | No (5%) | |
| Does CSR affect your decision when buying branded products? | Yes (37%) | No (32%) | Maybe (31%) |
| How much are Nike's factory workers in Vietnam paid? | £25 per day (7%) | £25 per week (28%) | £25 per month (65%) |

According to the labour rights organisation No Sweat,[42] the average wage for a Nike worker in Vietnam is just £25 a month. In 2005 Nike itself issued an audit of its factories,[43] admitting to problems of abusive treatment. Between 25 and 50 per cent of the factories in Asia deny workers a minimum one day off in seven, among various other abuses. In more than half of Nike's factories, the report said, employees worked more than 60 hours a week.

My straw poll is woefully unscientific, and Nike is admittedly a soft target for this purpose. Nevertheless, 65 per cent of Nike's customers guessed accurately how little their factory workers are paid. Moreover, they were happy to spend more than double the monthly salary of a Vietnamese worker on a single pair of trainers. Yet 95 per cent agreed that factory workers should be treated fairly. There is something preventing ethical rhetoric from turning into affirmative action at the till. It is the same thing that prevents customers from accepting that they are being overcharged for goods, goods that obviously cost so little to produce. It is the deep-rooted, emotional attachment to the brand that keeps us coming back for more.

## day 125

The ironic sting to this tale, as I have often been reminded, is that in publicly destroying my branded life, I simply create another new label

– Brand-Free Neil Boorman. Like any other pattern of consumption, my eschewing of branded products becomes a lifestyle. And like any other lifestyle, there are manufacturers who are eager to make and sell products to the demographic that adopt this standard of living, especially if this lifestyle is being discussed in the media. Confirmation of my marketability comes through the letterbox today, with the arrival of a trends prediction magazine that has picked up on my story. These magazines are produced exclusively for advertising and PR agencies, identifying emerging fashions in consumer lifestyle that can be implemented into marketing policy. According to the article,[44] I will be among 2007's key trend drivers in a minority swing towards *Nu Austerity*, a resurging conscience culture which will facilitate a rise of thrift chic. Twelve months ago, I would have been proud to feature in a trends dossier such as this, my lifestyle being worthy of mention in focus groups, my opinions accepted and thus validated by the brands. Now I feel rather depressed and angry that my little crusade has so quickly become a marketing tool to sell more stuff.

Naomi Klein asserted that brands are capable of co-opting any shift in culture or public opinion and turning it to their advantage. Household-name companies have inevitably begun to mirror the Western market's increasing drive towards sustainability in their branding. Following the *Stern Review*, many companies are offering the public pledges of efficiency, by way of carbon offsetting schemes. Perhaps this is no bad thing, if the promises in the press releases do indeed materialise into action. But how much of this is ethical re-packaging, or *greenwash*, as it is increasingly referred to? None of these corporate manifestos are pledging to manage growth. I see no pledges to phase out in-built obsolescence, or planned disposability, the two basic marketing gimmicks which help to drive consumerism and contribute to the mountains of consumer waste. I read in the papers that major car manufacturers are testing cars with engines made of plastic that are less expensive to replace than repair. Rebranding a company with a green colour scheme and a flower logo is not ethical consumption. It is a fig leaf behind which industry can carry on overproducing and overselling as normal.

My research at the British Library is drawing to a close. So much of the text that I have studied these past few months has been written from a theoretical perspective; the hyperbole of the brand manuals, the idealism of social politics; abstract ideologies that would seem inapplicable to the comfortable monotony of modern life. Each day the city rumbles into life, and Londoners repeat familiar consumer routines that would seem entirely natural, passing without any immediate negative consequence. And yet a day rarely goes by without the publication of a new report warning of the worsening environment, the mounting consumer debt or some new breakdown in society. For the average individual, there would seem to be little option but to shrug one's shoulders and get on with things as they are. Thus the isolation that I felt at the beginning of this project is still very real to me. But I have a clearer understanding of the environment that has led me to reject so many notions of 'normal' modern life.

It seems obvious to me that the constant pandering to self-interest, as pioneered by the likes of Edward Bernays, has taught us to behave less as a community, and more as individual consumers. Perhaps this is why we find it so difficult to alter our levels of consumption, even in the face of impending environmental doom. It is better to consume ethically packaged goods, perhaps using a credit card that donates money to Africa, than not to consume at all. The material good life, or the opportunity to pursue that life at least, has become a basic human right regardless of the social or environmental cost.

When the trade organisation War on Want accused Tesco and Asda, together with discount clothes retailer Primark, of using slave labour in Bangladesh, the news reports and consequent public reaction was one of shock and disgust.[45] These trusted 'family brands', it was claimed, were manufacturing clothes by workers paid on average 5p an hour. All three companies strongly denied the allegations.

For years, customers at these stores have enjoyed the fruits of this labour at what are commonly described as 'unbelievable prices'. Primark, in particular, has carved a niche on the British high streets as supplying clothes of high value at low prices (winner of 'Best shop in which to spend £50' award in the *Company* Magazine High Street Awards 2006, no less). One wonders how on earth these companies can afford to sell high-quality goods at such low prices. But we do know, because the news is full of stories of sweatshops in countries such as China and India. We know where the goods come from. This is one of the virtues of branding, that the companies who make the clothes are transparent and, in theory, accountable (Primark, Tesco and Asda have since signed up to a set of principles to provide decent working conditions and wages for workers in their supply chain). We know, and, as compassionate human beings, we most likely care. But we don't care enough to stop buying. It is terrible that people around the globe have to work 18-hour shifts in cramped conditions for very little money (the actual minimum wage in China is 30p, compared to £5.05 in Great Britain), but we could do with a new pair of jeans, and at such low prices, it's difficult to refuse. I believe that the constant pandering to desires by emotional branding is partly to blame for this selfishness.

Apologists for brand advertising often argue that to label consumers as manipulated dupes is to take a dim view of human nature. Surely it is a far dimmer view to admit that we Westerners would prefer a cheap new pair of jeans to the welfare of our fellow man. A far more positive view of human nature would be that, in the historical effort to provide ourselves with a better standard of living, we have created companies and institutions that promote the benefits of this comfort above all other, ultimately to the detriment of the wellbeing we so desire.

There is no caring family business to be found at the supermarket, although the friendly faces and the benevolent language – 'Every little helps' – on the adverts may suggest otherwise. There are only workers, businessmen and shareholders, who trade for profit, and profit alone. This is not a statement of condemnation. This is simply a statement of fact. Anything else is simply a myth constructed by the brand.

Brands have elevated the pursuit of personal pleasure to such a height that it takes precedence over all other concerns, and it has been achieved by emotional branding which appeals to the desires which reside within us all. That is why, despite the general trend towards corporate responsibility, we continue to spend money with companies who routinely ignore the ethics of production.

In August 2006, the Stop The War Coalition organised a march through Central London in protest at the renewed Israeli military action in Palestine, a cause supported by 63 per cent of the population.[46] Yet more people in London chose to attend the free Fruitstock Festival on the same day, organised by smoothie manufacturers Innocent.

The average turnout at Western elections over the last century has declined as consumerism has boomed. Turnout at the 2005 British general election was 61 per cent, three points above the all-time post-war low.[47] Only 37 per cent of adults under 25 bothered to vote. At the 2004 US elections, turnout was even worse at 55 per cent.[48] According to a Mori poll,[49] non-voters fail to turn up because they find voting inconvenient or simply because they are not interested in politics.

Shopping for happiness feels like a more satisfying way of spending time than worrying about politics or the environment. With so many seductive emotions bound up in branded consumption – identity, self-esteem, choice, freedom – it seems impossible to imagine any other way of life. In 1960, the philosopher Herbert Marcuse wrote in his seminal text, *One-Dimensional Man*, that 'the commodities of lodging, food and clothing, the irresistible output of the entertainment and information industry . . . bind the consumer more or less pleasantly to the producer. The products promote a false consciousness, which is immune against falsehood. And as these beneficial products become available to more individuals in more social classes, it becomes a way of life. It is a good life – much better than before.'[50]

To the disadvantaged around the world, giant brands are symbols of freedom from the oppression of poverty, the universal standard to which developing countries must aspire. In the booming economy of 21st-century China, the newly wealthy strive to acquire predominantly Western brands. According to one survey of China's Fortune 100,[51] BMW is the Chinese millionaires' luxury brand of choice, followed by Louis Vuitton, Mercedes-Benz, Rolex and Giorgio Armani. Ironically, many luxury goods are in fact manufactured in developing countries, shipped to the West, substantially marked up in price and then imported back, to be sold in the luxury boutiques of Shanghai. For the less wealthy, fake versions of the same products are good enough; they do not buy the things for their quality or origin, rather their value is the symbolic meaning of the brand itself; Western materialism.

Marcuse suggested that real freedom meant freedom from the economy, freedom from the daily struggle for existence, from earning a living. If this vision of life seems impossible, he argued, it was due to our emotional dependence on consumerism itself.

> The unrealistic sound of these propositions is indicative not of their utopian character, but of the strength of the forces which prevent their realisation. The most effective form of warfare against liberation is the implanting of material and intellectual needs that perpetuate obsolete forms of the struggle for existence.[52]

The endless cycle of working to live, and consuming to relieve the agonies of work, is a vicious one. The harder we work, the more we must spend to compensate for the toil. The more we spend on ourselves, the more we must work; a condition which Marcuse called 'the euphoria of unhappiness'.

> Most of the prevailing needs to relax, to have fun, to behave and consume in accordance with the advertisements, to love and hate what others love and hate, belong to this category of false needs.

For generations of Westerners such as my own, such a proposition is anathema. I grew up during the Thatcher era, with the repeated mantra that it was the right of man to 'work as he will and spend what he earns . . . freedom upon which all other freedoms depend'. Throughout my education, I was taught the values of consumerism, the sole purpose of work being to accumulate wealth for happiness. I am sure that I was never offered an alternative vision of life. It is not surprising then, that stumbling across Berger and Marcuse, their texts came as such an epiphany to me. It is not a comfortable feeling, being told that you might have been coerced into self-destructive dependency. Nobody likes to be called a sucker, but that is what I had become.

On coming to terms with my lot, I entered into a state of denial; perhaps anti-consumerism was just a hollow conspiracy theory. Denial turned to anger; anger at 'the system' for having commercialised my life; anger at myself for having been sucked in to such an extent. The brands became bogeymen, a means whereby I could shift the blame for my own selfishness. I tried to deal with the anger by bargaining with myself. I would purchase books such as *No Logo* to offset the guilt of consumption, but never really changed my behaviour. Then depression took hold, a struggle to come to terms with a culture that is dominated by consumerism.

It is becoming clear to me now that I spent the past few years in a state of grief, anxiously coming to terms with my loss of naïvety. Almost every aspect of the culture that I belonged to had become commodified, and there was very little that I could do to change it. The most basic elements of my life had become branded. Where my grandparents drank free water from fountains in the street, I paid for expensive packaged rations, the endless varieties of which were important symbols of my standing in life. Swathes of history, and nature, had been co-opted, stripped of any original meaning by brands. Nike, the Greek goddess of victory, no longer stands for victory. Blackberry is no longer an autumn fruit that grows wild along country lanes. Everything is for sale – or must be bought – and every sale is a statement of our lifestyle.

To be a successful consumer defines what it is to be normal. If I cannot afford the right gear, I become a failed consumer. Although my material living standards are immeasurably higher than in any previous generation, it is never enough. The constant aspiring to betterment never allows me to be grateful for my lot. Keeping up is everything. With branded consumerism encouraging us to better ourselves materially, each new generation experiences an inflation of needs. We expect everything that our parents had, and more.

My parents grew up in a period of rapidly growing prosperity, the like of which may never be seen again. They drew wages from jobs for life and received generous benefits from the welfare state. Education was free, and they had the option of buying a council property for below-market prices. During the 1970s and 1980s, inflation allowed them to pay off their mortgages effortlessly. Then Margaret Thatcher allowed aggressive American-style lenders into a deregulated market, causing house prices to rocket again. The rise in affluence allowed even working-class families to buy multiple new cars, colour televisions and holidays abroad. My mother returned to work as soon as she was able, not merely to cover the bills, but to improve the living standards of the family.

In the 21st century, a first-time buyer in the south of England needs to earn an above-average salary to afford an ex-council house. Their partner would need a full-time job just to cover basic living costs. Bringing up a child in this financial situation is a challenge. As many companies have downsized or transferred manpower overseas, younger workers have less chance of obtaining well-paid, long-term contracts, with university graduates settling for jobs for which they are vastly overqualified. In short, children of the baby boomer generation are struggling to maintain the living standards of the past.

The financial cost of this branded lifestyle is self-evident in the mountain of debt that Western consumers have accumulated. In 2004, consumer debt in the UK hit an historical peak of £1 trillion[53] rising to £1.25 trillion in 2006 (averaging £8,765 per head excluding mortgages). In the Netherlands, household debt is valued at almost 200 per cent of income. In the United States, the average debt to income ratio is 142 per cent.

The underlying message behind every consumer brand is the message of materialism. Adverts tell us that materialism is a central goal in life, that material goods are the main route to self-identity, success and happiness. Materialism is the yardstick for evaluating ourselves and those around us. All of our functional and emotional needs can be met by consuming things. In a sense, branding is materialism repackaged. The brand message manipulates our strongest desires and greatest fears to convince us to buy their products – to feel competent, to feel connected yet autonomous. We look to consumerism for short-term self-assurance, but in promising to transform our lives, the brands perpetuate the unachievable. In believing these promises, we give ourselves over to false hope. We become dependent on consumerism to construct our identities and self-worth, reliant to the convenience that these quick fixes offer.

And yet we are constantly reminded, by endless reports and by our own experience, that materialism fails to satisfy. According to the *Journal of Consumer Research*,[54] materialism as a life goal is less effective than affiliation and community feeling – the very things that brands have replaced – in producing wellbeing. Individuals who aspire to brand values have lower levels of vitality and self-actualisation. They suffer higher levels of anxiety, depression and behavioural disorders compared to those who aspire to more intrinsic values. In a 1996 study, it was proven that adolescents with a strong admiration for materialism suffer from attention deficit disorder, conduct disorder and narcissism.[55] A recent review of the summarised research on materialism concluded that, although people in richer nations are happier than people in poorer nations, people who strongly desire material wealth are unhappier than those who do not.[56] It has been proven that advertising has a substantial negative influence on child development and adult identity,[57] even the dreams of materialistic people are subject to greater insecurity.[58]

The notion that materialism is a reliable route to contentment in life is a fallacy, one of the many myths that constitute the language of branding. Having lived and worked with brands all my life, having both loved and hated the principles upon which they are founded, I believe that there are a number of basic myths upon which brands are sold. The sooner that I come to terms with these myths, the better my life will become.

**THE MYTHS OF BRANDING**

**Myth 1: Brand Value**
Consumer goods appear to be of greater value when they are attached to a brand. Often they are not. The brand adds nothing to the product beyond a perceived value, which is fabricated by the manufacturer.

Most goods halve in value the minute they are bought from the shop, regardless of the brand. They are designed that way.

*Fact*: BMW cars depreciate in value at the same rate as Citroëns.

## Myth 2: Brand Quality
The perceived quality of brand does not automatically relate to the actual quality of the product. Many 'quality' brands manufacture their goods in the same factories, using the same production techniques as brands with lower perceived quality.

*Fact*: Louis Vuitton manufacture their products at the same factory as Puma.

## Myth 3: Brand Origin
Products are often branded to denote cultural or geographical authenticity. In reality, they are mass-produced in factories far from their perceived place of origin.

*Fact*: The 'Italian' pasta sauce Dolmio is manufactured in the United Kingdom.

## Myth 4: Brand Heritage
Brands that trade off their cultural origins are rarely owned or operated by the original founders.

*Fact*: Since 1955, Burberry has been owned by GUS, the same conglomerate that owns Argos. It retains a stake to this day.

## Myth 5: Brand Science
The scientific breakthroughs that add value to a product are rarely validated by independent or government bodies.

*Fact*: There exists no scientific evidence to prove that Gillette Mach3 Turbo's five blades shave any closer or safer than razors with one blade.

### Myth 6: Brand Ambassadors

Public figures endorse brands because they are paid to, not because they use the things themselves.

*Fact*: Multimillionaire models tend not to use home-dying hair kits.

### Myth 7: Brand Aspiration

It is impossible to achieve a new lifestyle or become a new person simply by purchasing a product.

*Fact*: Lux soap does not transform the user into Sarah Jessica Parker.

### Myth 8: Brand Choice

Competing brands are often owned by the same company and produced to almost identical standards.

*Fact*: Proctor & Gamble manufactures Ariel, Bold, Fairy and Daz laundry detergents.

### Myth 9: Brand Individuality

Mass-produced goods are not unique. They cannot provide individuality to the owner.

*Fact*: Limited edition U2 iPods are available to buy in 71 countries.

### Myth 10: Brand Stakeholders

Although brands may claim to serve or even belong to the customer, they are run entirely to generate profit for their owners.

*Fact*: 'Your M&S' is owned by shareholders, not customers.

### Myth 11: Brand Professional

Expensive tools are rarely essential for the execution of a task. They are merely a confidence trick, no match for real skill.

*Fact*: Brazil's best footballers do not learn their skills wearing expensive boots, but barefoot on the beach.

### Myth 12: Brand Satisfaction

Brands never satisfy entirely or their producers would go out of business. Satisfaction through consumption relies on repeat purchasing, therefore never complete.

*Fact*: Lifetime guarantees are valid for the lifespan of the product, not the consumer.

### Myth 13: Brand Love

Regardless of the emotional messages to be found on the packet, the brand does not love you.

### Myth 14: Brand Message

There is but one message underlying all brands: materialism.

It would seem incredulous, insulting even, to suggest that as educated, media-savvy individuals, we should continue to buy into these crude myths. Yet one flick through a magazine or a glance at a television commercial break proves that brand advertising relies on these myths more than ever. The industry relies on a trick learnt by the pioneers of wartime propaganda; if you repeat a lie often enough, people eventually accept it as the truth. But the greatest trick of all has been to convince us that the lie doesn't work. Advertising is harmless fun, a welcome distraction, something which can be ignored. None of us likes to believe that branding works. And that suits the companies just fine.

There is no personal betterment or social mobility involved in buying an aspirational brand; they do not transform us into the people we would like to be. The people that we wish to become more like, if they exist at all, are unlikely to accept us into their world simply because we own the same products as them. If they did, they would be as materialistic as the brand messages themselves. To consume brands beyond our basic needs, conspicuously or not, is to buy into any one of the myths.

At the same time, as seductive as advertising has become, there exists no branding technique that forces us to consume against our will. Even though branding has penetrated to the core of Western culture, we consumers remain complicit in the business of supply and demand. In the words of Marcuse, the chains that bind us to consumerism are only as strong as we perceive them to be. The chains begin to weaken when we remember what brands really are – not symbols of meaning, not emotional crutches, but techniques of persuasion, Pavlovian devices that urge us to consume. There is no 'them and us' in this scenario, no shadowy organisation seeking to control our lives. We ourselves created this culture, and we can change it if we so wish.

It is unrealistic to expect the advertising industry to govern itself, for it is in the business of encouraging consumer growth where there is often no actual need. The advertising industry bible *Campaign* describes the right to advertise as a 'freedom of commercial speech'. Aside from restrictions to tobacco advertising and marketing pitched to adolescents, the industry enjoys almost total freedom, which, if anything, should be curtailed for the protection of the consumer. If we afforded greater power to our advertising standards authorities, we could begin to legislate the techniques of emotional branding. Products could be marketed more on the basis of their physical function, as most products were before the 1920s. To imagine a world without the fairytales of advertising is to imagine a life less glamorous, less sexy, less comforting, less life-affirming, but, as with all brand fairytales, these notions are simply myths themselves. Very rarely is life glamorous, or sexy, or comforting. Far from making our lives easier to live, brands make things more complicated. The sooner that we come to terms with this fact, the sooner we can live fulfilling lives.

The exercising of consumer freedom is not the choice between BMW or Mercedes. Consumer rebellion is not the boycotting of Esso in favour of BP. Sustainable consumption is not trading in the Range Rover for a Prius. It is choosing to consume only when necessary. The solution, I believe, is a lifestyle based on voluntary simplicity.

All we need do is downshift to a less complicated version of our lives. By consciously reducing our need for consumer goods, we need sell less of our time for money. With more time to ourselves, we can concentrate on doing things that make us happy. If this proposition appears naïve, it is only because we are accustomed to living complicated lives. As with branding, consumption of goods appears to promise to make our lives easier, but in fact makes it more complicated.

Do we really need so much meaning in the things we consume? Does this sophistication really make life any richer? I think that these complications make us poorer, both financially and emotionally. Writing in his book *The Value of Voluntary Simplicity*, the theologian Richard Gregg describes simplicity as a kind of mental hygiene:

> Just as eating too much is harmful to the body, so it seems that there may be a limit to the number of things or the amount of property which a person may own and yet keep himself psychologically healthy. The possession of many things and of great wealth creates so many possible choices and decisions to be made every day that it becomes a nervous strain. If a person lives among great possessions, they constitute an environment which influences him. His sensitiveness to certain important human relations is apt to become clogged and dulled, his imagination in regard to the subtle but important elements of personal relationships or in regard to lives in circumstances less fortunate than his own is apt to become less active and less keen.[59]

The simple life starts with the on-off switch of the television, a function that mercifully has yet to be phased out. When we stop looking at so much advertising and product placements, the desire to buy new things starts to recede. The same can be said of magazines. In fact, a concerted effort to avoid advertising-driven media has an almost immediate positive effect; less browbeaten to conform and consume, there is more time, physically and mentally, to get on with enjoying life. By the miracle of the Internet and podcasting, it is now entirely possible to enjoy entertainment media without watching a single advert.

With our minds relatively free of the buzz of advertising, the 'need' to consume is less urgent. When one does consume, it must be on the basis of real need as opposed to want, utility over symbolism, although much of that *want* evaporates when we are exposed to fewer manipulative messages. Every time we find ourselves standing at the checkout, we should ask ourselves, 'Do I *really* need this?' If the answer is no, then put it back and, sure enough, life goes on. Soon advertisements cease to appear as entertaining art forms, but vulgar propositions for needless expenditure; a newspaper ad for a luxury 4x4 sitting next to an article on the starving millions is all the perspective we need.

Simple living does not require us to starve ourselves of basic sustenance or even pleasure. It does not require us to abandon consumerism altogether. It only requires us to expect less from the act of consumption; mobiles are there to make calls, not to impress our friends; bars of soap are there to cleanse our skin, not to turn us into movie stars. The simple things we buy need not be enjoyable, or valuable, or beautiful, they simply need to mean less.

The 4th-century BC philosopher Epicurus upheld 'the untroubled life' as the paradigm of happiness, made possible by carefully considered choices and avoidances.[60] Specifically, he pointed out that troubles entailed by maintaining an extravagant lifestyle outweigh the pleasure of partaking in it. What was necessary for happiness, he concluded, was bodily comfort, and life itself should be maintained at minimal cost, while all things beyond the necessary should either be tempered by moderation or avoided completely.

Simple living is apolitical, and need not involve any religion, although many faiths from Hinduism to the Quakers have practised voluntarily simplified lifestyles. The Quaker text *Testimony of Simplicity* outlines that a person ought to live his or her life simply in order to focus on what is most important, and ignore or play down what is least important. Quakers are more concerned with one's inner condition than one's outward appearance, and with other people more than oneself (the kind of altruistic messages that are taught in citizenship classes these days).

There is no basic conflict between most political theories and living simply. We need not move from our cities into the wilderness. One could remain a capitalist and live simply, investing in ethical

220

stocks and shares for profit. With the will of the people, it could be relatively easy to enjoy an era of post-materialism, one in which we heap less strain upon ourselves and the environment. The only loss to ourselves would be anxiety, selfishness and debt.

I imagine myself enjoying a movie at home. Watching from a DVD, the picture will be much clearer than on VHS. On Blu-ray, the quality would be greater still. Yet the quality of the screenplay, the direction and the acting remain the same, regardless of the format. One could argue that the pleasure of watching the film with a finer picture is an enhanced pleasure. But by how much and at what cost?

Brands work on this same principle; the pleasure of consuming a product, they promise, will be higher for carrying that extra quality of the brand. Again, this may be true, but by how much and at what cost?

# EPILOGUE

# day 137

Pampers. Johnson's Baby Oil. Mothercare. I never thought I'd be a target customer for brands such as these, but as I stare at the baby TV screen in the maternity ward of University College Hospital, it dawns on me that I have indeed been promoted from an aspirational single to a working parent, the choice between Maclaren and Bugaboo pushchairs apparently being a pressing issue for people such as me. That Italian survey about sex life and TV in the bedroom turned out to be right; the less TV you watch in the home, the more you have sex and, of course, the more you have sex, the more likely you are to conceive.

Juliet is pregnant – unexpected news, which I am struggling to come to terms with. As we wait our turn in the hospital for a scan, it occurs to me that I took my self-centred journey just in time, for there is a dependent on the way, and there can be no more time for navel-gazing. I have often endured tedious conversations with new fathers who proclaim that their perspective on life changed once you had little ones to fend for, but they were of course right.

Juliet is assuming her role with aplomb, reading multiple baby books at any one time, and researching local services for before and after the birth. There will be no Pampers/Huggies dilemma, since we have found a reusable nappy service that picks up, cleans and delivers – in electric-powered cars, no less – straight to the doorstep. It is truly incredible how even the dirty business of nappies can be turned into an aspirational lifestyle option. Or is that simply ethical consumption? The spare room, which once served as my walk-in wardrobe is, fittingly, to become the baby's room. Luckily there is no longer much stuff in there for me to throw out.

Mother and baby magazines are scattered around the ward, free to pick up and take away. I didn't realise how ferocious the advertising in this market was until now; these magazines are packed full of advertorials and discount vouchers for Persil, Dettol, Andrex, Nestlé; all trying to establish customer loyalty before the thing is even born. Their earnest tone conveys a clear, and faintly threatening, message; that if you care for your baby, if you don't want to take any chances with their health (what parent would?) then you better buy their products, or else.

A whole new set of spending opportunities are unfolding before me, and a whole new set of challenges, if I am to remain non-branded beyond the life of this book. I don't think I'll ever really go back, and with a baby on the way, I probably couldn't afford to. Will I buy a bottle of Evian water again? Probably, if that's the cheapest bottle on the shelf. Will I buy a £50 T-shirt with a company's logo on the front again? Absolutely not. Will I buy a £50 T-shirt with a company's logo on the front for my child? That is another matter entirely.

The generational circle is almost complete; in a few years' time, I will be packing my child off to his or her first day at school, and I will face the exact same dilemma that my parents did, only with the materialistic law of the playground more intense than ever before, it could be worse. Back in 1982, all I wanted was an Adidas football and a Puma sports bag. Junior will be 'needing' all that, plus an iPod, a mobile phone and lord knows what other must-have gadgets Sony and Apple manage to invent in the meantime.

Do I stick firmly to my principles and deny them a television in their bedroom, ban them from eating junk food, refuse to clothe them from the high street? Do I send them into the playground without the status symbols I know they need to be accepted among their peers, and run the risk of them being bullied, possibly blaming me as a result? Or do I give in, let them have what they want and prey they don't fall foul of materialism in the same way that I did? It is an almost impossible overwhelming decision; the anger and frustration that I felt about my parents now seems terribly misplaced.

Perhaps I needn't have studied the psychology of consumption or the science of branding in order to come to terms with my addiction. I should have simply listened to the things that my mother used to tell me when I was young, because they are all true:

1. You are only paying for the brand.
2. Even worse, you are paying to advertise that brand.
3. Branded doesn't necessarily mean better.
4. You can often make it cheaper and better yourself, and it's more fun.
5. No matter how important it seems now, you'll want something newer and better soon after.
6. People who care about your brands don't really care about you.

I used to fly into rages when my mother repeated those mantras to me; I wonder if my children will react in any other way? Perhaps it's in the way I tell them. Rather than packing them off to school to find out for themselves, I should explain to them beforehand that the things we want aren't necessarily the things that we need, no matter how cool they look in the playground. Can a child of ten really understand a concept like that? It took me 20 years to work it out for myself.

If I do indeed talk to my children about consumerism, I'll be careful not to confuse branding with the benefits to be enjoyed by the product it is attached to. Driving a car through a country lane on a sunny afternoon is fun, regardless of who made the car. So too is listening to music, whether it is played on an old 1970s cassette player or an iPod Nano. Almost all of life's rituals and pleasures have been commodified but that doesn't mean you can't enjoy them for what they really are. With the benefit of five months' hindsight since the bonfire, I am beginning to wonder if I really needed to cut myself off from life's simple pleasures just because they had logos attached. Not every brand uses manipulative advertising, not every product is irresponsibly produced – although I'm having trouble naming names right now. It is most likely impossible to look at another person's possessions – even non-branded ones – and not make judgements about the people they are. Whether one acts upon those judgements is a different matter entirely.

## day 141

The final assessment of my therapy with Carol arrives in the letterbox, which is where it stays for the majority of the day, an ominous sort of report card that I cannot bring myself to open. What is there to fear? As long as she hasn't committed me, I should be fine. By the early evening, I finally manage to read the thing:

Psychological Assessment of Neil Boorman
by Carol Martin-Sperry

Neil came to see me because of his relationship with brands and consumerism. He told me that in order to make a break, he was planning to burn his belongings and then turn his back on branded goods of all types.

I asked Neil to tell me about this complex relationship and what it meant to him. It would appear that primarily his lifetime involvement with brands has been about a search for identity. This goes back to his childhood and his relationship with his parents and with his peer group at school. Being a somewhat shy underachiever, he felt a strong need to be cool at school, to find his identity in being stylish. This was rein-forced at home by his stylish parents and subsequently in the harsh competitive narcissistic media world that has become his workplace. But instead of feeling he belongs in the world, Neil feels marginalised and alienated, judged and judging. His constant self-criticism reinforces his lack of self-worth and the belief that he is not good enough. Neil is struggling with status anxiety, questioning his value system and wondering what his life goals really are.

There are splits in Neil's psychological constructs:

His private persona and his professional persona
His shyness and his exhibitionism
His lack of self-esteem and his confident appearance
The pressure to conform and the desire to stand out and
    be noticed

His involvement in brands and consumerism has made him uncomfortably aware of the contrasts between illusion and disillusion, the superficial and the profound, fantasy and reality.

Neil was seduced by the powerful messages of the brands, both conscious and unconscious. The unspoken promise was that ownership of the products would bring fulfilment, satisfaction and happiness. He would feel confident and effective, he would find his identity and his place in the world. He has been loyal to the brands, but they haven't delivered the real goods. This has reinforced his feelings of disappointment, disillusion and paranoia. His projected fantasies have not been fulfilled. His investment in the brands, both financial and psychological, has brought him no reward.

The symbolic role of the corporate brands is a paternal one. But, despite Neil's devotion, they have not been generous or benevolent, they have not made him feel special or unique. Neil's confusion and bewilderment has turned to anger and a desire for revenge. He decided to burn everything. This can be seen as a destructive act of anger, punishment and vengeance. It is also an expression of narcissistic pain and despair, and evidence of grandiose attention-seeking. On a more positive note, ritual burning is also a catharsis, an act of cleansing and purification, a mourning process and a rebirth. Like the phoenix rising from the ashes, he has a chance to make a new beginning and the freedom to make his own choices in future.

It is significant that Neil's father works in the fire-alarm business. The burning is also a rebellious act against a disapproving and punishing paternal figure in his inner world.

Neil has suffered from anxiety all his life. He also has an addictive personality. His first addiction was to alcohol, which he overcame. But now he is addicted to shopping.

An addict experiences the urgent need to relieve the pain of increasing anxiety. The addictive act starts with the tension of anticipation. Then come the rush, the high, the adrenaline surge, the endorphins, the feeling of satisfaction and relief and the brief sense of improved confidence and self-esteem. Unfortunately, this process is followed by a feeling of disappointment and letdown which invariably leads to depression and anxiety. Thus the compulsive vicious circle is repeated. Addicts generally suffer from strong feelings of anger, guilt and shame, emptiness, frustration and disappointment, vulnerability and fear.

There are no easy answers to coping with addiction. One needs to learn to accept the imperfection of the world, the sometimes ordinariness and banality of life. In order to confront the existential angst one needs to find meaning in one's personal relationships and creativity. One has to find a way of dealing with conflict and confrontation, of moving from emotional distance to intimate connection. One needs to own one's shadow and inner demons, not to repress or deny them. The splits have to be integrated in order to make one's inner world whole and heal the narcissistic wounds. This is the therapeutic work. It is a journey, not a destination and Neil is on that path.

## day 150

I woke today to find Central London covered in a blanket. Overnight, seemingly every billboard and bus shelter has been plastered with a new campaign for Apple. It reminds me of street scenes from VE Day or the Coronation, with every available space covered in posters and placards celebrating a momentous occasion. Perhaps today is Apple day.

The same ad pops up on my computer as I log on in the morning. Again, it appears on the back pages of newspapers, held aloft by commuters on the bus. In the advert, two men stand beside one another against a white backdrop. One man is dressed in a rather dull suit, looking bored with himself. The other guy is dressed casually in jeans and T-shirt; his posture is relaxed and he wears a broad, contented smile. They both hold a placard in front of them. The boring/smart guy's placard reads 'I AM A PC'. The happy/casual guy's placard reads 'I AM A MAC'.

Two years ago, I would have looked at that advert and felt proud to be a Mac person; someone who rejected conformity; a 'creative', as opposed to a 'worker'; a member of a community that thought outside the beige plastic PC box. Had I seen the ad six months ago, I would have been filled with loathing for both Apple's emotional branding and my own stupidity for having once bought into the dream. Looking at the ad today, I feel that some breathing space has grown between myself and the brand, the anger and disillusionment having subsided a little. I am no less mindful of the brand's allure, how easy it would be to slip back into the old routine. Yet I feel a greater confidence in my own ability to look away, to dwell on something a little more important.

People frequently ask me whether I shall ever return to branded consumption. For the time being, I answer no. I imagine I shall gradually allow myself a little convenience, an emergency shop at the supermarket perhaps. I miss the excitement of shopping, the glamour of fashion, the luxury of owning things that make me feel special but I doubt that I shall ever feel comfortable owning an iconic brand again. Emotionally, I feel more capable of standing on my own two feet without the crutches of status. I like to think that I no longer need to prove my self-worth through the owning of things, which comes as a huge relief to me.

I began this journey looking to establish an identity for myself beyond the brands. But I doubt I shall ever be able to discover who I really am. My values and my sense of self are constantly changing over time. What I can be sure of is the person that I am not. I am not an especially unique person that deserves the best at all costs. I am not and never will be the successful, contented guy in the adverts. I am not a member of any tribe dreamed up in a focus group. I am not a PC. I am not a Mac. I am just me.

# notes

1      *Ways of Seeing*, John Berger, Penguin, 1972

2      *Strategic Brand Management*, Kevin Lane Keller, Prentice Hall, 1998

3      *Emotional Branding*, Daryl Travis, Crown Business, 2000

4      *New York Times*, 8 November 1967

5      *Things To Know About Trademarks*, J W Thompson, J Walter Thompson Co Advertising, 1911

6      *Propaganda*, Edward Bernays, H Liveright, 1928

7      Fourth Edelman Study on Trust & Credibility, Brands & Branding, *Profile*, 2003

8      'Consumers and their Brands: Developing Relationship Theory in Consumer Research', Susan Fournier, *Journal of Consumer Research 24*, 1998

9      *Lovemarks: The Future Beyond Brands*, Kevin Roberts Powerhouse Books, 2005

10      'Generation Y speaks: it's all us, us, us', Robert Booth, *Sunday Times*, 4 February 2006

11      'Inclusion without cure will liberate us all', Adrian Faiers, *Journal of Mental Health Promotion*, March 2004

12     'A Meaning-based Model of Advertising Experiences',
D G Mick, C Buhl, *The Journal of Consumer Research*, 1992

13     *The Sense and Nonsense of Consumer Product Testing: Are Consumers Blindly Loyal?*, Haas School of Business, University of California, Berkeley 2005

14     'The new World Cup rule: take off your trousers, they're offending our sponsor', Luke Harding, *Guardian*, 19 June 2006

15     *Understanding Media: The Extensions of Man*, Marshall McLuhan, MIT Press, 1964

16     *What Is Brand Equity Anyway?*, Paul Feldwick, World Advertising Research Center, 2002

17     'Parents exercised over price of sports kit', Paul Lewis, *Guardian*, 16 December 2005

18     'Assessing the Emotional Drivers of Purchase: A Methodological Discussion', Dr Glenn Livingston, Livingston Research Group, 2004

19     *Building Strong Brands*, David Aacker, The Free Press, 1996

20     *The Culting of Brands: When Customers Become True Believers*, Douglas Atkin, Portfolio, 2004

21     *Chicago Sun-Times*, Kate N Grossman, 7 June 2003

22     *Carried Away: The Invention of Modern Shopping*, Rachel Bowlby, Columbia University Press, 2001

23     'Burberry Dumps "Lout Hat"', *Daily Mirror*, September 10 2004

24     'Style Counsel', Dylan Jones, *Mail on Sunday*, 6 August 2006

25     'Commodifying Space', www.freepress.net/issues/space

26     'Commodifying Space', www.freepress.net/issues/space

27     'Commodifying Space', www.freepress.net/issues/space

28     *Born to Buy: The Commercialized Child and the New Consumer Culture*, Juliet Schor, Scribner, 2004

29     'Worldwide Ad Spend 2007', Zenith Optimedia

30     *The Culture of Narcissism*, Christopher Lasch, W W Norton & Company, 1979

31     *Propaganda*, Edward Bernays, H Liveright, 1928

32     *Ways of Seeing*, John Berger, Penguin, 1972

33    'Brands Identity and Young People', Nick Anderson,
      University of Sussex
34    'Consuming Goods', Rosalind Minsky, from *Serious Shopping:
      Psychotherapy and Consumerism*, Adrienne Baker (ed),
      Free Association Books, 2000
35    'Bonfire of the Vanities', Neil Boorman, *Guardian*,
      13 September 2006
36    'The costs of consumer culture and the "cage within":
      the impact of the material "good life" and "body perfect"
      ideals on individuals' identity and well-being. Commentary
      on Kasser, T, cohn, S, Kanner, A D, & Ryan, R M: "Some
      Costs of American Corporate Capitalism: A Psychological
      Exploration of Value and Goal Conflicts"', Helga Dittmar,
      *Psychological Inquiry Vol. 18, No.1–9*, The Analytical Press,
      2007
37    *The Managed Heart: Commercialisation of Human Feeling*,
      Arlie Russell Hochschild, California Press, 1983
38    *Advertising Today*, Warren Berger, Phaidon Press, 2004
39    Today programme, Tony Juniper, BBC Radio 4,
      17 January 2007
40    *No Logo*, Naomi Klein, Picador 2000
41    'Current and Historical Earnings', www.nikebiz.com, 2007
42    'How to get involved', www.nosweat.org.uk/getinvolved
43    'Nike lists abuses at Asian factories', *Guardian*,
      14 April 2005
44    'Spring 2007 Trend Dossier', The Future Laboratory, 2007
45    'UK firms exploiting Bangladesh', BBC News website,
      8 December 2006
46    *Daily Telegraph*/Yougov poll, *Daily Telegraph*, 27 July 2006
47    'Election 2005: Turnout, How Many, Who And Why?',
      The Electoral Commission, www.electoralcommission.org.uk
48    'Voter Turnout 2004', United States Elections Project,
      www.elections.gmu.edu
49    'Post Party Politics: Can Participation Reconnect People And
      Government?', Richard Wilson, The Involve Foundation,
      2006

50 *One-Dimensional Man: Studies in the Ideology of Advanced Industrial Society*, Herbert Marcuse & Douglas Kellner, Routledge, 1964

51 'BMW is Chinese millionaires' favorite brand', www.chinadaily.com, 13 January 2007

52 *One-Dimensional Man: Studies in the Ideology of Advanced Industrial Society*, Herbert Marcuse & Douglas Kellner, Routledge, 1964

53 'Consumer Debt Report', Grant Thornton, 2007

54 'Materialism and wellbeing: a conflicting values perspective', James Burroughs, *Journal of Consumer Research*, 2002

55 'Life Values and Adolescent Mental Health' (Research Monographs in Adolescence), Patricia Cohen & Jacob Cohen, LEA Inc, 1995

56 'Would you be happier if you were richer? A focusing illusion', E Diener & R Biswas-Diener, *Science Magazine*, 2006

57 *Deadly Persuasion: Why Women and Girls Must Fight the Addictive Power of Advertising*, Jean Kilbourne, Free Press, 1999

58 *Insecurity*, Tim Kasser & Virginia Grow, Department of Psychology, Knox College 2002

59 *The Value of Voluntary Simplicity*, Richard B Gregg, Pendle Hill Publications, 1983

60 *The Essential Epicurus: Letters, Principal Doctrines, Vatican Sayings, and Fragments Epicurus*, Prometheus Books, 1993

# reading list

## Classic texts

Berger, John, *Ways of Seeing*, Penguin, 1972

Bernays, Edward, *Propaganda*, IG Publishing, 1928

Brown, J A C, *Techniques of Persuasion*, Penguin, 1963

Glasser, Ralph, *The New High Priesthood*, Macmillan, 1967

Goffman, Erving, *The Presentation of Self In Everyday Life*, Penguin, 1959

Lasch, Christopher, *The Minimal Self: Psychic Survival in Troubled Times*, Picador, 1984

Marcuse, Herbert & Douglas Kellner, *One-Dimensional Man: Studies in the Ideology of Advanced Industrial Society*, Routledge, 1964

Packard, Vance, *The Hidden Persuaders*, Penguin, 1957

Thoreau, Henry David, *Walden: Or A Life in the Woods*, Dover, 1995

Veblen, Thorstein, *The Theory of the Leisure Class*, Dodo Press, 1899

Williamson, Judith, *Consuming Passions*, Marion Boyars, 1988

Williamson, Judith, *Decoding Advertisements*, Marion Boyars, 1978

## Recent theory

Bauman, Zygmunt, *Identity*, Polity, 2004

Botton, Alain de, *Status Anxiety*, Hamish Hamilton, 2004

Clarke, David B, *The Consumption Reader*, Routledge, 2003

Dittmar, Helga, *The Social Psychology of Material Possessions: To Have Is To Be*, Taylor & Francis, 1992

— *Consumer Society, Identity and Well-Being: The Search for the 'Good Life' and the 'Body Perfect'*, European Monographs in Social Psychology Series, Hove and New York: Psychology Press, 2007

Frank, Robert H, *Luxury Fever: Why Money Fails to Satisfy in an Era of Excess*, Free Press, 1999

Gabriel, Yiannis & Tim Lang, *The Unmanageable Consumer*, Sage, 1995

Graff, John de, *Affluenza: The All-consuming Epidemic*, McGraw-Hill, 2001

Heath, Joseph & Andrew Potter, *The Rebel Sell: How the Counterculture Became Consumer Culture*, Capstone, 2005

Hodgkinson, Tom, *How To Be Free*, Hamish Hamilton, 2006

Kasser, Tim, *The High Price of Materialism*, MIT Press, 2002

Kilbourne, Jean, *Deadly Persuasion: Why Women and Girls Must Fight the Addictive Power of Advertising*, Free Press, 1999

Lasn, Kalle, *Culture Jam*, Quill, 2000

Patterson, Mark, *Consumption and Everyday Life*, Routledge, 2006

Schor, Juliet B, *Born to Buy*, Scribner, 2004

Smail, David, *Illusion and Reality: Meaning of Anxiety*, Constable, 1997

## Industry texts

Atkin, Douglas, *The Culting of Brands*, Portfolio, 2004

Clifton, Rita & John Simmons, *Brands and Branding*, Economist / Profile, 2003

Davis, Melissa, *More than a Brand*, EVA, 2005

Gobe, Marc, *Emotional Branding*, Allworth Press, 2001

Heath, Robert, *The Hidden Power of Advertising*, Admap, 2001
Keller, Kevin Lane, *Strategic Brand Management*, Prentice Hall, 1988
Ollins, Wally, *On Brand*, Thames & Hudson, 2003
Roberts, Kevin, *Lovemarks: The Future Beyond Brands*, Powerhouse, 2004

# biographies

Adam Curtis is a British television documentary maker who has during the course of his television career worked as a writer, producer, director and narrator. He currently works for BBC Current Affairs. His documentaries include *The Mayfair Set, Century of the Self, The Power of Nightmares* and *The Trap*.

Helga Dittmar is Reader in Psychology at the University of Sussex. Her research (funded by ESRC, Department of Health, Office of Fair Trading) examines the impact of consumer society on individuals' identity and wellbeing. She was the first social psychologist in Europe to study the role of material goods for identity, and has since extended her work to include motives in conventional and online buying, dysfunctional buying behaviours, and media influences on body image and eating behaviours in children, adolescents and adults. Her work is reported in two books, *The Social Psychology of Material Possessions: To Have Is To Be* (1992) and the recently published *Consumer Culture, Identity and Wellbeing: The Search for the Good Life and Body Perfect*, as well as numerous articles in scientific journals.

Tom Hodgkinson is a British writer and the editor of the *Idler*. He was educated at Westminster School. He has contributed to articles to the *Sunday Telegraph*, the *Guardian* and the *Sunday Times*, as well as being the author of the *Idler* magazine spin-off *How To Be Idle*. His latest book is entitled *How To Be Free*.

Phillip Hodson is a Fellow of the British Association for Counselling. He is the author of 11 books including *Men: An Investigation into the Emotional Male*. Widely known on UK television as both a writer and a presenter, he also presented the much acclaimed Phillip Hodson Hour on LBC radio for over 15 years. Phillip has written problem pages for five UK newspapers and nine magazines, and he has been a contributing editor to *Psychology Today*. He is head of media and chief spokesperson for the British Association for Counselling and Psychotherapy.

Carol Martin-Sperry is a counsellor and psychosexual therapist of 20 years. She trained with Relate and London Marriage Guidance, and now manages a private practice in London. She is accredited and registered with the British Association for Counsellors and Psychotherapists. Carol is a broadcaster, writer and consultant on counselling issues and represents the British Association for Counselling and Psychotherapy as a media spokesperson. She is the author of *Couples and Sex: An Introduction to Relationship Dynamics and Psychosexual Concepts*.

Clare Short was Secretary of State for International Development from 1997 to May 2003, a ministry created after the 1997 British general election to promote policies for sustainable development and the elimination of poverty; the ministry is responsible for Britain's programme of assistance to developing countries. From 1996 until the 1997 general election she was Opposition spokesperson on Overseas Development. She was Shadow Minister for Women from 1993 to 1995 and Shadow Secretary of State for Transport from 1995 to 1996. She has been Opposition spokesperson on Environment Protection, Social Security and Employment. Clare Short is the author of *An Honourable Deception? New Labour, Iraq and the Misuse of Power*.

## acknowledgements

Many thanks to Clare Conville and all at Conville & Walsh for placing such faith in me. Thanks to Jamie Byng, Anya Serota, Andy Miller and all at Canongate for their editorial vision. Thanks to Tom Hodgkinson, Kalle Lasn, Adam Curtis, John Berger, Carol Martin-Sperry, Phillip Hodson and Clare Short for magnificent inspiration. Thanks to Rana Reeves, Kate Statham and Erin Manger for such sound advice. Thanks to Ros and all at Fantastic Fireworks for handling the bonfire so well. Thanks to all the friends who pitched in and lent support, including Tim Parker, Tom Awad, Daniel Pemberton, Kevin Braddock, Russell Davies, James House, Micha Gilbert, Emma Tutty & James Grant, Glyn & Jim at ESP and Ekow Eshun. Thanks to Alan Clarke and Ashley Bingham for the photography. I am indebted to Libby Brooks, William Briely and Lottie Moggach for their support in the press. For their undoubting support and incredible warmth I thank Dee, Barry and Debbie Bingham together with Jane, OW and the extended Riegel family. I thank my parents Bob and Margaret Boorman and my sister Lindsay and her husband David for their understanding, selflessness and love for all these years. Most importantly of all, I thank my partner Juliet Bingham for transforming my life and loving me without question.